W9-BTQ-967

811

**DATE DUE**

| | | | |
|---|---|---|---|
| | | | |
| | | | |
| | | | |
| | | | |
| | | | |
| | | | |
| | | | |
| | | | |
| | | | |
| | | | |
| | | | |
| | | | |
| | | | |

McCarthy, John
   After the game

OEMCO

# AFTER THE GAME

*A Collection of the Best Sports Writing*

# AFTER

# THE GAME

*A Collection of the Best*

*Sports Writing*

*Selected by John McCarthy*

**DODD, MEAD & COMPANY** · *NEW YORK*

Second Printing

ISBN: 0-396-06600-3
Library of Congress Catalog Card Number: 72-1531
Printed in the United States of America
by The Cornwall Press, Inc., Cornwall, N.Y.

Thanks are due to the following for permission to reprint this material:
Saturday Review for "The Age of Willie Mays" by Peter Schrag, Copyright
© 1971 Saturday Review, Inc. The Sterling Lord Agency, Inc. for "Racing's
Angriest Young Man" by Jimmy Breslin, Copyright © 1960 by Jimmy Bes-
lin. Harper & Row, Publishers, Inc. for extracts from THE BOGEY MAN
by George Plimpton, Copyright © 1967, 1968 by George Plimpton; and
"The Fallen Idol: The Harlem Tragedy of Earl Manigault" from THE CITY
GAME by Pete Axthelm, Copyright © 1970 by Pete Axthelm. The Atlantic
Monthly and Gerald Holland for "Lunches With Luce" by Gerald Holland,
Copyright © 1971 by Gerald Holland. Dodd, Mead & Company, Inc. for
"The Man Who Was Cut Out for the Job" from BLACK COACH by Pat
Jordan, Copyright © 1971 by Pat Jordan; and excerpt from HIGH STICK
by Ted Green with Al Hirshberg, Copyright © 1971 by Ted Green and Al
Hirshberg. Little, Brown and Company for "The Disciples of Saint Darrell"
from SATURDAY'S AMERICA by Dan Jenkins, Copyright © 1970 by Dan
Jenkins. The New York Times for "The Silent Mr. Stengel" by Arthur
Daley, © 1955 by The New York Times Company. A.S. Barnes & Company,
Inc. for "The Big Fellow, Babe Ruth" from THE TUMULT AND THE
SHOUTING by Grantland Rice. William Barry Furlong for "Where the
Action Is" from the June, 1966 issue of Harper's Magazine, Copyright ©
1966, by Minneapolis Star and Tribune Co., Inc. Rex Lardner for "The Assault
and Battery of Lacrosse" from the April, 1969 issue of Holiday, Copyright
© 1969 The Curtis Publishing Co. The Saturday Evening Post for "Rasslin'
Was My Act" by Herman Hickman, Copyright © 1954 by Curtis Publishing Company. Harold Ober Associates Incorporated for "Farewell to the
Babe" by Paul Gallico, Copyright © 1956 by Time, Inc. Norman Mailer
and his agent, Scott Meredith Literary Agency, Inc., 580 Fifth Avenue, New
York, N.Y. 10036 for "King of the Hill" by Norman Mailer, text Copyright
© 1971 by Norman Mailer.

*To our twelve grandchildren, sportsmen all*

# Introduction

Sports writing has matured in recent years—partly out of need and partly because everyone now has more leisure time. With our increased participation in sport, whether as player or spectator, the reporter has also been called on to put forth a little something extra. Especially since his by-line, which once appeared only on the back pages of newspapers, has moved onto bookshelves and into mass circulation magazines.

A few short years ago, I sat in the press box on warm summer afternoons next to Ring Lardner or Damon Runyon or Grantland Rice—giants in the field. No present sportswriter has yet developed the historical stature of these three. But the talent today is just as remarkable; and the writing every bit as excellent.

Here then is a collection of my recent favorites together with an occasional voice from the past—a more gentle though still very competitive time. It's not just a pleasant selection. For some of these people will prove quite challenging. So should you find yourself otherwise alone after the game, relax and share with me these moments of excitement and quality. Containing, perhaps, even a measure of importance.

—JOHN McCARTHY

# Contents

ix

# AFTER THE GAME

*A Collection of the Best Sports Writing*

PETER SCHRAG

# The Age of Willie Mays

Time is of the essence. The shadow moves
From the plate to the box, from the box to second base,
From second to the outfield, to the bleachers.
Time is of the essence. The crowd and players
Are the same age always, but the man in the crowd
Is older every season. Come on, play ball! *

IT WAS ALWAYS A GAME of myth and memory. The ritual transcended the moment of play, tested performance against im-
mortality, and allowed otherwise ordinary men to place themselves in something larger than conventional time. Each
spring brought its own renewal and each summer its moments of truth. The word came from Vero Beach and St. Pete
and Scottsdale, where the big leaguers trained before the season: new faces and new ballyhoo, and new predictions of
who would be greater (someday) than Mantle, who could
throw like Koufax, and who could run like Cobb. But there
was more; there was the man in the crowd, his memories, his
moments, his brush with greatness, and, above all, his return,

---

* From Rolfe Humphries's "Polo Grounds" in *The Collected Poems of
Rolfe Humphries*, © 1965 by Indiana University Press.

1

year after year, to the places where the idols of the past, the anticipated glory of the future, and the remembrance of youth came together against the clipped green grass of the field in the afternoon sun, against the crowd, and against a ritual that, despite its historical brevity, seemed as old as time.

Those of us who came to know baseball when there was little television and no big-time professional football or basketball talked its language, heard its lore, and were taken with its special sense before we had ever played an organized game or pondered its beautiful mystery. There were giants on the field, men of legend whose voices we had never heard, whose faces we knew only from newspaper photographs or from the murky images on our bubblegum cards, and whose records—batting average, home runs, runs batted in—suggested meaning beyond anything we understood. "Facts" supported myth, and myth magnified the facts on which it was supposed to be based.

It was always a game of argument. The action on the field was never sufficient to fill the time, and it therefore required of its spectators something more than catcalls and cheers. After every play we confronted not only the opportunity but the necessity for discussion, analysis, and comparison, and it was in those long moments of inaction—when the teams changed sides, when the relief pitchers ambled in from the bullpen (in the days before they rode on golf carts), in the winter hiatus, in the stretches when nothing might ever happen again—that we, the fans, chose our idols and elected our heroes.

*Time is of the essence. The crowd and players are the same age always, but the man in the crowd is older every season.*

Perhaps it will always be that way; perhaps the ritual will survive conditions that have destroyed other American perennials, and will live a charmed life into eternity. And yet something has changed: The crowd, too, is getting older; it is losing its small-town innocence and its capacity to believe without ambivalence, and the half-life of demigods becomes shorter with each passing year. We make and discard them according to the requirements of the television schedule; we demand action—violent action—to fill the anxious moments, and we seem no longer capable of creating idols in our idleness.

There is nothing new in the argument that something is destroying baseball—avaricious major league club owners buying and selling franchises, moving teams, abandoning old fans, and wooing new ones with cast-off bush league players who should be selling sporting goods or life insurance; mounting expenses; the competition of other activities; and the influence of television itself. But these things—though they are, for some of us, matters of concern—are hardly as significant as the fate of the hero himself. Each generation likes to say that there will never be another Ruth, another DiMaggio, another Ted Williams, congratulating itself (as mythology must have it) that it lived in the last great age of heroism and achievement. Ask any big league manager and he will remind you that the eclipse of one generation of stars always heralds the rise of another. It is only the man in the crowd who is older every season. The players are more skilled—are larger, faster, stronger—than any in history.

And yet this time they are wrong. We will have great players, but we have left the age of the mythic hero. The immortals were forged in innocence, products of the belief that this was one nation with a single set of values, that any boy might succeed, of the ability to say "Wow" without embarrassment, and of the nearly magical capacity of big league baseball to preserve its small-town qualities within the secure confines of big-city stadiums. Once we walked through the turnstiles, we all became boys again, breathed a little easier, and enjoyed the protection of the ritual, the memories, the immersion in another dimension of time.

For many of us who came to our baseball in those more innocent days, only one great man is left, and his name is Willie Mays. This week—on May 6—he became forty years old, and he should, therefore, be well past his prime, an aging star dogged by fragile legs, trick knees, fatigue, and the other assorted aches and pains that the flesh of annuating athletes is supposed to suffer. But Mays moves with the grace of memory, defying time, defying the inexorable erosion of fantasies, defying age itself. He remains unequivocally our man. To see him now is like watching the instant replay of a generation, the crowds of twenty years, the old ball parks with their erratic dimensions and their even more erratic fans, Hilda Chester and the Dodger Symphony at Ebbets Field, the short right field foul line in the Polo Grounds, where Mel Ott, among others, once hit his "Chinese" home runs. And, of course, there is the image of Mays himself: the unbelievable catches, the 3,000 base hits, the 630-odd home runs (second only to Babe Ruth's lifetime total), the elegance that, when we first saw it in 1951, could hardly be comprehended. Mays always moved differently from other players, started instinctively toward the place where the ball was hit— moving from his center field position almost, it seemed, before the batter swung—and he caught fly balls against his belt with the palm of his glove turned up, playing with a casual defiance of error, a disdain for security, and with an emphasis on style that repudiated mere professional competence.

When Mays came to the Giants in 1951, Jackie Robinson, who broke the color line in major league baseball, already had been with the Dodgers for four years; in the meantime, moreover, a handful of other Negro players had been signed, and they were being cautiously accepted by the fans and players. But Mays brought with him something that I imagine the game rarely enjoyed before, and that can only be described as aristocratic class. Despite his notorious disregard for the official causes of civil rights (for which he was later attacked by Robinson himself), Mays was not merely a ballplayer who happened to be Negro; he was a black athlete. He ran black, swung black, and caught black. He did not play the man's game but his own, and his every move disparaged the tight-assed honkies who did things by the book. William Goldman, in a book about the theater, recalled what Mays had done for him: "It was about time he arrived on my horizon, because during all those years of being bored by baseball, of sitting on bleacher seats for pitchers' battles, or dying from the heat while the manager brought in some slow reliever, I'd been waiting for Willie. He was what it was all about." There are countless thousands of us who felt the same way. Mention Mays now and you find more people who claim to have seen his first game with the Giants than could ever have squeezed into the Polo Grounds that day; more who remember his impossible catch of Vic Wertz's 440-foot drive in the 1954 World Series than ever attended a Series game. Of such stuff are legends made.

This spring, for the first time, I made the pilgrimage, a

forty-year-old man pursuing another forty-year-old who was the idol of the boy. Instant replay—what every kid used to dream about, and what many still do—sitting in the Arizona sun, or leaning against the batting cage to feel the intensity of the pitch and the opposing concentration of the hitter, or, again, standing in the locker room to watch the man who preserves the fantasy. Spring training. The symbols of time come together, old players and young, Hall of Famers and rookies, welding a continuity that goes back beyond remembrance: Carl Hubbell, Hall of Fame pitcher who won 253 games between 1928 and 1943, the man who struck out Ruth, Gehrig, Foxx, Simmons, and Cronin—one after another—in the 1934 All-Star game (now director of the Giants' farm system) sitting by the dugout; Wes Westrum, who managed the Mets in leaner days, hitting ground balls to the infield; Larry Jansen, who helped pitch the Giants into the World Series in 1951, watching the young pitchers warming up—kids just up from Fresno and Amarillo and St. Cloud.

Around the field the sports writers are trying to grab a few crumbs for tomorrow's paper, looking for another rookie of promise, escalating every solid drive into a slugger's future, and in the bleachers people with memories longer than mine are discussing games played twenty years before I was born. Juan Marichal, another player of supreme elegance, is pitching batting practice. (High kick, the left foot higher than the head, the ball coming from some deep recess of motion, the glove brushing the knee as the ball is thrown, and turning an ordinary man of six feet into a fantastic engine of power.) Mays, his right foot dug in at the rear of the batter's box, hits a couple to the fence in left center, then takes a pitch low and away.

"I can't hit that," he says to Marichal. "Can't hit that no way."

Marichal pitches another, again low and a little outside, and Mays smokes it on a line over the head of the shortstop.

"That was the same pitch," Marichal says. "The same pitch."

"I had to hit it," Mays answers, his voice rising and, at the same time, a little resigned. Logic loses to performance, and Charlie Fox, the Giants' manager, turns from his position behind the batting cage with an expression of futile amazement: What can you say when you are supervising a genius?

Mays still plays the same game. After the first two weeks of the 1971 season, he led the league in runs batted in and was among the leaders in batting average and home runs. Twenty years and three thousand games later the style hasn't changed. He will run a little less this year, steal fewer bases, skip—with Charlie Fox's blessings—the fatiguing Tuesday and Friday night games at Candlestick Park, the Giants' home field in San Francisco, but the moves are all the same, and the virtuosity is unblemished. He protects himself in a dozen different ways: He does not drink or smoke; throws underhand whenever possible to protect the arm and shoulder; takes his meals in his room when the team is on the road; walks onto the Arizona practice field wearing a warmup jacket so the autograph hunters, failing to recognize his face, won't swarm to his number; melts away from practice before the other players and slips into his pink Imperial, license number SAY HEY, to drive to lunch and then to a round of golf. "He never stands when he can sit," says Fox, "and he never sits when he can lie down."

In the locker room he is a person—or, better, a kid, shifting moods from highpitched exuberance to petulance—and in the stadium he is a demigod, but between them he becomes an apparition that materializes and evaporates according to its own impulse. Perhaps, you say, he is hurting, suffering the anguish of exploitation, of too many games, too many pitchmen, too many sellers of clothes, bats, gloves, buttons, pictures, and causes, too many journalists asking questions—how much did he sign for? how much does he want?—too much pressure, but he has no intention of thinking about himself as a man of complexity or as the aging star (like Mantle) whose every painful move becomes a heroic act. His public role is to remain a player only—a man who plays—because he seems incapable of any other part.

And yet it is hard for anyone to tell how much is man, how much boy, and how much the distillation of idolatry. We are sitting in the team dining room at the Francisco Grande, an Arizona hotel owned by the Giants: Mays, wearing asparagus-green trousers, a green turtle-neck shirt, and a green cardigan sweater; Sy Berger of New York, the king of the bubble-gum cards—which, he explains, are bigger than ever with the kids—and the boy from New York. Somewhere else another presence of Mays is negotiating a new contract with the Giants—he has asked for $75,000 a year for ten years, but the reporters, after the contract is signed, guess $165,000 a year for two years—and he is clearly concerned about something that other people would call the future. But here at lunch Mays talks only about playing ball—"I'm not thinking about five years from now"—and complaining about the old photographs that Berger uses on his bubble-gum cards. Berger answers that Mays looks the same as ever, and Mays screws up his face and says sheeit . . . . Somehow, I tell myself, he seems to make it possible to contemplate the old days without confronting the matter of age itself, but I am not really sure. Which one of us is the kid, and which one the man of maturity? (A good businessman, say the flacks around the field—investments, endorsements, he's got a bundle—but the speculation in the swamp between myth and reality is so rank that anything goes.) I do not know, therefore, just how the fantasies lodge between us, but I do sense some regret (mine, perhaps; yet possibly his) about the past.

Before the Giants moved from New York to San Francisco, Mays spent part of his free time playing stickball with the kids in Harlem, going from the Polo Grounds to the streets not as an act of charity but as an activity of natural joy. (Although he was good there, too, he was not the best; but that may indeed have been an act of charity.) He does not do such things anymore—they don't play stickball in California, he said—nor has he ever become the idol in San Francisco that he had been in New York. They have a show-me attitude out there, one of the sports writers explained, very sophisticated compared to the hayseeds in New York, and that, too, seems a pity. How can one tell them—for the sake of everything, for Mays, for the game, for the nation—that the height of baseball sophistication is exuberance and the instinct to understand the subtle line between the ingenuous and the hyperbolic, and between the serious and the comic?

You leave your reservations and ambivalence at the gate. This is a conservative game that sometimes oozes with unbounded chauvinism—about the country, the flag, and itself—and that cannot tolerate even the most minimal expressions of dissent. There are players—Joe Pepitone of the Cubs, for example—who wear their hair long, and others who have associated themselves with the peace movement, or who read Dostoevsky, but most clubs and players regard every manifestation of independent thought with suspicion. In this monopolistic business where athletes are chattel, the image of the well-dressed, well-groomed, politically benign player is regarded as a matter of importance. The injunction to regard ballplayers as interesting human beings is therefore self-defeating: What they do in their moments off the field is the same sort of thing that might interest any ordinary man whose means outrun his imagination. They play cards, watch television, go hunting, and discuss their sexual exploits.

At the Francisco Grande one night, the Giant management showed a film of the team's 1970 season to a crowd of balding boosters and their wives, people who spend much of their time in VIP lounges and not in the bleachers. On the screen there was flash and glamour—Gaylord Perry winning twenty-three games; Marichal striking out the side; Willie McCovey, described by the film narrator as the most feared hitter in baseball, lining one over the fence in right while the crowd cheered and the background orchestra played a few measures of Beethoven. Just outside the room where the film was shown, Marichal and McCovey, in sports shirts and slacks, were watching a John Wayne film on television while Perry was beginning the sixth hour of a card game that had been in progress since early afternoon—ordinary men attempting to fill tedious moments in lonely cities.

*You leave your ambivalence at the gate.* It does not matter what kind of person Willie Mays "really" is, nor does the question mean very much. He is what he does, a ballplayer and then something more, a man who has—like most highly talented performers in other fields—transcended his trade. In the locker room he is one of the boys, needling other players, denying any knowledge about who might have placed Tito Fuentes's missing socks into his locker, tossing a football down the aisle, lending a couple of bats to Bobby Bonds, discussing his golf scores. And beyond the locker room there are endless theories, each of them fit for a moment: that he has dollar signs in his eyes, that he is supremely generous ("There was this sick kid in the hospital . . ."), that he is interested in nothing but baseball and women, that he will play two more years and then become the first black manager in baseball, that he expects too much of other players to manage a club. . . .

Mays never has been even remotely political, and if you ask him what he has done for the cause of racial justice—where he has marched or what organizations he supports—he will tell you (if he answers at all) that he does things his own way, without publicity and without making himself a politically marked man. Long ago his ebullience earned him the nickname Say Hey (which by contemporary sensibilities, might suggest something just this side of "boy"), but in recent years he has become more cautious, a man who seems to have learned that everything has its price and that he himself (as the highest paid player in the game, as an endorser of bats, automobiles, clothes, and cosmetics) is a highly valuable piece of property.

But none of that matters. The "contribution" is more subtle and profound, a contribution of style. Mays has become a sports hero by doing things his own way, and if few other athletes can do that, it is all the more a tribute to his skill. One morning in Phoenix, at Charlie Fox's request, he took a

group of young outfielders to a corner of the ball park to
work on some of the finer points. Although Mays always has
been comfortable with kids, it is not something he does very
often, and it turned into an extended disquisition on style.
(All of them were black, which may have added to the ur-
gency, however subtle, of the message.) "You don't play it by
the book," he said. "You play it opposite; you come up with
the ball on the side you're going to throw. . . ." (Going
through the motions now, picking up a ball from the grass,
always moving, the bare hand sweeping the ball out of the
glove, the arm cocking. . . .) "Don't get directly in front of
it; if you want to make money, get the ball on the side; if
you get in front of it you're playing it safe. You have to move
everything, your arm, your legs, your body, keep it all moving; you're like a ballet dancer out there; don't short-arm it,
don't be afraid to let it go, and don't ever figure the ball's
going to get by you."

One of them asked a question about a play last year in
which the crowd in San Francisco hooted its disapproval.
"Don't worry about the fans, fuck the fans. They don't know
anything about what you're trying to do." They all watch
him again, the legs moving, the glove, the hand, the arm, the
whole dance that we have seen a thousand times on the field
performed in slow motion. (You can remember it all, hear the
announcers, the crowd, see the fielder going back, back to a
forgotten fence, taking the ball with his back to the plate,
driving his spikes against the wall, putting his shoulder
against it, throwing on a line toward the infield if there are
runners on base, or if there are none heaving it underhand,
nonchalantly, and walking back to retrieve his cap where it
had fallen during the chase.) "I've studied the game," he is

saying to them now, trying to explain his imposition on them, "but nobody ever showed me. My father started me, but nobody showed me." Later in the day I will see one of them, George Foster, carrying a baseball through the lobby of the motel, practicing the two-fingered, across-the-seams grip that Mays had explained that morning.

Mays was nineteen when the Giants bought his contract from the Birmingham Barons, a Negro team, and brought him up to the white man's big game. He played one season of minor league ball at Trenton and part of another at Minneapolis before arriving at the Polo Grounds. Harry Truman was President, Joe DiMaggio was still playing for the Yankees, and the presence of Negro players in the major leagues was, on the one hand, a matter of caution (whom would they room with? how would they travel? could they take the pressure?) and, on the other, an occasion for liberal self-congratulation.

Every black player, therefore, was something of a secret agent; a man had to express himself on the field and nowhere else. Mays arrived in New York in the same year that Mantle started his career with the Yankees, and comparisons were therefore inevitable: who was the better hitter? who was faster? who could hit more home runs? Mantle was, in every respect, the hero of tradition—a big, strong, attractive kid from a small town in Oklahoma, the kind of player about whom they write books for boys. But what was Mays? The myth had no place for him; all it offered was the possibility of limited integration—the hope that he might become one of the boys, might be good, and might be liked. The one chance of transcending those limitations was style itself, and the style became like a signature.

*If you want to make money, don't play it safe.* He runs out every hit, the legs flowing, long smooth strides, the feet slightly pigeon-toed (Dr. Spock says somewhere that pigeon-toed babies are more likely than others to be athletes), making the turn at first as if he might go for two—the convincing performance—making the fielder throw, making him think, and adding a beat to a play that might otherwise be routine. At such moments you feel the possibilities, the suspended tremor, the delicacy of time in the balance. Time is of the essence: The difference between a single and a double is a fraction of a second and a cloud of dust; the difference between an infield out and a single is the blink of an umpire's eye.

When Mays first came up, he said a great deal about learning from Joe DiMaggio—the ritual probably demanded it, especially of an athlete playing in New York at the time—but he owed more to talent than to any coach or player. In Arizona this spring, Leo Durocher, who managed the Giants in Mays's first season, observed that he didn't teach Mays anything: "He could do it all." The ability, Durocher said, pointing a bat at the heavens, came from *there*. But the triumph exceeded competence. Just at the moment when everything in America was going corporate, when the old idols of Americanism were entering their declining years, and when baseball itself seemed to be dulled by tepid professionalism, he appeared to us as the new romantic individualist, a man of the ritual, but a man who also enriched it. He brought jazz to the game.

In the decade that followed there would be others, Henry Aaron of the Braves, Bob Gibson of the Cardinals, Ernie Banks of the Cubs—all of them suffering the misfortune of having to play outside the New York limelight—but Mays was the symbol. He expressed on the field what James Baldwin and others would later try to say in words: if you would retrieve your humanity from the fear of death, the fear of defeat, the fear of vulnerability, you need us as much as we need you, need to learn something again about joy and suffering, about risk, and about those possibilities of uninhibited expression without which neither life nor art can survive. "Something very sinister happens to the people of a country," Baldwin wrote, "when they distrust their own reactions as deeply as they do here, and become as joyless as they have become."

The tragedy lies in our own limitations. We loved the player but failed too often to appreciate the message, did not understand the significance of the play. We missed the lesson of improvisation—"all human effort beyond the lowest level of the struggle for animal existence," wrote Albert Murray, "is motivated by the need to live in style"—and thus Mays may himself become a transitory kind of figure. There will never be—not for many years, at any rate—a black Babe Ruth or a black Charles Lindbergh, men who can lead the celebration of national achievement, because our racism still runs too deep and because—in any case—we have outgrown our hope and innocence. At the very moment when Mays became the greatest player in baseball the game was diminished; even as he enriched it, and thereby promised to enrich us all, it lost its symbolic pre-eminence, ceased to be the intimate common possession it once had been, and became just another big-time sport. Black players now dominate professional sports—basketball, football, and baseball—but we switch channels too fast to permit them to become our own; after this game there will be another, and another, people jumping, tackling, blocking, running, throwing, catching. Everything is taken with a touch of detachment—a little "sophistication"; we are here and they are out there, and we thus create barriers against fantasy and destroy the ability to identify without equivocation. Every black kid may understand, but the rest of us have reservations.

The game, of course, goes on, but the possibility that we will ever again have common, integrating heroes seems more remote than ever. The people we admire now are, almost without exception, symbols of particularism—baseball stars, football stars, track stars, heroes of the black, heroes of the young, heroes of division: Muhammad Ali, César Chavez, John Lennon, the Berrigans, people of style and distinction in an age that lacks the rituals and values of community. We failed in the great effort to syntheticize a national adventure in the space program because it required (for technical and political reasons) a group of courageous, proficient, but totally indistinguishable individuals, men with nearly identical profiles, styles, and personalities. They took risks, too, but the risk was in trusting someone else's technology, in betting on the competence of thousands of anonymous technicians on the ground. They could not possibly transcend their medium or play it opposite from the book, and no one will ever turn to his neighbor in front of the television set and say "Conrad? [Or Cooper or Glenn or Schirra or Sheppard?] Conrad? He *stinks.*" No one will ever stand on the sidelines pointing at the heavens to explain where they got their phenomenal talents.

Perhaps it was appropriate that I saw Mays at close range in that Arizona setting of retired cardiac cases, development houses, and plastic. On the field the dream was preserved—

if you play ball you must continue to believe in the permanence of the ritual—but in the surroundings something had gone sour. The world was threatening to come through the turnstiles in pursuit of the fans, and not even the reveries that flourish in the sunshine seemed quite secure anymore. Every day the old people came to the field to sit in the warm sun, watch practice, and collect autographs, but even the autograph collecting was indiscriminate. Anything in uniform would do, and when they saw a face they remembered from television—the face of an actor or an announcer—they asked for his autograph, too. Only the kids knew better; they wanted Mays and Marichal and McCovey. (One elderly man got Mays's signature on a ball, but didn't recognize the face or the number, and couldn't read the writing: "I just got number 24," he said to his friend, "do you know who he is?") Here in the sunshine of the Southwest, the dream was coming to an end and people were gathering its remains like squirrels before the winter.

But what the head observes the heart resists. We are still in the presence of a beautiful mystery; style always defies time, and all the sociology in the world isn't worth a moment of poetry. In the hotel the old players and the coaches tell stories about athletes and games most of us have long forgotten or never knew, and on the field young men create the fantasies out of which new stories may someday be told. It is a good time to be forty—old enough to remember and young enough to believe—a good time to sit in the sun with someone you love. If the ritual is no longer for everyone, one can only regret what others are missing. For me the game goes on; Willie Mays is still playing.

JIMMY BRESLIN

# *Racing's Angriest Young Man*

THE SHACK was on stilts so the floor wouldn't be against the ground in wintertime. But it didn't matter because when you went out to the creek for drinking water and brought it back in a basin, the way Bill Hartack had to before dinner every night, any of it that would drip on the floor quickly turned to ice. A potbellied stove was the only warm thing in shack number 371 and this does not constitute a heating system, even for a tiny three-room shack. But it was all they had because Hartack's father worked at soft coal in the mines around Colver, Pennsylvania, and there was no money in this. Nor was there much of a life in the shack. Hartack's mother had been killed when he was seven and he had to raise his two sisters while his father dug coal.

You always remember this when you tell about Bill Hartack, the talented jockey who is one of the most controversial people in sports. It might make him easier to understand, you think.

But then Hartack will be at a race track, acting the way he did at Churchill Downs last May 7, and you forget everything because there is only one way to describe him. You say, simply, that his attitude is *to hell with everybody* and you have captured Hartack.

At 4:30 that afternoon, a guy in khaki work shirt and pants who is an assistant starter at Churchill Downs came up to Hartack's horse, a blaze-faced colt named Venetian Way. The guy took the horse by the bit, let him prance for a moment, then led him into stall number nine of the starting gate so they could begin the Kentucky Derby.

When the 14 horses all were locked into the gate, they slammed nervously into the tin sides and fronts of the stalls and the jockeys were calling "Not yet" and "No chance, boss" to the starter and there was a lot of noise and tension. Then the bell rang and the gate clacked open and, with riders yelping, the horses came out. Each made a leap first, because a race horse always is surprised to see the ground when the gate opens and he jumps at it. Then the horses started to run with the long, beautiful stride of a thoroughbred and there was a roar from the big crowd.

Hartack pushed Venetian Way into fourth, then took a snug hold on the reins. His horse was full of run, but Hartack wanted to keep him fourth, just off the leaders, and he stayed there until they were running down the backstretch. Then it turned into no contest. Bally Ache, one of the favorites, was leading. But not by enough. Tompion, the top choice, was in third position but he was creaking. On the final turn, Hartack let his horse out. Venetian Way made a big move and simply ran past Bally Ache as they swung by the five-sixteenth pole and headed into the long stretch.

With the thousands of people screaming from the three-decked stands, Venetian Way began widening the space. Hartack seemed to become frantic as his horse took over the race.

He was whipping with his left hand and rolling from side to side in the saddle, the way the book says a jockey should not ride but the way Hartack always does. At the eight-pole Venetian Way had four lengths and Hartack was a wild, all-out jock giving the horse the kind of ride you must have when the purse is $160,000. Venetian Way won big.

After the winner's circle ceremonies, Hartack came into the crowded jockeys' room. At Churchill Downs, everything is a rotting, soot-covered mess and the jocks' room isn't much better. It is cluttered and steamy and, at this moment, was mobbed with reporters. It didn't look like much of a place, but it always has been one of the great sights in a jockey's life. You love everything when you win a Derby and it is all one big thrill of money.

But Hartack came into the room with that quick, long stride of his and his brown eyes flashed. He gave the reporters a dark look and said nothing as he went to his locker. He was obviously about to make a scene. There was no sense trying to relate him to a shack in Pennsylvania now.

The explosion came the moment the first newsman opened his mouth. "Willie," he began, "when did you think you had the race won?"

"Jeeez!" Hartack snapped. "Don't call me Willie. That's disrespectful. The name is Bill. And *that* is a stupid question. I stopped answering that one 40 years ago. When you ask me an intelligent question I'll answer you."

People are encountered in all walks of life with a chip on their shoulder because of harsh backgrounds. But you would have to be born of Murder, Inc. to be this angry after winning a Kentucky Derby.

For those who did not walk out on this blast, Hartack had

a short description of the race, along with his usual course in journalism for those present. Reporters, he said, misquote him. And, he made it clear, newspapermen bother him. In fact, he didn't want to be bothered by anything except riding. Then he left to ride a horse in the eighth race. He finished second and was even madder after that. *To hell with everything, Hartack says, except getting home first on a horse.*

Winning horse races is something he can do. He has had two winners and a second in four Kentucky Derby rides. He won a Belmont Stakes, a Preakness, two Florida Derbys, the Flamingo, the Woodward, Arlington Classic. He has won virtually every major race the sport has and you can tap out that this is going to be the story for years to come. Just as big as the story they will go on making out of Hartack's behavior. For this is a kid who simply will not bend. It is either his way or you can go home, and most people don't like his way.

Two days after the Kentucky Derby, Hartack was sitting in the coffee shop of the Bo-Bet Motel, which is a short distance away from the Garden State Race Track in Camden, New Jersey. He had on a black sports jacket and gray slacks and a crisp white shirt which was open at the collar. He is 27, but he looks younger because he is only 5 feet, 4 inches and weighs 114 pounds. But when he toyed with the cup of coffee in front of him and started to talk you could see this was no little kid who could be moved around easily. And the guys at the table with him—Felix Bocchicchio, the old fight manager who owns the motel, Scratch Sheet Pestano, the jockey's agent, and a couple of newspapermen—did all the listening.

"There's only one thing that counts," Hartack was saying. "Words don't mean anything. They can misquote me all they want or write something bad about me, but the only thing that counts is the chart of last Saturday's race. It says Venetian Way, number one. It don't say nothing else. And nobody can change it. Everything else, they can have. The only thing I'm accountable for in this business is the race I ride. I have to stand up for the owner of the horse, the trainer, and the people who bet on him. And I have to see another jock doesn't get hurt because of me. I don't have to worry about anything else. And I wish they wouldn't worry about me. Everybody is trying to run my life so hard they haven't got time to run their own."

He jammed a filter-tip cigarette between his teeth and started to light it. His speech was over. And he had left very little room for rebuttal. No matter what he was like, he had just brought home a 6–1 shot in the biggest race in America, and you had no argument.

You rarely do. Six weeks later, he came out of the gate in the Belmont Stakes aboard an 8–1 shot named Celtic Ash and for a half-mile he held Celtic Ash back ten lengths off the leaders. That was how he had been told to ride the late-running horse and Hartack followed instructions to the stride. First money was $96,785 and Hartack would get 10 per cent of it, but this didn't cause him to get jumpy and move up his horse too early, as nearly all of them do. He just sat there, way out of it. It took strong nerves. At the half-mile pole he moved to the outside to get a clear path in front of him. Going into the last big turn, he finally let Celtic Ash out. Then he started to slam and kick and push at the horse and it all worked out. Hartack came into the stretch with a live horse under him and won by five and a half lengths over Venetian Way—with whom Hartack had parted company after the Preakness because of a disagreement with the trainer. It's hard to argue against winners that pay 8–1.

Vic Sovinski, Venetian Way's trainer, found this out. He is a big ex-baker from Kankakee, Illinois, who has been accused of training a horse as if he were slapping together a tray of prune Danish. At Louisville, before the Derby, Sovinski was around knocking Hartack's brains out over the way Bill had ridden the horse in a warm-up race the week before. Sovinski wanted the horse worked out an extra two furlongs after the finish. Hartack, who found the muddy going was bothering the horse, didn't push Venetian Way during the work. Sovinski said he loafed. Hartack thought he had saved the horse from being senselessly worn out. The press, always receptive to knocks on Hartack, trumpeted Sovinski's views. The Derby, of course, took care of that argument.

But after Venetian Way ran a poor fifth in the Preakness, Sovinski blew up again and yanked Hartack off him. The jockey promptly jumped on Celtic Ash. Then he explained the case of Venetian Way.

"Horses reach a peak, then they need a layoff," he said after the Preakness. "Venetian Way needed a freshener. He didn't get it. So he ran two races back in the pack. Then he was up again and ran second in the Belmont. Was I glad to beat him in the Belmont? What do I care? I don't have time to worry about particular horses I beat. I just want to beat them all."

In the Venetian Way case, Hartack was mostly silent for one of the few times in his career. This was because there was a steady stream of talk around the tracks that Venetian Way had been a sore-footed horse and only an analgesic called butazolidin had soothed him at Churchill Downs. It was ruled illegal at the Preakness and elsewhere. Hartack did not care to get into any discussion of this.

But in just about every other storm to come up during his career, he has been in there saying exactly what was on his mind. Because of this, people constantly compare him to baseball's Ted Williams. This is an untrue comparison. Williams is nasty in general only to sports writers and spectators. When stacked against Hartack's style, this is like hating Russia. Anybody can do it.

Hartack goes all the way. He takes on anybody, from a groom to a steward or an owner of horses or a track itself and if he thinks he is right you can throw in Eisenhower, too, because while he can be tough and unmannerly and anything else they say about him he is not afraid.

He is a little package of nerves who has been suspended for using abusive language to stewards, for fighting with another jockey, for leaving the track and not finishing his day's riding because he lost a photo finish. He snaps at writers, agents, owners, or anybody else in sight. The people who have anything good to say about him are few.

But nobody ever can say Hartack doesn't try. When he rides a race horse, he is going to do one thing. He is going to get down flat on his belly and slash whip streaks into the horse's side and try to get home first. Which is all anybody could want from a jockey.

But even those few people who have a good relationship with him will tell you that he is no fun when he loses. He is unbearable, no matter who is around. Since jockeys lose more often than they win, meetings with Hartack are on a catch-it-right basis. Most people don't like him because of this. But if there is anybody in sports who can afford to act this way, it is Hartack. He comes honest.

"Bill can walk on any part of a race track," Chick Lang, who used to be his agent, said one day last summer, "and he doesn't have to duck anybody. He can look everybody in the eye. There is nobody, no place, who can come up with a story on him about larceny or betting or something like that. How many can you say that about?"

Lang was extolling the rider while having a drink at a bar near Pimlico Race Track, where he now is employed. After six years of doing business with Hartack and taking down $50,000 a year for it, Lang found even the money couldn't soothe his nerves any more.

"It became just one big squabble," Lang said. "Bill would be fighting with me, then with an owner or a newspaperman or a trainer and it just got to be too much for both of us. He acts unhappy all the time. He acts as if he hates everything about what he's doing. I don't know what it is."

This drive, which makes Hartack a person who wants to win so badly he upsets you, comes from classic reasons. A boyhood in a Pennsylvania coal town during the depression does not make you easygoing and philosophical about life. For a year and a half the family lived on the 50-cents-a-day credit at the company store which Bill's father earned by digging soft coal. For 50 cents a day, you lived on potatoes.

On December 13, 1940, Hartack's mother, father, and year-old sister Maxine got into a battered car his father had borrowed so he could make the 30-mile drive to the mine company office where he was to be paid. By this time, miners were being paid money instead of potatoes. On the way, a trailer truck slammed into the car, throwing it down a hill. Bill's father was in the hospital for ten weeks. Maxine, the baby, had to stay for a year. Bill's mother died on Christmas morning. He and his sister Florence, who was six then, were taken care of by neighbors. It was not a good day for a kid.

"I barely remember it," Hartack says. But you figure he carries it with him someplace, whether he knows it or not.

A year later, the Hartacks' shack caught fire and the four of them barely escaped the flames. They moved in with some other people while his father built a new house.

With his father working the long hours of a miner, Hartack took over the job of raising his two sisters. He saw they were up in the morning and had breakfast and made school. At night he cooked dinner for the family. As for himself, school in Black Lick Township was rough; Bill was small and the other kids, big-necked sons of miners, beat hell out of him.

So Hartack took it out on schoolbooks. He was valedictorian of his high-school class.

When he graduated, at 18, Bill was thinking about an office job in Johnstown. Anything but the mines. When the office job didn't materialize, Hartack's father spoke to Andy Bruno, a friend who was a jockeys' agent. Bruno agreed to get Bill a job with horses. Hartack gave his son a dollar and let him drive away with Bruno to the Charlestown, West Virginia, track. Hartack picked up horses quickly. After he rode that first winner, he never stopped.

With this background, you'd think, it would be impossible for Hartack to miss. He had all the hunger and sorrow and hardness a kid ever would need to drive him to the top. It is the standard formula for successful athletes. But there have been fighters who have come out of the slums and they quit when you come into them and there are jockeys who had hunger and should be all out, but when it gets tough they shy away from the rail and take the easy way home.

Hartack, when he first came to the track, brought more than hunger with him. You can find that out by talking to his father. Bill Hartack, Sr., is a slight man with close-cropped brown hair which has only a little gray in it, a thin mustache, and a slight European accent. He was asked if Bill's early years were what made him so tough when he loses.

"Part of it," his father said, "but not all. I see him today how he acts and I don't say anything because he's just the same as I was. When I worked it was piece work. You got paid for the amount of coal you loaded. I set a record for soft coal that lasted until they brought in machines. I worked from when the sun came up to when the sun came down. And even when I was getting only that 50 cents a day for food I worked like that. I'd come to work with only some water in my lunch pail, not even a piece of bread, but I couldn't let anybody dig more coal than me. Once, another fella dug more than me during a week. I was so mad that when I went home I couldn't sleep nights. I couldn't wait to get back and dig more coal than him. It had me crazy. You couldn't talk to me."

"The boy is just like him," Bocchicchio said. "When he first came to stay with me here, I'm looking for him one day. It's a Sunday. He ain't been out of his room for dinner the night before and now breakfast and lunch has gone by and I don't see him. It's getting dark and I'm worried. I go over to his room and knock on the door and he let me in. He was still in bed. He don't want to talk. So I leave him alone. But I get right on the phone with Bill here and I ask him what he wants me to do. He says, 'Did he have any winners yesterday?' I says no. So he laughs. 'He'll be all right in time for the track,' he tells me. That's what this kid is like. If he don't win, you can't talk to him."

"When I was young," Mr. Hartack said, "I had a terrible temper. I fight. In the mines I argue with anybody. But you find when you get older, you mellow and you're not so mad any more. Bill will be like that. It will take a little while, but he'll mellow. But he'll still want to win. That he'll never get over."

This win-or-shoot-yourself attitude of Hartack's comes out, during a race, in the form of a rail-brushing, whip-slamming kid who will take any chance on a horse to win. Regarded on form alone, Hartack seems to be a poor rider. The secret of being a jockey is to keep a good-looking seat on a horse. Hartack, on the other hand, does it all wrong. He rolls from side to side in such a pronounced manner that even an amateur from the stands can see it.

"The form doesn't look classic," Jimmy Jones of Calumet tells you, "but it really doesn't matter none, because he has a way of making horses run for him. And that's what the business is."

Horses ran for Hartack from the start. When Bill came to Charlestown, Bruno, the agent friend of his father's, turned him over to trainer Junie Corbin, a verteran trainer on the small, half-mile track circuit. Hartack had no particular interest in becoming a jockey when he arrived, but under Corbin he learned the business.

On October 10, 1952, with just two races behind him, he held onto a horse named Nickleby for dear life and came home on top to pay $18.40 at Waterford Park, West Virginia. Since then, he has never stopped. By 1954 he was one of the top jockeys on the half-mile circuit. A year later Corbin ran into trouble with his stable—a groom had given caffein to a horse. When Corbin was suspended for this, his bankroll couldn't take the layover. So he sold Hartack's contract for $15,000 to the big Ada L. Rice Stable. Chick Lang was in the picture as agent now and at the first opportunity, a year and a half later, he and Hartack went free-lance, meaning they could take whatever mounts were open. Calumet Farm asked for a first call on Hartack—and got it because of the horse-flesh they were putting under Bill's rear end each day.

From then on he made it big. In 1957 his horses won a total of $3,331,257 in purses. This is a record for a jockey. He also won 43 stakes, which topped a mark set by Eddie Arcaro. As a rider he is in a special little class with Arcaro and Willie Shoemaker. And in three of the last six years Hartack has been off by himself as national riding champion.

He has taken his father out of the mines and put him on a farm he bought at Charlestown, West Virginia. He has his younger sister in college. And life for him has become a series of new hi-fi sets, a different date whenever he picks up a phone, plenty of money—and live horses.

Hartack, like most people who don't have to live with women, is not against them. "There must be 150 girls around Miami I can call up for dates," he says. The situation is similar in Louisville or Oceanport, New Jersey, or wherever else he rides for a living. But it is strictly on a spur-of-the-moment basis. Riding horses and winning on them is basically his whole life.

Money or acclaim never will change his attitude. A look at him in his own surroundings shows this. One warm Tuesday morning last February, for example, Hartack stepped out of his $50,000 brick-and-redwood ranch house in Miami Springs and walked across the lawn to a beige, spoke-wheeled Cadillac which was in the driveway. He keeps the car outside because the big garage has been turned into a closet to hold his 150 suits.

It was 11:45 A.M. when Hartack pulled away from the house and started for Hialeah. The street was lined with palm trees and expensive houses. Sprinklers played on the lawns and the sun glinted on the wet grass. Hartack was fresh-eyed. He had slept for 11 hours and when Paul Foley, a guy who stays with him, woke him up, Bill took a shower, swallowed orange juice and coffee, and left for the job of riding horses. For the last five years he has been going to his business like this and making anywhere from $150,000 to $200,000 a year. For anybody who ever has had to go to work hours earlier each morning, packed into a train with nervous, bleak-faced commuters who spend most of their time at home two-stepping with bill collectors, Hartack's way of life is the kind of thing you would steal for.

Hartack didn't talk as he drove to the track. He was thinking about the horses he would ride that day. At night, he reads the *Racing Form* and carefully goes over every horse in each race and as he does this he tries to remember their habits. One will swing wide on a turn, he will tell himself, so if he gets a chance he will stay behind that one and then move inside him on the turn. This reading and remembering is something a jockey must do or he isn't worth a quarter Hartack, as he drove to the track, ran over the horses in his mind. He was mute as he pulled the car into the officials' lot at the track. His face was solemn as he walked through the gate and into the jockeys' room. Inside, he undressed, put on a white T-shirt and whipcord riding pants, then sat quietly while a valet tugged on his riding boots. The other jockeys paid no attention to him except for a nod here and there and Hartack returned it. Then he took out the program and the *Racing Form* and began to look at them again.

"How do you feel?" a guy asked him.

"Terrible," he said. "My stomach bothers me. It always bothers me." He kept reading the paper. It was the best you ever will get in the way of conversation when Hartack is on a track.

Outside, Chick Lang was standing on the gravel walk in front of the racing secretary's office. He was shaking his head. Lang is a heavy, round-faced, blond-haired guy of 32. He had been at the barns at 5:45 A.M. talking to trainers and owners and making deals with them for Hartack to ride their mounts.

"I don't know whether life is worth all this," Lang was saying. "You saw how he was today? Concentrating, serious. Nobody allowed to talk. That's fine. It's the way he wants it and that's the way it should be. But what about other people? Don't you think he should give them something, too? Last week, on Wednesday, he went to the coast to ride Amerigo in the San Juan Capistrano Handicap.

"Before he left we talked and decided that he wouldn't take any mounts here until Monday. That was yesterday. So I went out and booked him on seven horses. What happens? Sunday night he calls me from Las Vegas. 'I can't get a plane out of here,' he said.

"Well, you've been to Vegas. They run planes out of there like they were streetcars. But that's what he tells me. Now I've go to get on the phone and start trying to find trainers and tell them Hartack can't ride the next day. It embarrasses hell out of me. Here I make commitments and then I have to break them. It's terrible."

Trouble is something Hartack will take—or he will make—and he doesn't care about it. And while carrying around this winning-is-all-that-matters attitude he has had plenty of jams.

The business of newspapermen, for example. Hartack has one of the worst relationships any athlete ever has had with newspapers and he is not about to improve it.

Now many people do not like sports writers, particularly the wives of sports writers, and in many athletic circles it is considered a common, decent hatred for a person to have. But most sports writers whom Hartack dislikes couldn't care less. And, the notion is, neither does the reading public. Ofttimes, the public is having enough trouble deciphering what sports writers write without having to take on the additional burden of remembering that there is a feud between Hartack and the press box. But it is important to Hartack that he does not like the writers. And they put in the papers that his name is "Willie" and he blows up at them.

Hartack has troubles with officials, too, and these cost him. Suspensions dot his career. Last year, for example, he snarled at Garden State stewards—they insisted he cursed—and was set down for the remainder of the meeting. In 1958 he was set down for 15 days by Atlantic City stewards when he was first under the wire on a horse called Nitrophy. But Jimmy Johnson, who finished second on Tote All, lodged a foul claim against Hartack, saying his horse had been interfered with. The stewards allowed the claim and took down Hartack's horse. Hartack tried to take down Johnson with a left hand in the jocks' room. For his troubles both on the track and off it, Bill was given 15 days. In the last two years, Bill has been set down to a total of 61 days. And he has been fined and reprimanded several times. At Hialeah in February he lost a photo with a horse called Cozy Ada and after it he was in a rage. "What do I have to do to get a shake here?" he snapped, walking out on the rest of his riding commitments. He was fined $100 for this. This is a kid who simply cannot stand losing, even to a camera.

His temperament does not make him a hero with the other jockeys. There was a night last summer in the bar of the International Hotel, which is at New York's Idlewild Airport, and Willie Shoemaker and Sammy Boulmetis and some other horse guys were sitting around over a drink and Hartack's name was mentioned.

"I can't figure him out," Boulmetis was saying. "One day he seems nice to you. Next day he won't even talk to you."

Walter Blum, another rider, had an opinion, too. "You know," he said, "you can't live with him. He just wants to make you hate him. I mean, he really works at it."

Through all this, Hartack's outlook has been the same. "I do my job," he says. "I do what I think best. If I make a mistake, that's that. But the only place a mistake shows is the official chart of a race. If I didn't win, that's a mistake. Nothing else counts. Not you or anybody else. Only that result."

To get down and wrestle with the truth, Hartack's attitude is, on many occasions, the only right one in racing.

Take, for example, the warm afternoon in February of 1959 at Hialeah when Hartack started jogging a horse called Greek Circle to the starting gate. To Hartack, the parade to the post is all-important. He gets the feel of his mount by tugging on one rein, then the other, and watching the horse's reaction. He tries to find out if the horse is favoring one foot or another or likes to be held tightly or with a normal pressure on the bit. Greek Circle responded to nothing. The horse seemed to have no coordination at all and that was enough for Hartack.

"My horse isn't right," he yelled to the starter. "He can't coordinate himself. He's almost falling down right now. I'm getting off him."

The starter called for a veterinarian and Hartack jogged the horse for the vet, Dr. George Barksdale.

"The horse is fine," Dr. Barksdale said. "Take him into the gate. He'll run fine."

Hartack's answer was simple. He stopped the horse and swung his fanny off him and dropped to the ground. The veterinarian shrugged. Across the way, in the stands, they were adding up figures and a neat little sum of $5,443.56 had been set aside as the track's share of the $136,089 bet on Greek Circle. Because the next race, the Widener, was on television and time was a problem now, the track stewards had to order the horse scratched and the money bet on him returned.

They knocked Hartack's brains out on this one. He was in headlines across the nation the next day as a little grandstander who should have been suspended for his actions.

But when the smoke cleared and you could think about it objectively, you could see who was wrong. Eddie Arcaro, over many glasses of a thing called Blue Sunoco in the Miami Airport bar a week later, talked about it. "Nobody in his right mind, the vet included, could knock Hartack for that. Do you know how many jocks have been killed because they were on broken-down horses? And they tell me this horse has been sore all year. Bad sore, too. Hartack was right. It took a little guts, too."

Then on May 16, 1959, Hartack was aboard Vegeo at Garden State and as he got into the gate, the horse was nervous and reared up and Bill yelled to Cecil Phillips, the starter, that he wasn't ready to go. Phillips' answer was to press the sticks of wood in his hand together and they completed the electric circuit which made the gate open and the race start. Hartack's horse was rearing in the air and by the time he got him straightened out the field was up the track and the race was lost.

Hartack went to the track stewards with this complaint. Now Hartack coming off a loser is bad enough. But a Hartack coming off a loser that he felt is somebody else's fault is really something. This is a Khrushchev who rides horses. He called the stewards and snapped at them. Their version was that he cursed. They set him down for the remainder of the meeting.

"I get in trouble because of these things," Hartack tells you. "But I'm never going to stop because I'm right. I'm doing it honestly. The only reason I get my name around is that I'm the only one who does it. When I have a horse under me that's broken down, I won't ride him. And if the starter blows my chances in a race, I yell about it. It doesn't just happen to me. It happens to everybody else. But the rest of these riders are afraid to say anything about it. They get on a horse that's broken down and they keep quiet. Then they give him an easy ride, so they won't take any chances of getting hurt, and when they come back they give some ridiculous excuse to satisfy the trainer. You know, 'The horse lugged in' or 'he propped on me' or 'he tried to get out on me.' In the meantime, the public has bet its money on the horse and they didn't get a fair shake. But the jocks feel you won't have to make an excuse to them. They don't count. Well, I look on it differently. I owe loyalty to anybody who bets on my horse. The person who does that is going to get the best I can give him. Nothing is going to stop me from doing that."

If you have been around Hartack on race tracks, and watched him as he tries to win, you would know how far he is willing to carry his fight. Like the dark, rain-flecked Saturday in Louisville in 1958.

The driver moved his ambulance slowly through the filth of Churchill Downs' grandstand betting area and he had his hand on the horn to make people get out of the way as he headed for the gate.

Hartack was on a stretcher in the back of the ambulance. He had a wooden ice-cream spoon stuck between his teeth so when the pain hit him he could bite into it. The stick doesn't help take pain away, but you do not bite your lip when pain comes if you have a stick between your teeth, so Hartack could grimace and tighten his teeth on the wood each time the ambulance hit a bump.

His body was covered with mud and his left leg was propped on a pillow. He looked tiny and helpless, the way jockeys always do when they are hurt. A few minutes before, a two-year-old filly named Quail Egg had become frightened in the starting gate and she flipped Hartack. As he rolled around in the mud under the horse, Quail Egg started to thrash at the ground with her hoofs. Then the horse fell heavily on Hartack and a bone in his leg snapped.

As the ambulance moved into a main street, where it was smoother riding. Hartack put the stick to the side of his mouth and muttered some words to Chick Lang.

"Nothing heavy on this leg," he said. "Don't let him put a

heavy cast on this leg, Chick. We got to ride that horse next week."

The Kentucky Derby was to be run on the next Saturday and Hartack was contracted to ride Tim Tam. Now he was flattened out on a stretcher in an ambulance and his leg was broken, but he still was talking about riding the horse.

Then he called a company in Chicago which makes special braces. "I want a real light one. Aluminum," he told them. "Make it special. It has to go inside a riding boot. I need it by Wednesday."

"He won't listen to me," the staff doctor from the hospital in Louisville said quietly. "The fibula is snapped and there are some ripped ligaments around it. That leg will need a long time."

It did. Hartack was out for six weeks. But if you had seen him with a stick in his mouth and pain waving through his body and heard him talking about trying to ride a horse, then you had to say that he is a kid with something to him.

Every time Hartack has been hurt he has been like this. On July 10, 1957, he was moving around the last turn at Arlington Park on a horse called Smoke-Me-Now. The one in front, Spy Boss, had been running steadily, but he became tired and started to fall apart all at once and Smoke-Me-Now ran up his heels. With a thoroughbred horse in full motion, it only takes the slightest flick against his ankles to cause a spill. This time Smoke-Me-Now caught it good and he went down in a crash. Hartack was tossed into the air. His little body flipped in a somersault and he landed on his back. Nobody would pick him up until an ambulance came.

They took him to a hospital in Elgin, Illinois, and the doctors said Hartack had a badly sprained back and muscles were torn and he'd be out for a couple of weeks at a minimum. This was on a Thursday. On Saturday, Hartack was scheduled to ride Iron Liege, for the Calumet Farm, in the $100,000 Arlington Classic. Hartack likes $100,000 races.

At eight o'clock Friday night, Dogwagon, who is an exercise boy for Calumet, was sitting in a camp chair in front of the barn at Arlington Park and a guy came over and asked who was riding a stable pony around the area at this time of night.

"That is Mr. Bill Hartack," Dogwagon said. "Mr. Bill Hartack has a fine feeling for money and right now he is teaching his back to feel the same way. He strapped up like he was a fat ole woman trying to keep the rolls in. But he goin' be ridin' Iron Liege tomorrow and he'll be therebouts when they pass out the money, too."

Hartack was jogging back and forth across the stable area on a painted pony. He came back to the barn, after 45 minutes of this. He hopped off and went to a phone to tell Calumet's Jimmy Jones that he could ride the next day. He was beat a nose on Iron Liege and he went into a rage because he lost the race.

In the tack room, somebody passed by and said, "You did a wonderful job getting second. I mean, you're lucky you can walk, much less ride."

"I don't care if I have one leg," Hartack snapped. "That's no excuse. I wanted to win the race."

Which is the whole game with Hartack. There isn't a thing in the world you can say is wrong with him except he cannot stand to lose. And he does not think anything else in the world matters except not losing.

Last June, for example, Hartack was at Monmouth Park

and was due in New York to see Floyd Patterson fight Ingemar Johanson. Scratch Sheet Pestano, his agent, was at the bar in Jack Dempsey's Restaurant on Broadway, Hartack's ringside seats in his pocket.

"You meeting Hartack?" somebody asked him.

"When I get the race results, I'll let you know," Pestano said.

He went into a phone booth and called a newspaper office for the day's results at Monmouth. Hartack was on seven horses. As Pestano listened to the guy on the other end, his face became longer. He came out of the phone booth with the tickets in his hand.

"You meet him and give them to him," he told somebody with him. "He lost on seven horses today. Every one of them should have been up there. He won't be fit to live with tonight. I'm going home. I don't want to be anywhere near him. He just can't stand losing."

Mr. Harry (Champ) Segal, dean of Broadway horse players, was listening to the conversation.

"If all them jockeys was like that maybe you could cash a bet now and then," the Champ said.

Which is what everybody has to say about Hartack, whether they care for him or not.

GEORGE PLIMPTON

# from *The Bogey Man*

MY WOES IN GOLF, I have felt, have been largely psychological. When I am playing well, in the low 90's (my handicap is 18), I am still plagued with small quirks—a suspicion that, for example, just as I begin my downswing, my eyes straining with concentration, a bug or a beetle is going to suddenly materialize on the golf ball.

When I am playing badly, far more massive speculation occurs: I often sense as I commit myself to a golf swing that my body changes its corporeal status completely and becomes a *mechanical* entity, built of tubes and conduits, and boiler rooms here and there, with big dials and gauges to check, a Brobdingnagian structure put together by a team of brilliant engineers but manned largely by a dispirited, eccentric group of dissolutes—men with drinking problems, who do not see very well, and who are plagued by liver complaints.

The structure they work in is enormous. I see myself as a monstrous, manned colossus poised high over the golf ball, a spheroid that is barely discernible 14 stories down on its tee. From above, staring through the windows of the eyes, which bulge like great bay porches, is an unsteady group (as

I see them) of Japanese navymen—admirals, most of them. In their hands they hold ancient and useless voice tubes into which they yell the familiar orders: "Eye on the ball! Chin steady! Left arm stiff! Flex the knees! Swing from the inside out! Follow through! Keep head down!" Since the voice tubes are useless, the cries drift down the long corridors and shaftways between the iron tendons and muscles, and echo into vacant chambers and out, until finally, as a burble of sound, they reach the control centers. These posts are situated at the joints, and in charge are the dissolutes I mentioned— typical of them a cantankerous elder perched on a metal stool, half a bottle of rye on the floor beside him, his ear cocked for the orders that he acknowledges with ancient epithets, yelling back up the corridors, "Ah, your father's mustache!" and such things, and if he's of a mind, he'll reach for the controls (like the banks of tall levers one remembers from a railroad-yard switch house) and perhaps he'll pull the proper lever and perhaps not. So that, in sum, the whole apparatus, bent on hitting a golf ball smartly, tips and convolutes and lunges, the Japanese admirals clutching each other for support in the main control center up in the head as the structure rocks and creaks. And when the golf shot is on its way the navymen get to their feet and peer out through the eyes and report: "A shank! A shank! My God, we've hit another shank!" They stir about in the control center drinking paper-thin cups of rice wine, consoling themselves, and every once in a while one of them will reach for a voice tube and shout:

"Smarten up down there!"

Down below, in the dark reaches of the structure, the dissolutes reach for their rye, tittering, and they've got their feet up on the levers and perhaps soon it will be time to read the evening newspaper.

It was a discouraging image to carry around in one's mind; but I had an interesting notion: a month on the professional golf tour (I had been invited to three tournaments), competing steadily and under tournament conditions before crowds and under the scrutiny of the pros with whom I would be playing, might result in 5, perhaps even 6, strokes being pruned from my 18 handicap. An overhaul would result. My Japanese admirals would be politely asked to leave, and they would, bowing and smiling. The dissolutes would be removed from the control centers, grumbling, clutching their bottles of rye, many of them evicted bodily, being carried out in their chairs.

The replacements would appear—a squad of scientific blokes dressed in white smocks. Not too many of them. But a great tonnage of equipment would arrive with them—automatic equipment in gray-green boxes and computer devices that would be placed about and plugged in and set to clicking and whirring. The great structure would become almost entirely automatized. Life in the control center would change—boring, really, with the scientists looking out on the golf course at the ball and then twiddling with dials and working out estimations, wind resistance, and such things, and finally locking everything into the big computers; and with yawns working at the corners of their mouths because it was all so simple, they would push the "activate" buttons to generate the smooth motion in the great structure that would whip the golf ball out toward the distant green far and true. Very dull and predictable. The scientists would scarcely find very much to say to each other after a shot. Per-

haps "Y-e-s," very drawn out. "Y-e-s. Very nice." Occasionally
someone down in the innards of the structure would appear
down the long glistening corridors with an oil can, or perhaps
with some brass polish to sparkle up the pipes.

That was the vision I had. I began the overhaul myself. I
would obviously have to look the part. A month before I left
on the tour, I outfitted myself completely and expensively
with new golf equipment. I had played golf since I began
(which was when I was twelve or so) with a white cloth golf
bag that bore the trade name "Canvasback" for some reason;
if the clubs were removed it collapsed on itself like an accor-
dion, or like a pair of trousers being stepped out of. It was
light as a feather, and caddies always looked jaunty and super-
cilious under its weight. I often carried it myself. It had a
small pocket with room for three balls and some tees. It had
eight clubs in it, perhaps nine—two woods and a putter and
the rest, of course, irons with two or three missing—an outfit
hardly suitable for tournament play.

So I bought the works. Clubs and a new bag. Sweaters.
Argyll socks. A small plastic bag of gold golf tees. I bought
some gold shoes with flaps that came down over the laces—
my first pair; I had always used sneakers. The golf bag was
enormous. It seemed a dull conservative color when I saw it
in the late afternoon gloom of a Florida golf shop. But when
I took it out on practice round the next day, it glowed a rich
oxblood color, like a vast sausage. It was very heavy with a
metal bottom with brass studs around it, and when I first
went out I felt guilty seeing it on a caddy's back. But the
clubs let off a fine chinking sound as the bag was carried, as
expensive and exclusive as the sound of a Cadillac door shut-
ting to, and the fact that porters, caddies, and I myself, who-

ever carried it, were bent nearly double by its weight only seemed to add to its stature.

It was proper to have such an enormous bag. I thought of the caddies coming up the long hills of the Congressional on television, wearing the white coveralls with the numbers, and those huge bags—MacGregors, Haigs or Wilsons, with the pros' names stamped down the front—with the wiping towels dangling, and the bags nearly slantwise across their shoulders, with one hand back to steady it so the weight would be more properly distributed.

Still, I never really got accustomed to my great golf bag. The woods had brown woolen covers on them. In my early practice rounds in the East I used to follow the clubs at quite a distance, and off to one side, as they were carried down the fairway, as one might circle at a distance workmen moving a harpsichord into one's home—self-conscious and a little embarrassed.

I was particularly aware of the big bag on trips—particularly lugging it around in a railroad station or an air terminal, where intense men with briefcases hurry past, and there are tearful farewell going on, and melancholy groups of military people stand around with plastic name tags on their tunics to tell us who they are. A golf bag is such an immense symbol of frivolity in these parlous times, so much bigger than a tennis racket. When I arrived in Los Angeles by plane to head upstate for the Crosby tournament, the terminal seemed filled with soldiers. There had been many on my plane. At the baggage claim counter the gray-green military duffel bags began coming down the conveyor belt, one after another, and the soldiers would heft them off and set them to one side in a great mound. My golf bag appeared among them with its rich oxblood glow, obscene, jingling slightly as it came toward me on the conveyor.

A porter gave me a hand with it. We got it outside to the traffic ramp with the rest of my luggage and he waited while I arranged to rent a car for the long ride up to Monterey.

"You must be going up to the tournament," the porter said.

"Why, yes," I said gratefully. "The Crosby."

"George Knudson just came through a while ago," he said. "And George Archer. Always tell him 'cause he's, man, *tall.*"

"That's right," I said. "He's as tall as they come."

He hefted the bag into the trunk of the car.

"They set you up with a new bag, I see."

The bag was so new that a strong odor drifted from it—a tang of furniture polish.

"A great big one," I said. "They're getting bigger, it seems."

I fished in my pocket for a tip.

"Well, good luck up there," he said. He wanted me to tell him my name, some name he would recognize from the tour so he could announce to them back in the terminal, "Well, you know, So-and-so just came through . . . on his way up to the Crosby."

"I guess I just head *north,*" I said. I waved an arm, and stepped into the car.

"Yes, that's where it is. Up the coast." He smiled. "Well, good luck," he said. "I play to a 5 myself."

"No kidding?" I said.

"Well, that's nothing compared to you guys. I play out on the municipal course. And at Ramble Beach."

"A 5 handicap is nothing to be sneezed at," I said.

"I wish it was a 4," he said.

"Sure," I said. "Well . . ." I tried hard to think of an appropriate golf term.

"Well, *pop it*," I said.

He looked startled.

"I mean really *pop* it out there."

A tentative smile of appreciation began to work at his features. I put the car in gear and started off. As I looked in the rear-view mirror I could see him staring after the car.

The final hours of the drive go through the high country of the Big Sur, the sea lying flat and unroiled to the west. It was calm and warm, which was welcome golfing weather, but unexpected; the vagaries of the weather during the Crosby are famous: in 1962 it snowed; in 1967 gale winds swept in from the sea and made the play of the ocean holes almost a senseless procedure—like a sort of lunatic golf played between the crews of fishing trawlers bobbing in a storm.

I stopped overnight and it was still easy weather by the early afternoon of the next day when I drove onto the scenic Seventeen Mile Drive that winds along the edge of that pine-covered coastal country.

The Crosby is played on the three golf courses of the Monterey Peninsula—Cypress Point (which is a private club within a club, with only one hundred and fifty members); Pebble Beach, where the headquarters of the tournament are set up; and the Monterey Peninsula Country Club, which, while impressive enough, is the least spectacular of the courses and considered the easiest. (In the last year or so a public course named Spyglass Hill—to commemorate Treasure Island's hill and Robert Louis Stevenson, who lived nearby—has been completed and has displaced the Monterey Peninsula Country Club as the third leg of the Crosby.) All the courses are part of a development known as the Del Monte Properties, which was started in 1915 by Samuel Finley Brown Morse, the captain of the Yale 1906 football team and a grand-nephew of the telegraph inventor. I met him by chance years ago in his house in Monterey. I can remember the powerful presence of the man, and how odd it seemed that such a man of vigor lived in a home full of delicate Oriental art and compartmentalized by pale-yellow gauze-thin Japanese screens that were slid to and fro on metal runners, just barely audibly, by servants as we moved through the house. He was a very physical man. He thought nothing of ripping a telephone directory apart, and he often challenged his guests to a boxing match. When they demurred, he would groan, and he would say, "Well, all right, then, let's do some Indian wrestling."

He was an inventor in his own right, or at least of an inventive turn of mind: in 1931 he used the guano from the cormorant rocks in Carmel Bay to fertilize the golf courses—a misdirected plan which turned out to be almost fatal to the grass on the courses, but had the pleasant compensation that the more picturesque sea lions took over the rocks, newly cleansed, and would not let the birds back. There the seals remain, just offshore, making a honking, quite derisive sound —clearly audible to the golfers working the ocean holes.

I parked my car and went into the Del Monte Lodge to register. The place was crowded. People were checking in— the amateur contingent of golfers, I assumed, since all of them were keyed up, as if they'd been belting down drinks of Scotch. They seemed everywhere in the lobby, in their gaudy golfing outfits, back-slapping, and calling out to each other: "Hey, old buddy, been out on the track yet? Been out there myself and had a gorgeous round, absolutely gorgeous."

Bing Crosby was standing by the registration desk, very calm in that hubbub, smiling at people, and shaking hands. He was wearing a Scotch-plaid hat with an Alpine brush in the band; he had a very long thin-stemmed pipe in his mouth, which he would take out from time to time to speak his fancy brand of talk, as formal as a litany: "Ah, Brother So-and-so, the authorities inform me that you have ambulated across our fair acres and invited yourself a sizable 7 on the 8th. What transpired, Brother So-and-so? Did you happen to traffic with the cruel sea?"

Close by was Crosby's friend and lieutenant, Maurie Luxford, the man who actually runs the tournament. He has been doing it for twenty-one years. I went up and introduced myself, and we went off to a corner where it was quiet and he talked for a moment or so about his difficulties as a tournament director. In the months preceding he had received over 9,000 applications from those who wanted to play in Bing's tournament. There was only room for 168 amateurs, Luxford said, shaking his head; of that number Crosby had reserved about 120 places for his own friends whose names were from what Luxford referred to as "Crosby's Black Book"— Bing's golfing friends—and that left a maximum of 48 places for Luxford to fill from those thousands of applications stacked in the big cardboard containers in the corner of his office.

"It's quite a privilege," Luxford said. "You'd be surprised what people will do to get an invitation to the Crosby. I had a man come up to me in a country-club locker room and offer $20,000 in cash for an invitation. Very embarrassing."

I whistled in awe; I took the opportunity to thank Luxford for sending *me* an invitation. I had written Crosby a few months earlier saying that I hoped to do a series of articles on playing on the tour and how grateful I would be if he were to extend the privileges of his tournament.

"I hadn't realized *what* a privilege," I said. "What a temptation for the unprincipled—to trade off an invitation for some of that hard cash."

Luxford looked at me carefully.

"Oh, I'm who I say I am," I assured him.

"Well, I *hope* so," he said.

When I asked him how the tournament worked, he said that this was the twenty-fifth, the Silver Anniversary of the tournament—what Bing called his "clambake"—and that the proceeds (television fees, entry fees, and the rest of it) were to be split up among local charities.

"The pro-am event is one of the biggest sources of income for a golf tournament," Luxford said. "The entry fee here for the pro-am is $150. For some tournaments it's much more. It costs $1,000 to play in the pro-am of the Florida Citrus Open. So those guys down there are close to $150,000 before they *begin* thinking about income from ticket sales and television."

The Crosby is quite unlike any other pro-am tournament. Most tournaments have a pro-am event on the first day—each professional playing with three amateurs, who play to their handicaps, the foursome's best ball on each hole being recorded. In the Crosby each pro is paired with one amateur and the two play together as a team for the entire four-day event.

"Who's your partner?" Luxford asked.

"I don't know," I said.

"You better go to headquarters and check in."

On the way up to the tournament headquarters, I kept thinking about the television on the last day—my stomach tightening as I thought of being paired with a great professonal, which would mean a big gallery following, and someone carryng a sign with the team names on it, and the women sitting on the shooting sticks in rows ready to make clucking sounds if a shot was scraped along the ground.

"I don't suppose I have Hogan, or Palmer, or anyone like that," I said to the ladies behind the tables at headquarters.

"No," they said. "Mr. Hogan is not playing in the Crosby this year. Your partner is—" they looked it up on the pairing sheets—"Bob Bruno."

"Oh yes," I said.

"You're scheduled to go off with him at 10:10 tomorrow morning at the Monterey Peninsula Country Club. Manuel de la Torre is the other pro in your foursome and his amateur partner is Bill Henley."

They gave me Bruno's telephone number. He was staying at a small motel in Monterey. I called him and we talked briefly. He had finished his day's practice. He would meet me tomorrow on the first tee. I told him about my golf, my 18 handicap, and I said I hoped he wouldn't mind being saddled with such a thing. He sounded very pleasant. He said, No, that for "ham 'n' egging"—that is to say, combining in a good partnership—a player with a high handicap, if he got onto his game, could be tremendously useful.

Afterward I asked around about him. No one knew much except that he was tall. He turned out to be 6 feet 5½ inches tall, about the tallest professional on the tour—up there with George Archer and George Bayer. His best paydays had been a tenth at St. Paul in 1964, where he won $1,675, and a twelfth at Seattle that same year, for which he won $1,100.

Bruno's status as a golfer (and he would admit it, if ruefully) was in the lower echelons of the touring pros—in the category known as "rabbits." These were the golfers on the tour who were beginning their careers, or whose play was erratic or in the doldrums. They had to play in a qualifying tournament, usually held on a Monday, and fight it out among themselves for the available slots in the draw of the regular tournament. In the Los Angeles Open, for example, which preceded the Crosby, there had been about 20 open slots in the draw for which about 250 rabbits had been forced to compete. The PGA publishes a complete money list every year, which is uncomfortable reading down toward the end: Jim Hart made $11 in 1967; Reynolds Faber, Norman Rach and Arthur Jones each made $4; a golfer named Alex Antonio played in a number of tournaments, often making the Sunday cuts, yet he never won any money at all.

It is expensive to join the tour. Bruno told me later that $250 a week was a conservative figure, and when I looked startled he explained that the average entry fee for a tournament is $50; any motel room with a plain white bedspread and a window looking on the truck park in back is $50 to $60 a week; a caddy would look awfully sour if he didn't get $50 for a tournament's work; and then one had to set aside $8 to $10 a day to eat. That's $230-odd right there—not taking into consideration travel expenses, or a movie and a haircut from time to time. The PGA itself warns any golfer that he cannot expect to play the tour for less than $300 a week.

To make ends meet, most professionals starting their careers on the tour sell stock in themselves—half their winnings over a stipulated time, usually five years, perhaps ten. Backing a pro is a speculative risk, and assistance comes largely from club members or friends willing to help a young club pro without much hope of financial return.

In a sense I was relieved to be paired with Bruno—a relative unknown. It was bad luck for him, but at least the irregularities of my game would not be disturbing a truly great player, someone making a run for the tournament win.

After checking in I went around to the pro shop at Del Monte Lodge and inquired about getting a caddy for the tournament. Almost all the golfers, I was told, both professional and amateur, had already checked in, and most of the caddies had been assigned. There might be somebody left out back, they said.

I looked out there, and a somewhat elderly caddy got up off a bench and hurried up and introduced himself. Abe, his name was—a very small man encased in oversized clothes, an extra-long windbreaker over a worn dark sweater, the baggy pants of a top-banana comedian hanging loosely on him and making him look, from afar, like a waif. He had a dark wind-creased face and a rather gloomy set to his mouth.

He said, "You looking for someone to pack your bag?"

"Absolutely," I said.

He went on to say that I was lucky to get him. Abe wasn't just any old "bag-toter." He knew the Monterey courses from

twenty, maybe thirty years' experience and had "packed"
bags for some of the "great ones."

"Marty Furgol—packed for him," he said.

"Oh yes," I said.

"You ain't a pro?" he asked hopefully.

"I'm afraid not," I said.

"Who is your pro?"

"Bob Bruno."

"Who's he?"

"Well, for one thing he's just about the tallest pro on the
tour."

"Well, that's something," Abe said.

We went out that afternoon to get in as much of a practice
round as we could before darkness fell. We played the ocean
holes of Pebble Beach under a setting sun. Out in the sea
hundreds of whales were moving north, so that sometimes,
looking out, one could spot a dozen or so spouts at the same
time, a feather of spray, pink in the dying sun, and then the
distant dark roll of the body beneath.

Abe said as we walked along that he was originally a sea-
faring man. He had come west from Massachusetts, and he
had been with the sardine fleets out of Monterey in the days
when the schools were thick and lay out beyond the kelp
beds. He had become a furniture mover after that, caddying
when he had the time. In the evening, years before, when the
tides were right, he went down to the rocks and beaches
where the sea boiled in at the famous oceanside holes of
Pebble Beach and, equipped with a long pole and a sack, he
scraped around for lost balls, which he would then sell.

He told me that on a good day he would come up out of
the sea with his sack full-up with balls. This activity was not

quite legal because of the trespassing laws, so he would set out for home across the golf course with his coat buttoned and straining across the bulge of the sack. His odd notion was that the club officials, if they saw him out there, might take him for a pregnant woman out for a stroll in the twilight.

"They'd've had to be pretty nearsighted, Abe," I said, looking at him. We were waiting on the 6th for a pair in front of us. He was so short that he had to carry my golf bag slantwise on his back, like a soldier carrying a bazooka, and I noticed that the clubs often began to slide out as he walked. He smoked incessantly, never flicking at his cigarette, so that it developed long curved ashes that wavered and finally dropped whole to lie on the grass like gray cicada husks. He had a terrific smoker's cough and wheeze.

"What was the best day?" I asked.

"The top day I ever had on the beaches," he said, "was 350 balls. I dragged myself across the course *that* day."

"What would that day be worth to you?" I asked.

"In the golf shops I could count on getting 50 cents a ball if they weren't too sea-logged. Then the price was 20 cents."

The wait continued on the 6th. I asked Abe if he had ever played golf. He thought about it and said that in twenty-five years he had played three holes. In fact, he had played the last of the holes not more than two weeks before. I asked him how it had gone. He said that for someone just keeping his hand in, he wasn't so bad.

Abe said you didn't have to play golf to be a good caddy. You had to know the courses, that was all, and he certainly knew them. He had been involved in the Crosby tournaments for years. One year he had carried a scorer's signboard down the fairways—one of the years of the bad weather, when the wind had ripped in off the Pacific at gale force. "Man, that was an experience," he went on to say. They paid him ten dollars for carrying the board. He hadn't been able to find a bag to pack that year, and he said that carrying the board behind the foursome, which he thought was going to be duck-soup easy, just changing the numbers from time to time to show where the two players and their teams stood in relationship to par, well, it had been worse than packing *two* bags. It was the wind, catching and flailing at the board and turning it in Abe's hands, and then hauling and jockeying him around the fairway, so that in the big gusts he felt like a man controlled by his umbrella in a windstorm. One of the pros' names on his board was Al Besselink; he couldn't remember the other one. When they got to the sea holes of Pebble Beach—the 7th, 8th—the board became almost completely unmanageable; it kept bearing Abe off inland, toward the eucalyptus forests. He would turn the board's edge into the wind and tack back up toward his group, but the wind would catch and turn the board broadside to, like a sail, and Abe would be scurried off before the wind, hauling to and doing what he could. In my mind's eye I could see Abe careering Al Besselink's name through distant foursomes while galleries turned to stare after him. Finally, he lost his foursome completely, so he tried going inland where he thought he had a better chance of getting the board back to the caddy house by traveling through the natural windscreens of the pines.

"I had to get that sign back up there," said Abe. "If I don't come back in with the sign, maybe I don't get my ten dollars."

I had a good first 9 that afternoon, playing relaxed golf,

and Abe, when I told him my handicap was 18, whistled and said "we" would have an interesting tournament. He said maybe we'd even get to have someone carrying a signboard behind us! That's what we would have if we were in contention.

Like many caddies, Abe referred to his golfer as "we" when things were going well. After a good drive he would say, "We're right down the middle. Yessir, we're right down the goddam pike." In adversity, the first person "we" was dropped and the second and third person would appear. A caddy would say after gazing at a duck hook: "You're dead. You're off there way to the left." Or in reminiscing to another caddy after a day's round, he would shift gears in midsentence: "So we're right down the fairway, lying one, and what does he do but hit it fat."

When we got to the inland holes the deer were moving— materializing in the shadows of the eucalyptus trees, occasionally bounding in quick long stiff-legged leaps across the fairways. Abe said that one year a whole herd of them had idled across the fairway in front of Tommy Bolt, one of the most tempestuous and colorful players on the tour.

"I reckon every deer on the peninsula lined up and passed in front of Bolt," Abe said. "He got good and red in the ears waiting for them, and finally he shouted, 'Hey, get those marshals outa there!' "

It was dark when we got in. Our starting time in the tournament was 10:10 the next morning. Abe said that he would come and fetch me very early for some work on the practice tee. He told me to get a good rest.

A friend at the lodge had seen the two of us walk in from the course. "Who's that little guy with you?" he asked.

"My caddy," I said.

"You're in trouble. He doesn't look like he can lift a golf ball, much less a bag. And what are those noises he makes?"

"He wheezes somewhat," I said, "but he gets around O.K. Hell, he's a professional furniture mover."

"What does he carry, tea tables?" my friend asked. "You remember Ogden Nash's caddy—the one who had chronic hiccups, hay fever, whistled through his teeth, and who had large shoes that squeaked?"

"Yes," I said.

"Well, that's your caddy."

"Not Abe. Not good Abe," I said. "He's been on these courses for thirty years. You wait," I said. "You just wait."

There was time at sunrise to get in a touch of practice. One item I had not thought to bring on the tour was a bag of practice balls. The Del Monte Lodge did not supply the familiar wire pails filled with red-circled practice balls that one is able to rent at almost all country clubs. Abe had told me not to mind. He had said he would scrounge around his house and bring some practice balls with him the next morning so that we could get some "loosening up" before the first round started. He said he had some balls "down cellar," he thought, from his shoreline collecting days, and he would fetch them up.

Early the next morning he banged on the door of my room at the lodge, and I could hear him wheezing and clearing his throat, and he called out, "Don't be keeping too long."

I got ready. Just before coming out I bathed my hands in the hottest water I could stand. I had read and remembered that it was a preparatory device Gene Sarazen had often used in brisk weather to get his finger muscles loose and his hands supple.

It was chilly outside. Abe was wearing a huntsman's cap with flaps that came over his ears. The street lamps were still on.

"Mornin', Abe," I said.

My hands began to smoke from their hot-water bath.

Abe noticed.

I was somewhat surprised myself by the volume of condensation that rose from my hands into the crisp air. I waved them to get them dry.

"Let it go!" Abe said. "You ain't putting it out that way."

He must have thought I was trying to extinguish a runaway cigarette, or a cigar, or something that had caught fire in my hands.

"It's all right, it's all right," I said noncommittally. The steam rose. "They're a bit wet, that's all. It's all right."

We started for the practice range. After a few seconds, the hands stopped smoking.

"You bring some balls?" I asked.

"Ten," Abe said.

There was a faint ground mist easing off the grass and a chill in the air that reminded one of duck-shooting dawns. When we got to the tee it was still so dark that one *heard* rather than saw the few golfers already practicing—the quick swish of the wet-weather gear as a golfer went through his swing, the click of the club head connecting with the ball, and then the hum of the ball as it flew out over the dark field. Far in the distance the caddies, just dark shapes from where we were, could look up and see the ball against the sky, which was light, so they could follow its flight and move accordingly. Pretty soon, with the sun coming quickly, the balls sailing out would, at the top of their trajectory, glow gold suddenly, like planets, then wink off as they dropped into shadow. Down below, where we stood, it was still dark. A tall line of pines close behind us cut the light, and in the grass one could hardly see the tee on which to place the ball.

Abe had a fishnet bag with him; a small clutch of balls bunched in the bottom. We found a place in the line, and he rolled the practice balls out. Even in the gloom I could see their condition—one of the balls rolled erratically, like a pear—and I asked, "Abe, is that a gutta-percha you've got in there? Those seem a mite shopworn."

"Well," Abe said, "I keep things down cellar I can't get rid of easy."

He strolled out across the practice field, his fishnet bag dangling loosely. I hit some eight and nine irons, just to get limber, and the rickety balls fluttered out to him noisily, like paper in a windstream. I noticed Abe ranged after them with great agility, and even when I was teeing up a ball he seemed to be moving around out there in the gloom, looking and darting about like a cattle egret.

Paul Christman, the former football star, was down the line from me, also hitting out short irons. He had an eye on Abe.

"That caddy of yours has great range," he called to me, a gentle dig in his voice. "He's moving around like a free safety."

I hit all the balls out to Abe except the one that had rolled like a pear. It had done so, as I now could see in the brightening light, because a portion of its interior protruded like a polyp. I waved for Abe. He trotted in. He gave a glance at the remaining ball.

"I thought it might explode if I hit it," I said.

"No mind," he said. He poured the contents of his fishnet bag out on the grass. There were now about twenty balls, many of them bright and pristine, with not a mark on them except, perhaps, as I imagined suddenly, a small PC for Paul Christman stamped on the cover. Christman was a very serious amateur golfer, the sort who might stamp his practice balls. He was always on the practice tee when I looked out there.

I peered warily down the line toward him. Abe was wheezing loudly with pleasure. "I got us some," he announced.

"Yes," I said, softly. "So I see."

When the sun pulled up over the pines and the practice field shone in its light, Abe had to cut down on his activities. But his fishnet bag was always bulkier when we had finished a morning's practice. I suspected that he thinned out the crop when he got home, picking out the best ones, because each morning he would arrive with his "down-cellar" balls, the original ten, the ball with the polyp among them.

"I thought we had more of these," I said one morning.

"I found ten balls down cellar. You lost one when you hooked it that time. Now there are nine," he said to me, reproachfully.

Just before setting out for the Monterey course, we checked the bag and took out two clubs—the four wood and the three iron—to get down to the fourteen-club limit. I told Abe I felt more comfortable with the woods, even though I knew a wood shot off the fairway was riskier than a long iron. The pros usually carry only two woods in their bag—the driver and the brassie—and they supplement the irons with a one iron. In the old days, until the fourteen-club restriction, pros carried many more clubs, one for every conceivable situation, including such oddities as left-handed clubs for lies where a right-handed swing was impossible. Harry Cooper carried twenty-six clubs and Lawson Little's caddy had to struggle through a round carrying *thirty* clubs. Leo Diegel had four drivers in his bag—one that had a hook built into it, another with a slice, and then he had a pair of drivers especially tailored for wind conditions, one with a high loft for taking advantage of a prevailing wind, and the other with an almost flat face so the ball would bore low into an oncoming wind.

Abe shook his head over the number of woods we kept. I said I believed in them. The irons seemed dinky to me—I never could believe the thin blade could drive the ball very far, and I was apt to press, whereas the wood club seemed so much more of a weapon.

I had on a pair of green golfing slacks. The Pro-Shu shoes were shined. I didn't wear a golf glove, though I should have. It had been my impression that a golf glove was to keep the hands from getting sore and blistering, and since my hands were relatively tough from pre-tournament practice I had not bothered to buy a glove. I learned later that the glove is used mainly to improve the grip.

As for the golf hat I had at hand, I looked carefully at it. It was one of the items that came in the gift kit amateurs received when they checked in at the headquarters. I don't usually wear hats, but it was gray with red piping that read Bing-Crosby-Pro-Am and there was a tab in the back for adjusting the head size so the wearer could either have it sit up jauntily on top of the head, or pull it low and shield the face in brooding shadow. I decided against it finally. Afterward I noticed that the golf professional rarely wore the golfing cap that came with his kit. He would almost invariably wear the golf hat received in the kit from the previous tournament which would indicate that he was an established figure on the circuit and a regular tour performer. Many of the golfers at the Crosby wore Los Angeles and San Diego Open hats, which were the two tournaments that preceded the Crosby.

We drove out to Monterey. It was easy to find Bob Bruno. He was on the practice putting green, a very tall man bending in mournful, prayerful study over a putter that seemed undersized, a child's toy. We chatted a while. He seemed serious and well-meaning, a big-featured man with a slightly pock-marked face. He was wearing a black golfer's glove. He wore a San Diego Open cap. He said he had gone to bed quite early the night before. He was very difficult to get up in the morning, he went on. People really had to work on him, pummel and pull him, and sometimes they just gave up. He didn't want that to happen, so he had had a long night's rest. And there he was, he said smiling, ready to tear the course apart.

The first hole at Monterey was a par 5, an easy one, perhaps the easiest hole in the tournament, downhill off an elevated tee, onto a wide fairway through the pines, mottled with the slants of the early-morning sun flickering through, and the shadows blue-green.

The pro shop is set right behind the first tee. A small crowd was on hand. It was cold, and many of them were in the pro shop looking out through the plate-glass window. I avoided looking at their faces.

There were a number of foursomes in front of us. Bob Tuthill, an assistant PGA tournament director, was standing by the first tee. I fell into nervous conversation with him. He had the comforting opinion that an amateur's shots off the first tee were likely to be good, whatever the pressure: having done nothing wrong or right, and yet to indulge in a streak of bad habit, the second-rate golfer had an excellent chance of stroking a decent shot.

"That reminds me," said Tuthill. "There was this important occasion, opening this European golf course, when the officials prevailed on a German prince, big corpulent fellow, to tee off and hit the first ball. He stepped up, with all these witnesses and newspaper people standing around, and a caddy way down the fairway to retrieve that first ceremonial ball, easing in a bit, perhaps, guessing what was to come, and the prince took a lunge at the ball and missed it completely. Very embarrassing. But there was an old British professional who found the exact words, to say: "And now," he said, "if your Royal Highness is ready, I think the opening stroke should now be made."

"Great tact," I said. "I trust you'll produce the same line if by chance I imitate his Royal Highness. It's quite likely."

"For a small price," Tuthill said.

Maurie Luxford was at the starter's table. He held a bull-horn, and announced each foursome as the players approached the tee and prepared to drive. "And now, about to drive, playing out of Burning Tree Golf Club, the very personable . . ."

Luxford's introductions were famous on the tour, especially for their hyperbole, which was as flamboyant as a prize-fight announcer's. Over the years many contestants found that their stature bloomed at Luxford's hands. Pandel Savic, for example, who usually played with Jack Nicklaus in the pro-ams, was the Ohio State quarterback, quite a good one, who took his team to the Rose Bowl in 1950. That was his highest honor. In his first Crosby, he was introduced by Luxford as being chosen All-Big Ten. Then through the years he rose to Honorable Mention All-America, then All-America, and finally he reached a pinnacle of sorts when Luxford announced him as 1950's Heisman Trophy winner.

Luxford was particularly famous for his gift of embroidering the reputations of obscure amateur golfers. He would announce a contestant: "the world's greatest Dodge dealer in San Bernardino!" Or of an obscure stock company actor: "And now, as Bing Crosby himself would surely say, an actor's actor! A *great* actor's actor. Ted Bong."

The crowd would stir and crane forward.

"Who?"

"I think he said Ted Bong. Or Wong. Something like that."

"Oh yes."

My own introduction was short. Luxford announced my name and he added that I was playing out of the Piping Rock Golf Club of Long Island. "He is a . . . *the* writer from Long Island," he stuck on as an embellishment. "His playing partner is Bob Bruno, the very personable long-ball hitter from San Diego, playing partner of Andy Williams last year, nearly *seven* feet tall, ladies and gentlemen . . ." etc., etc.

Bruno and I won the honor. I drove first. "Keep it easy," I kept telling myself. The shot boomed down the fairway, long and straight, and behind the bay window a few spectators clicked their rings and knuckles against the glass in appreciation.

Bruno was delighted. "Holy smoke!" he said.

I took an apple from the bowl on the starter's table, and our foursome set off down the course.

I had a good lie, and my second shot was nearly as long as the first, and straight, rolling up to within 40 yards of the green.

"We're moving," said Abe.

As we walked along, I began to feel guilty about my 18 handicap. Would the golf committee complain? Would fingers be pointed and voices lowered when I entered the Del Monte Lodge with six natural birdies on my score card—our team score some 17 or 18 strokes ahead of the nearest competitor?

Bruno came up and walked alongside to encourage me. "You're in great shape," he said. "A good approach, and you've got a chance at a birdie. With your handicap stroke, that'll start us off great—two under par."

I studied the next shot with care. I took out a pitching wedge, a club I felt easy with; but as I stood over the ball, bringing back the club, my old terror of being an unwieldy machine swept over me, and I *shanked* the shot, dumping it into a trap off to one side of the green. The ball skidded off almost at a diagonal. The silence was absolute until I broke it with a strained cry, as if after the first two superb shots the absurdity of the third was unbelievable—like two graceful ballet steps, and then a splay-legged pratfall, a thump and a high squawk of dismay.

I stalked miserably into the trap, and, not catching enough sand with my wedge, I lifted the ball into a grove of pines on the other side of the green. I was still about 40 years away, just the distance I'd been two strokes back. The ball was stymied in the pines, and it took me two more strokes to get out.

"Pick it up," Bruno called petulantly. "There's no use." He himself had bogeyed the hole. We had started off the tournament by losing one stroke to par on the easiest hole on the peninsula.

"I'm awful sorry," I said to Bruno.

"I told your caddy to stick that pitching wedge in the bag and leave it there," he said. "You had a clear line. You should've rolled it up there with a four or a five iron—a pitch-and-run shot." He shook his head.

"I'm not so hot on those," I said. "I've always felt comfortable with that wedge."

"We'll get going," he said more cheerfully. "Hell, we've got 53 holes to go."

GERALD HOLLAND

# Lunches with Luce

Born: To Henry R. Luce,
quizzical-browed, Midas-touched tycoon,
a new magazine on August 16, 1954,
his fouth. Its name: *Sports Illustrated.*

THE OFFICIAL HISTORY of Time Inc., Volume II, is scheduled for publication late this year, and it is promised that this volume will set down the full, inside story of how Henry Robinson Luce's last magazine, *Sports Illustrated,* came into being seventeen years ago.

Having been present at the creation, I find myself speculating not so much about what will be told in the official version, as about what will be left out. I doubt, for instance, that the historians will have very much to say about the Luce editorial luncheons which began a year before publication of *SI.* This is a great pity because the luncheons showed Luce at a time when he was still, at fifty-five, in excellent health, when almost all his properties were flourishing, company profits were at an all-time high, and he himself was at the height of his powers.

Furthermore, the *Sports Illustrated* luncheons dealt in depth with a subject about which Luce was almost totally uninformed. He appeared to have given only passing attention to the sports stories in *Time* and *Life*. Now, because there was so much that was new to him. Luce took great delight in the luncheons. There seemed to be no end of things to be learned, and like all instinctively good reporters, Luce never made a pretense of knowing something with the mental reservation to have someone explain it to him later. He grasped at everything he did not understand and pursued and probed it on the spot until he had it made perfectly clear to him. It was this unflagging, frequently uninterruptible curiosity, sometimes superficially comic, that was his hallmark as the last of the great founding journalists, the quality that made him to his last day more curious and inquiring than most of his writers and editors.

Not all of the luncheon guests who were involved in the new magazine were knowledgeable sports fans, and many of us learned along with Luce, without having to appear as naïve as he was willing to be. Thus, his contributions to the magazine may have been greater than anyone recognized at the time. At any rate, it is too bad there are not minutes to be studied now when *Sports Illustrated* appears to have a chance of being his most substantial financial success. In the absence of minutes, I feel that people like myself ought to set down what they can remember of the lunches against the day when someone comes to grips with the definitive Luce biography.

The forthcoming Volume II of the official history will also be forced, I fear, to omit mention of an exciting prologue to the drama of the lunches with Luce. There was, for instance, the matter of the first task force assigned to explore the possibilities of the new magazine. This small group, recruited from *Life,* was headed by Ernest Havemann, the ace of its writing staff. His conclusion, after several months of study, was eloquently negative. Among Havemann's points, contained in a long, single-spaced memo, tendered with his resignation from the project and the company, was his opinion that there was not enough going on in sports to fill a weekly magazine all year. "What," asked Havemann, "is there to write about in the wintertime? Sleds?" This was a question of some pertinence early in 1953 when nobody foresaw today's great sporting boom with basketball, hockey, and professional football expanded throughout the country and solid sellouts all winter long.

At the time of the Havemann memo, Luce was in residence with the American ambassadress in Rome and was expected home in six weeks or so, confident that a paste-up dummy prepared by Havemann and his aides would await him. Now the men of the executive suite suddenly found themselves with nothing but Havemann's damnably persuasive memo. The crisis was met by the drafting of Sidney L. James, an assistant managing editor of *Life,* who had a considerable reputation as a troubleshooter with a special enthusiasm for apparently lost causes.

Where Havemann's view of the project had been dim, James saw the brightest prospect in modern magazine journalism. Sports, he proclaimed, were the wave of the future. Packing his papers and his secretary, he moved at once to the seventeenth floor, retaining Havemann's small staff, recruiting spare talent from *Time* and *Life* editorial and layout rooms, and offering a tryout to almost every young man who stormed the offices as rumors spread that Time Inc. was hiring.

Along about here, I believe, the official history may well begin its story of *SI*. But I doubt that it will mention one most unusual young man who was taken on and given a chance to prove himself. He was tall and lean and soft-spoken when he spoke at all. On the morning he reported for duty, he was assigned to a remote office, and given a desk, a typewriter, a frayed newspaper clipping ("see what you can do with this"), but no chair. He seemed either too shy or too bewildered by the feverish activity around him to ask for one.

I remember seeing him standing at his desk, examining the clipping carefully, turning it over and over as if he were not sure which side he was expected to see what he could do something about. Occasionally, he would sit on the edge of the desk, but jump up at once as from a hot stove. It did not seem to occur to him to ask for a chair, and no one, not even James himself on his tours of the offices, appeared to notice that he did not have one. Finally, on the third day, he leaned over the typewriter from a standing position and typed a line slowly, consulting the tattered clipping between taps. When he had finished, he placed the typed page and the clipping on top of the typewriter, weighted them down with a box of paper clips, turned on his heel and walked out, and was not seen on the premises again.

Having observed his leave-taking, I made it a point to look at the result of his labors. The tired old clipping told of a horse which had jumped over the fence during a race and gone galloping around the infield of a local track. The typed rewrite read simply, "The horse jumped over the fucking fence." The episode, as it spread around the office, enlivened our labors, but it was quickly forgotten as we worked almost around the clock to meet the six-week deadline for our paste-up dummy.

I did not think of the young man without a chair again until 1969 when I came upon a picture spread in *Life* about Kurt Vonnegut, Jr., his *Slaughterhouse-Five,* his play, and other triumphs. Something about Vonnegut's face in *Life* haunted me. I held a finger over his mustachio, still was puzzled, finally sat down and wrote a letter to his home on Cape Cod and asked him if he, by any wild chance, had once worked for three days without a chair and had written a curt, clear, complete story about a racehorse for a nonexistent magazine. I had an answer by return mail. Our young man was indeed the now famed Kurt Vonnegut, Jr., who, if he had been given a chair, might at this moment be writing horse racing for *Sports Illustrated* and piling up Time Inc. profit sharings, insofar as there are any these days. In his prompt reply to my note, Vonnegut gave no hint that he felt he had let opportunity pass him by in the old Time-Life Building.

Many another young man came and went along with Kurt Vonnegut as the Sid James team began to show results. Typewriters clattered day and night in every available corner of the seventeenth floor, and artists' razor blades flew as dummy-type layouts filled the walls. There was never any doubt in James's mind that the short deadline would be met. Writers made up stories out of their heads; others went on flying trips to get them. Outside writers, artists, and photographers were assigned at whatever fees it took to get them. Every sundown, waiters from the best Rockefeller Center restaurants wheeled in trays of hors d'oeuvres and great quantities of spirits, and these were followed by other teams from the kitchens who set up steam tables offering a choice of entrées and other tables laden with rich desserts. This high living claimed a few casualties who fancied the drinks more than the solid nourishment, but they were swiftly replaced, and the work went on at top speed as the paste-up dummy grew steadily fatter. With only hours to spare, it was ready and waiting when Luce returned from Rome. He was delighted with it, and after exhaustive questioning of James and his top aides, he gave the command, "Print it!" It was so done, filled with unpaid-for ads and mailed to advertisers and ad agencies everywhere.

At this point in his career, it was said that there were hundreds of Time Inc. employees who had never seen Luce. Not so our little band of pioneers. Sometimes it seemed that we saw more of Luce than we did of our wives. Some of us were assigned to escort him to sporting events and explain the action and identify the players. For others of us there began the era of the lunch.

There was one I shall never forget. I wince at the memory of it even today. It was held in a second-floor private dining room of the old building. Copies of the Sid James printed dummy were at every place, but Sid James himself was not there. Luce, impressed by James's great save of the Havemann project, had ordered him to take a vacation at the Luce home in Charleston, South Carolina. A vacation was the last thing James wanted, but he could scarcely turn down such a signal honor.

In his place, at Luce's right, sat Edward K. Thompson, *Life's* managing editor, puffing on a big fat cigar with an air of assurance becoming his position as editorial chief of the company's then biggest moneymaker. There were some *Time* editors there, and the men who were to rank high on the new sports magazine, as well as John Shaw Billings, *Life's* first editor.

I had a place at the foot of the table. I was not exactly at ease. For one thing, the printed dummy was getting bad notices around the building. People on *Time* and *Life* professed to find it below their editorial standards, and even the researchers and secretaries were against it, because, if published, it was sure to lose money at the start and thus would eat into their profit-sharing, then 10 percent of their annual wages. Adding to my uneasiness was the fear that some article I had written for the dummy would come up for comment. I was scarcely able to touch my food. Instead, I gulped coffee and an overzealous waiter kept filling my cup. Chain-smoking the while, I must have had eight or ten cups of coffee before I suddenly became aware I had to go to the bathroom.

I tried to put the matter out of my mind. I strained to hear what was being said at the head of the table. As I got it, Luce was saying that he had been interested in a story in the dummy about wrestling, signed by a college professor. It was supposed to be a satire, and the professor's point was that when vast numbers of people agreed on anything (in this case that wrestling was 100 percent fake), the chances were that half of them were wrong. Thus, the professor reasoned, wrestling was probably more honest than most people said. I had rewritten all this, believing myself to be sharpening the satire. Instead, as Luce himself read aloud from the story, I was horrified to hear that I had lost the satire and made it appear that wrestling was mostly honest. In my dismay, I drained a cup of cold coffee.

I heard Thompson say to Luce, "The story is naïve."

I heard Luce say to Thompson, "Why, I believed it."

I turned to my neighbor, whom I had never seen before. "Where's the can in here?"

"That door right behind Luce."

"I got to go. Would it be all right, do you think?"

My neighbor looked at me coldly. "No. You stay put until Luce gives the word to adjourn."

"How long will that be, do you think?"

"Could be hours."

"What am I going to do?"

"Hold it, pal."

I tried to concentrate on the head of the table again. Luce had apparently gone on to something else, but I could not make out what he was saying. I saw John Shaw Billings slap his leg, throw back his head, and laugh heartily (I had heard he was noted for this). I looked wildly around the room. There was the door we had come through when we had entered. It was halfway across the room. There were the swinging doors into the kitchen. What if I were to get up, shout "I quit!" and run into the kitchen? Or say nothing and make for the entry door? Or rise with dignity, address Luce directly, something like "Back teeth are floating, sir, if you don't mind?" and stride manfully for the can directly behind him? Abruptly, I took off. My neighbor grabbed at my sleeve as I got up, but I shook him off and started for Luce and the blessed can. As I advanced I saw heads swivel and faces turn toward me in horror. It was plain that the luncheon guests, rising in importance as I pogoed along, considered that I had gone mad and was advancing on Luce as an assassin.

Somehow, the face of Luce impressed itself on my mind in an image that remains with me to this day. He could not have appeared more disinterested. He did not even look at me directly. But the others appeared to be frozen by the awful spectacle of my staggering progress toward my goal.

I returned to the room a new man, fearing neither man nor beast nor Luce nor Thompson. I smiled broadly as I walked back to my lowly seat, staring down the frowning faces of the editors, reached my chair safely, and prepared to give my full attention to whatever matter was by that time under discussion. I heard Luce say, "And then there are the many humble tasks of magazine-making, the little things that contribute so much to its character. I am often struck as I leaf through *Reader's Digest* by the small items scattered through the book, reflecting, as they do, the infinite care that went into their writing and editing, each one the work of many hands with not a word wasted, every word precisely right."

John Shaw Billings slapped his leg and nodded vigorously. Thompson lit another cigar. A *Time* man pulled a sheaf of paper from his inside coat pocket and made a small note. Two other editors exchanged whispers and nodded in unison with John Shaw Billings across the table.

Luce resumed, "I must get up to see my friends, the Wallaces. What is that town of theirs?"

Ed Thompson puffed on his fresh cigar as he turned to Luce, who waved the smoke away. "Pleasantville," said Thompson. Pleasantville was indeed the post office address of the *Digest* according to its masthead page.

"No, no," said Luce, "I don't mean Pleasantville."

John Shaw Billings half-rose from his chair, slapping his leg. "Mount Kisco!" he cried.

Luce frowned and shook his head.

Out of somewhere came a voice, "North White Plains!"

"No," said Luce firmly.

Relaxed in my chair, I could sense a growing panic as voices shouted over each other, "Hawthorne! Thornwood! Bedford Village! Dobbs Ferry!"

Again and again Luce shook his head, his face darkening with irritation.

Suddenly they ran out of names.

I could hear my neighbor hiss, "I could swear it's Pleasantville."

I could not resist hissing back, "Hold it, pal."

Luce's fingers drummed the table. The sheer drama of the moment gripped me. Here, the editor in chief had sought a tiny morsel of information which his highly paid editors were unable to supply. Freed from my own crisis, I sensed great odds at stake here. Was it out of the question to imagine that careers were hanging in the balance? Would husbands be telling their wives tonight, "We sell the station wagon. Peter has got to come out of St. Paul's. He'll have to settle for high school here in Greenwich. We're out of the Yacht Club, the boat goes for what we can get. And unless there's something at *Newsweek,* the house is on the market as of now."

Now there was complete silence. It was plain that Luce was not going to proceed until he got the name of the Westchester town he wanted.

As for myself, I felt no anxiety whatever. My principal investment at the moment was a Simmons Hide-a-Bed being puchased on time payments at Bloomingdale's Department Store. Furthermore, I knew the town Luce wanted. I had spent a summer in a rented house near the *Digest,* and there was absolutely no doubt in my mind. During my bladder crisis, I would not have considered uttering a word. I also knew that to do so now would denigrate every editor at the table. If I had learned one lesson as an itinerant journalist it was this, "Never make the man ahead of you look bad." But in my euphoria, brought back from the can. I could not resist. Loudly and firmly, I uttered my one word contribution to the luncheon:

"Chappaqua!"

Luce peered down the table. He beamed. "Right!" he cried, "Chappaqua!" He leaned over and whispered to Thompson. Thompson looked down the table to me. He whispered back to Luce, probably identifying me, for we had once worked together on the Milwaukee *Journal.*

Of course, I was right. The *Digest* was and still is in the limits of Chappaqua township. Somebody, I think, made up the name of Pleasantville as being more appropriate.

I felt I had committed the unforgivable sin. Happily, it was not held against me. As weeks passed, I established a reputation for being so inept in the art of journalistic politicking as to be a threat to no one. My ridiculous trip to the can while Luce was speaking reassured all my colleagues that I could safely be written off as a rival of any consequence.

So I continued on the guest list for the regular Luce luncheons. But I had learned my lesson. I drank no liquids of any kind, and I volunteered no answers, although Luce came to every luncheon equipped with questions large and small. One challenged the table to come up with article ideas for men of world importance. I did not stick my neck out. I heard one man suggest a piece on golf by Eisenhower. Another, in a bold ploy, said, "Harry, how about Churchill on polo?" Luce shook his head. "I was privileged to see my old friend Winston recently and he is not well. He's still bright and alert, but I would not ask him to undertake such a commission."

"How about Herbert Hoover on fishing? He's a great fisherman."

Luce smiled wryly. "No. Hoover doesn't like me." He paused and added brightly, "He likes my wife, but he doesn't like me."

Names flew thick and fast, but Luce was unimpressed. He let them run on, then suddenly held up a hand.

"Wait," he said, "I've got it."

He smiled faintly as hands slipped into inside coat pockets for copy paper and pencils. Editors leaned forward, tense, waiting for the magic decision, for it was clear that the subject was beyond further debate. Luce seemed to savor the scene. He let them wait, looking up and down the table, searching faces, apparently certain that he had a bigger bombshell than any one of his men suspected. He drew a cigarette from the pack at his plate. There was a rumor that he had only lately become informed of the cigarette scare. I reasoned that he had probably ordered exhaustive research on the subject and had come up with the least harmful brand. I took a piece of paper from my pocket, waited with ball-point poised.

The suspense was unbearable. Nobody drew a breath except me. With my wretched luck at these affairs I coughed.

Nobody looked at me, but I saw lips tighten and jaw muscles twitch. At last Luce spoke:

"Khrushchev!"

There was a burst of admiring comment from those editors who addressed Luce as "Harry." John Shaw Billings was not there, but if he had been, I am sure he would have slapped his leg. The others shook their heads in helpless admiration. Luce developed his theme as he tossed off orders.

"Draft a cable outlining the idea, make clear Khrushchev is to have complete freedom, article will lead the magazine, offer suggestions, place of sports modern world, importance of Olympics, invite comment on charge Russian athletes are paid employees of state."

Pencils fairly flew. Luce went on:

"Say detailed letter follows. Have Washington bureau clear with State."

This was all far beyond my depth. My ball-point still at the ready, I had written nothing. But looking at Luce puffing on his cigarette, I had an inspiration. I wrote, "HRL smokes Winstons."

Although Khrushchev was not heard from, it was probably this luncheon and its exercise in thinking big that led to the signing up of William Faulkner, Robert Frost, Catherine Drinker Bowen, John P. Marquand, William Saroyan, John O'Hara, and others of their stature to write about such subjects as horse racing, hockey, baseball, and golf. (Later on, President Kennedy and his brother Robert were contributors.)

The high mark of my lunches with Luce came just before publication in August, 1954. I was amazed when Sid James came into my office and said that we were having lunch with Luce alone—just the three of us.

It seems that Luce was quite pleased with a long, long story I had written for the first issue. It traced the history of sports back to the caveman and was crammed with odd facts that fascinated Luce and apparently made him curious about the author.

I made several trips to the men's room to prepare myself for this private audience, moistened my lips with water, and remembering the crisis at my first luncheon, probably brought myself to the brink of dehydration.

Somehow, when we were seated at the table of a private dining room high in the RCA Building, I felt completely comfortable—this probably, as I look back, due to another, little-known talent of the editor in chief for putting people at ease if he wanted to. He asked me how I got into journalism, and I found myself saying that I had started on the St. Louis *Post-Dispatch* with Sid.

Luce smiled, "Well, there used to be a Yale tradition around here, but it's turned into a *Post-Dispatch* tradition." (Roy Alexander, then managing editor of *Time,* Otto Fuerbringer, then Alexander's assistant, Larry Laybourne of the news bureau, Ernie Havemann, again writing for *Life* under contract, were all *P-D* men. Sid James had been the first.)

It was the best Luce luncheon I ever had. We talked of this and that over coffee, and Luce said, "Now let's just gas." He made a complimentary remark about my long history of sports.

I thanked him and said I regarded the assignment as the clutch, a story we simply had to have in the first issue.

Luce pounced on the word.

"Clutch, clutch? What's that?" he demanded.

"Why, in baseball," I said, "when a hitter is up with two out and the winning run is on third base, he is said to be in the clutch. In other words, he's simply got to come through with a hit, to get that winning run home."

Luce seemed astonished by this information.

We gassed on, and he mentioned a story that had appeared in that morning's New York *Times*. I am not positive, but I think it had something to do with the quality of current literature. Luce disagreed with the argument of the *Times* man, and finally said, "If I were managing editor of *Life*, I'd have an editorial on that subject next week." He shrugged his shoulders and stopped there, indicating that since he was not *Life's* managing editor, he was powerless to do anything about it.

He must have mentioned his concern elsewhere, because next week in *Life* there was the editorial reciting precisely the points he had made.

This was my first chance to observe how Luce could reveal his preferences without making a great point of it. I saw him exhibit his technique in this area at another luncheon after the practice of getting big-name writers to cover big-time sporting events had been established as a regular policy.

Luce asked a text editor, "Who do we have doing the Kentucky Derby this year?" The editor replied confidently, "Why, I thought it would be interesting to see what [he mentioned a well-known Chicago writer] could do with it, Harry."

The bushy Luce eyebrows raised ever so slightly.

"You've given him the assignment, have you?" asked Luce.

"Yes, I have, Harry," the editor said, "and he's agreed to

take it on." Luce lit a Winston, and said casually, "Well, I can't imagine anything good coming of that." He quickly went on to another subject.

He issued no order. None was necessary. A half hour after the luncheon, a letter canceling the assignment was on its way to Chicago, promising a check for the full amount agreed upon under separate cover.

For all the usually high level of enthusiasm at the luncheons, *Sports Illustrated* was not prospering. Profit-sharing at Time Inc. dropped from 10 to 5 percent because of it. Madison Avenue was not impressed, bracketing it in their budgets with cheap-paper men's magazines. Nobody foresaw today's turnabout, when the big general-circulation magazines, with their millions of readers, would be in trouble and the limited-audience journals would be prospering.

*Sports Illustrated* started with 450,000 subscribers, drawn from the gold-plated *Time-Life-Fortune* mailing list. Those first readers bought the magazine sight unseen. The circulation was carefully controlled at this point, and the talk was of slow progress that would level off at a million.

This was the thinking when Luce brought another blockbuster to lunch one day long before the magazine was within sight of the planned magic million. He tossed his bomb out on the table and said he wanted everyone present to hazard a prediction as to how *Sports Illustrated* would appear when it had not one- but *two*-million circulation.

All eyes turned to Sid James. With his never-failing high spirts, James came up to each week's deadline, no matter what near catastrophes had been averted along the way, with the exultant declaration over the late Sunday night drinks that we were sending to press the finest issue of *Sports Il-lustrated* up to that moment. If this were so, how were we to envisage for Luce a better magazine than the one on the stands? Luce nodded to the man on my right, throwing me into a panic, for it meant that I was next. Forgetting my lesson of long ago, I drained my coffee cup, which was promptly refilled by a hovering waiter. I heard the man on my right begin, "As Sid was saying when we were closing this issue. . . ." He wandered off into a vague dissertation picturing the magazine with two-million subscribers as being essentially identical to our current one, except, of course, that it would have more of the same kind of stories and features as it grew fatter with ads than the *New Yorker*.

Luce nodded to me. I said, "My idea exactly. I couldn't agree more. Writing will get better and better, of course, as contributors adapt to our style. As Sid was saying. . . ." I trailed off into incoherence, and Luce pointed to the man next in line.

This young man apparently had dreamed of finding himself confronted with just this opportunity. Probably he had not dared to imagine himself getting the rapt attention of Luce himself, but one could almost see him hunched over his typewriter late at night, writing and rewriting memos detailing his ideas for the sports magazine of the future. Perhaps he planned to send them to Sid James (Sid gave all such memos his close attention and forwarded some to Luce with full credit to the author). But that was channels. This was not, by miles.

The young man, once he had the floor, obviously decided to go for broke. He said flatly that the two-million readers of the future would receive a magazine bearing almost no resemblance to the present product. As we grew, the man said, we would *educate* our readers to a new sporting world, instruct them, take them into places and behind scenes such as no sports chroniclers had ever done.

He went into great, exciting detail. Luce leaned forward, carried away by it all. Sid James smiled faintly, tapping the tablecloth lightly with his right forefinger.

Luce broke in now and then to ask a question. The young man fired back answers without a second's hesitation. The others still to be heard from appeared flabbergasted by this display of audacity. In my mind, the young man had committed the greatest error since my now-legendary trip to the bathroom. Luce at last passed on to the next man, exchanging a meaningful glance with Sid James, but there were no further flights of fancy from the other speakers about the magazine of two million. The Sid James line prevailed.

As for the daring young man, he apparently did himself no real harm with James (who genuinely admired respectful spunk *in channels*) nor any spectacular good. But he had impressed Luce, and it was perhaps for this reason that he was, after a proper interval, given an office with cross ventilation (a plum, since the old building was not air-conditioned) and a secretary. Eventually, he saw that this was to be the limit of his reward, and maneuvered himself into a better-paying post in another division of the empire.

Meanwhile, Luce's talk at the lunches began to reflect his growing knowledgeability about sports. He attended every sporting event he could. His guides included Sid James, Ed Thompson, Paul O'Neil (a top writer then on loan to *Sports Illustrated* from *Time*), Clay Felker, now editor of *New York* magazine, and Don Schanche, who was later managing editor of the *Saturday Evening Post* and *Holiday*.

Luce had a lot to learn. Sid James undertook his reeducation in baseball. At every event he witnessed, Luce admitted that mediocrity bored him, but that excellence excited him as much as it did any other fan.

Paul O'Neil escorted him to a fight card at Madison Square Garden. Luce sat glumly through the dull preliminaries, but when the main event came on, featuring Floyd Patterson, then only nineteen but already picked by *Sports Illustrated* as the next heavyweight champion, Luce began to show interest. Suddenly, he grasped O'Neil's arm and demanded, "What's a left hook?" O'Neil explained and demonstrated the punch, and for the balance of the twelve-round fight, Luce was on the edge of his aisle seat at ringside, throwing left hooks until the final bell.

Ed Thompson took him to a college basketball game at the Garden. Late in the game, the team with a 13-point lead began freezing the ball. Luce wanted to know why.

"They're protecting their lead," Thompson said. "They're holding on to the ball until the clock runs out."

"That's no good," said Luce, "You can't survive by hoarding. It's like making money. Any small boy can save money, but you've got to spend money to make money. The team that's ahead now is going to lose." And it did.

Therein lies one key to Luce's skill as a publisher. At the luncheon during which he called for ideas for a *Sports Illustrated* with two-million circulation, he was not making idle talk. He truly believed that the day of the two million would come, and he kept spending until his dying day to bring the day closer. By 1960, Time Inc. had lost $23 million on *SI* and was prepared to go on for as long as necessary. He believed in his last book completely. At a luncheon one day, he said, "We're going to make it. We just need time and people."

As has been told in countless places, Luce was a master at picking people and then maneuvering them like chessmen. Essentially a great competitor himself, he was always looking for the competitive spirit in others. He liked to throw two competitive men against each other.

When the brought Andre Laguerre, who had been chief of the Time-Life bureaus in Paris and London, to New York as assistant managing editor of *Sports Illustrated,* it was plain that such a competition was in progress. A man of Laguerre's stature clearly was not to be assistant anything for long. Both competitors were masters at intramural maneuvering, but on May 19, 1960, the decision came by mimeograph to all hands. Luce appointed Laguerre managing editor of *SI* and Sid James its publisher, with high praise for both men (in Luce's mind, a managing editor's job at Time Inc. was superior to that of a publisher). Sometime later, James received his final reward, a vice presidency of the company with which he had started as a stringer in St. Louis some thirty-odd years before.

About two weeks before Luce died in Phoenix on February 28, 1967, he attended his last board of directors meeting in New York. He heard glowing accounts from all sides. *Life's* circulation and ad revenue was up, ditto for *Time;* and the book division had doubled its sales to $16 million. Altogether, with investments of one kind and another, the company that Harry Luce and Britton Hadden had founded with $86,000 reported revenue of $503 million. Its net profit was $37,300,000. Now, four years after Luce's death, the great Time Inc. pillars wobble. *Life* has eliminated its international editions entirely, and firings go on there and in other divisions of the company as well. Some investments have gone poorly, notably in MGM stock. Radio and television stations have been sold to McGraw-Hill with returns earmarked for CATV.

The future is dubious in many sectors save one. Henry Robinson Luce's last book continues to thrive. Under Laguerre's remarkably effective editorship, it reached Luce's goal of two-million circulation on January 1, 1970. On January 1 of this year, it went to 2,150,000. It will go on gaining, if anything goes on. It is good that *Sports Illustrated* furnishes the brightest outlook among all the properties, for Luce was strictly a magazine man. He was for spending, but not for building a conglomerate with scores of entirely unrelated diversifications.

One point should be emphasized about Luce and the success of his last magazine. This success owed a great deal to his overall attitude toward it and his publishing philosophy in general—but not too much more. *Sports Illustrated* bears the marks of many hands. In the beginning, its most valuable asset was the enthusiasm and unshakable confidence of Sid James. It was under James that a staff was assembled almost overnight and actually trained on the job. A whole copy room was made up of girls who had never worked in any branch of journalism before. Under James, color for covers and inside pages had to be selected five to six weeks in advance. Under Laguerre, fast color came in and was so developed that today, sports action photographed in color on

Sunday is in the magazine three days later. Under Laguerre, the writing staff was strengthened by recruiting some of the best young newspapermen from all over the country and spending the money to send teams of them all around the world.

Other ingredients were the great sporting booms and the expansion of professional baseball, basketball, football, and hockey, the tremendous growth of the professional golf circuit, and the finding of sports stories in places where no one had thought to look for them before. Finally, and frankly, *Sports Illustrated* became the great success it is as more and more people turned to its handsome pages eagerly and desperately because they could not bear to read—or long ponder—the dreadful tidings of the news on the front pages of newspapers, on radio and television—and, yes, in the newsmagazines.

What would Luce do if he were in his prime again in today's world? Hard times alone would not bother him: he founded *Fortune* during the Depression and risked his every dollar to save *Life* from suffocation by premature success.

But what of the other troubles? Would the disintegration of his values, the calamities in the educational structure, and in what he knew as manners—would these and the scores of other frightening portents distress him to the point of despair? One of his surviving colleagues says yes, it would be too much for him. Others say no, he would have a go at it. Confident that solutions lay somewhere, and urged on by that insatiable curiosity of his, he would set out to find them— which, of course, would call for many a luncheon with Henry

Robinson Luce in one of those plush private dining rooms atop the new Time-Life Building or, if the temple should totter, at one of those overpriced, overdecorated, and under-serviced eateries downstairs.

PAT JORDAN

# The Man Who Was Cut Out
# for the Job

JEROME EVANS IS 40, with skin the color of milk chocolate.
His weight has not varied a pound in 20 years. His body is
so lean and tight that his muscles, veins and bones are visible
as distinct elements through the thin cloth of his skin. His
body is so taut that it seems to have no potential to give but
only to rip.

Evans is constantly aware of the condition of his body, his
clothes, the way he walks, talks and eats, all his natural man-
nerisms because, as he says, "Everyone's looking at me." As
a black man operating in a white world, Evans realizes eyes
are turned on him, and so he has turned his own eyes inward
to insure that nothing of Jerome Evans is visible to others
that is not first visible to himself. To Evans the most repre-
hensible weakness would be for some trait or mannerism to
slip out without his consent. Though he is constantly and
consciously sifting possibilities and deciding what to reveal
or conceal, Evans' selections are not based on any desire to
deceive. Rather, he wants to create the self he thinks he
should be. All his life he has been confronted by two cultures: black and white. And when they are in contradiction,

he has not always been sure which to choose. If Evans were a romantic he would simply choose that which is most natural to him rather than that which is foreign. But what is natural and what is best in a given society are not necessarily the same. Because of his wish to pick and choose the best from each culture, Evans' life is a precarious balancing act. He never seems to relax. Every decision, no matter how insignificant, must be debated thoroughly before being acted upon. For instance, when a white football player on the Williams team scores a touchdown and Evans is about to congratulate the boy, one can almost hear the whirrings in the coach's mind. He raises his arm to put it on the boy's shoulder, the arm suspended in midair, and then lets it fall to his side as he rejects that possibility and instead shakes the player's hand.

"I've built up in my mind what a man should be," he says. "This ability not to let down in front of people, whether they're black or white, is part of it. Some things I may want to do, but I won't. If I get drunk once in a while, lots of blacks will take comfort from that because it will prove I'm no better than them, and whites will take comfort too, because it'll prove I'm just 'like every other nigger.' But I won't be just any other nigger. I'm a man like anybody else."

If the black community in Burlington has any complaint about Evans, it is that he is too much his own man. He is too aloof and so, in a way, inaccessible to their pressures. He does not view problems externally. His solutions are arrived at in relation to himself, his wife and his two young children, and not in relation to "his people." He has said many times, "I don't trust leaders of 'people.' You have to beware of saints —they're dangerous. I want only to lead myself and my family."

Upon his graduation from North Carolina Central University in 1955 Evans decided to coach at primarily black schools throughout North Carolina. He had no desire to penetrate the white world. However, after moving from one black high school to another, year after year as the tide of integration rolled through the state, Evans began to see himself as a prehistoric mammal fleeing evolution and faced with extinction. Soon he would have to quit coaching, for there would be no black schools left to hire him. However, quite another choice —and a surprising one—presented itself in 1970 when he was asked to take the job at Williams High. He decided to accept the position and with it the pressures of integration.

Before the Burlington school board offered that position, however, it had had to oust C. A. Frye. A decade before, Frye's teams had been among the most powerful in North Carolina, but as other schools accepted integration, and with it large numbers of swift, elusive black football players, Williams remained a bastion of white supremacy. Its teams began to win less frequently, and the fortunes of their fiery coach declined accordingly. During these years Jerome Evans was molding well-disciplined black teams at Jordan Sellers that posted records such as 7–2 and 8–1, while Frye's players were struggling through seasons of 3–6–1 and 2–8.

Even so, Frye remained feared and respected as the Williams coach. His violent outbursts toward players were legendary among the townspeople, half of whom thought them a disgrace while the other half reveled in their ferociousness. He was known to tear the shirts off the backs of players and swear with such vehemence that the school's cheerleaders would run for shelter.

"There were times, if I had a knife I would have killed

coach Frye," said Mike Pierce, a white player. "He had no patience with anyone. When I was on the junior varsity I could hear him yelling from the other field and I was scared at the thought of ever playing for such a man. But one day in school he called me Mike and said how the team would need me the following year, and after that I was crazy about him. He screamed and cussed all right, and when you stunk he made a little raspberry sound and did a war dance around you like you were burning at the stake. He made you want to quit football and just grow your hair. And a lot of boys did quit, but maybe Frye gave them an excuse to do what they wanted. He brought out a lot of things in you that you never knew existed—both the best and the worst." Frye might have retained his coaching job indefinitely had it not been for a number of incidents, a few of which he was involved in, but some of which he took no part in whatsoever. Like Jerome Evans, he too was a victim of the times.

One night as he was about to go to bed he heard a commotion on his front lawn. Since he lived in a section of Burlington that was being encroached upon by the Negro population, Frye immediately assumed it was a "nigger prowler." He grabbed his gun, flung open the door and fired at the first thing that moved. He discovered that he had "winged" a white boy who had come to the house to see his pretty daughter, Cathy. The incident did not sit well with members of the school board, who noted that he could have handled the situation in "a less volatile way." A short while later, Frye was taken to court by a youth who claimed the coach had punched him on discovering him in the school gym at an hour it was supposed to be closed. Frye was eventually exonerated, but a few months afterward he was rumored to have pushed another boy down a flight of stairs at Williams in a fit of anger. It was said that the boy was paralyzed for life and that the police were hunting Frye. The rumors were simply untrue, but it no longer really mattered. Many of the city's residents felt they had had enough of C. A. Frye.

"The point was," said Craig White, a recent Williams graduate, that "everyone believed those rumors about Frye. That was the kind of man he was. There were vestiges of fanaticism about him. When he played basketball he took more pleasure in knocking you over than in going around you. But still, I was fascinated by him. You had to accept him for what he was because if you thought about it, that would ruin him for you."

Frye could not be removed without sufficient cause, but school officials found that. In the spring of 1969, black citizens in Burlington rioted and a good deal of their anger was over the fact that Williams High would not have a single black cheerleader during the following football season. Later that year a black citizens' committee demanded that upon the full integration of Williams, a black head coach should be appointed for one of the school's three major sports. The superintendent of schools, Dr. Brank Proffitt, saw in this demand an opportunity not only to satisfy the town's 8,000 blacks, but also the whites clamoring for Frye's dismissal. Early in 1970 Proffit called Frye to his office and informed him that he was being elevated to the administrative position of athletic director of the Burlington senior high schools. Frye accepted Proffitt's offer, but privately he remained determined to fight what amounted to his dismissal as Williams' football coach.

The school superintendent was relieved. He felt the success or failure of the integration of the Williams team would directly affect the mood of the town. "And I decided we needed a black man as coach," said Dr. Proffitt. "One who was controlled and disciplined. Jerome Evans was constructive and not bitchin' about the past sins of whites. He had a sense of what the long haul was. Although Frye believed he was a just man, I knew justice wasn't only a matter of black and white. There was a lot of gray in it, and Frye never could see gray in any situation. He was too simplistic."

When news hit Burlington that Frye had been removed as coach, a number of his supporters threatened to call a town meeting to get him reinstated. Two hundred white students walked out of classes at Williams in support of Frye. They were led by a number of football players. After several tense hours, during which the blacks threatened a counterdemonstration, the situation was resolved. Frye called off his supporters on being warned by Dr. Proffitt that if Burlington had another riot his credibility as a coach would be seriously jeopardized throughout the state.

The football players returned meekly to classes the following day and Frye dropped out of sight until midsummer, when it was announced he had accepted the post of football coach and athletic director at small Gibsonville High School, only 10 miles west of Burlington. "I wish he had gone to Florida as he threatened," said Dr. Proffitt, "rather than hanging like a shadow over the town and Jerome Evans."

When Evans started football practice in late August he did not have to prove anything to the black players who had known him at Sellers and would now be playing for Williams. His challenge lay with the team's whites. "I worried about how I should treat those boys who had supported Frye," said

Evans. "Then I decided to make believe nothing had happened and treat everyone fair. I wasn't very forceful at first
because I didn't want to scare anyone off. The whites had to
be shown that all the things they'd been brought up to be-
live about blacks were false. And to build their confidence
in me, and my own in myself, I had to show them a black
coach could win games. The Williams 4-A conference was
supposedly a lot tougher than the 3-A conference that Sellers
had played in, but I found it wasn't. After we won a few
games I could afford to get tougher with some of the white
boys."

Evans' white players and white assistant coaches began
accepting him, at least superficially. They did not see, however, that his fairness was tipped in their favor, since he
showed more tolerance for the failures of white players than
he did of the blacks, many of whom thought the coach was
"a man possessed this year."

"When Evans first came to Williams," said Mike Pierce,
"I thought he wouldn't even look at guys like me who had
walked out in support of Frye. But the first time I met him
he gave me a big smile and shook my hand and told me he
was relying on me, and after that I knocked myself out liking
him. All us whites did. But it wasn't real. We were always
wondering when we'd get shafted for one of his blacks. Soon
it occurred to us that maybe we wouldn't. If Evans had been
an emotional type of guy, like Frye, we never would have relaxed. Another problem was that it was always there in the
back of our minds that maybe Evans wasn't as good a coach
as Frye. We never admitted it, probably not even to ourselves,
but maybe it was because he was a black man. After we won
a few games we accepted him more. I guess it's a shame that

before we did, he had to prove he could win in this conference. If he was white he would have been accepted first, but because he's black he's accepted only for what he does, not for what he is."

Pierce and other whites were surprised by the cool way Evans handled situations that would have had Frye's neck deep red. One day while Evans was giving orders to his offensive team a white player, William Whitley, was staring off into space.

"If Frye caught anyone daydreaming like that," said Pierce, "the guy would still be picking Frye's cleats out of his mouth. But Evans just gave Whitley that pained smile of his and said, 'William Whitley, whatever am I gonna do with you, boy?' I guess Whitley wouldn't even be on the team if Frye was coaching. Frye had no patience for dreamers, quitters or anyone, really. If Frye doesn't like someone they don't exist anymore so far as he's concerned. Evans is the opposite. He's very decent to people he doesn't like, maybe even more decent than to people he does like."

But Evans was less than successful with two players. One was a black halfback from Jordan Sellers, Larry Matkins; the other was the team's white quarterback, Fred Long, who had been one of Frye's stars. There is a picture of Larry Matkins in the 1969 Jordan Sellers yearbook. It shows a lean, intense black youth with a completely shaven head sweeping by the outstretched arms of a would-be tackler. As a 5' 10", 175-pound sophomore, Matkins was considered one of the best prospects in the South. It was reported that the University of Alabama was interested in him. He was 15 years old. In 1970 he was elected a Williams co-captain, along with a white player, David Coleman, and he was expected to carry the team. But Matkins was to have a mediocre year. He was Evans' biggest disappointment. The coach said of him, "I see so much of myself in that boy and I want him to excel so bad it hurts." To bring out the best in Matkins, Evans was unmerciful with him in practice. If Matkins gained 20 yards on a run, Evans berated him for not gaining 30. Many whites felt Evans was expecting too much of the boy, who was now competing against more efficient defenses than he had at Sellers. Evans could not see this. He said: "Matkins' difficulty, among other things, is that girl of his."

The girl was a pretty, black cheerleader who had been going steady with Matkins since he had arrived at Williams from Sellers. Evans' complaint was that the girl had been trying "to act white, and she's trying to get Matkins to do the same thing." One day Evans caught the pair cuddled in each other's arms (a popular stance among white Willams couples) in the hallway at a time when Matkins was supposed to be at practice. When Evans told the halfback to go to his office, the girl said, "He's with me now." Evans was furious. "Well, he may be with you permanent," he declared, and left. Matkins' other difficulty was that he had always looked up to Evans in a fatherly way, and at Williams the coach was not able to devote as much attention to his star player. He was often aloof with the boy, which confused him. "I couldn't spend as much time with him as I did at Sellers," said Evans, "because the whites would think I was playing favorites. But I don't know whether Larry understood this or not."

The problem with Freddy Long was more touchy. Long was a stocky youngster with a perpetually dazed, openmouthed expression. Thanks to Frye's constant badgering, Long had produced startling offensive performances during the previous year. But he did this by calling hardly a play at the line of scrimmage himself; he was simply acting as his coach's alter ego. During the 1970 season Jerome Evans failed to get the same performances from Freddy Long. In fact, without Frye's hassling, Long seemed unable to function in the most elementary manner. When Evans gave him the freedom to call most of the plays, Long became confused. He would drop back for a pass, see a man clear and then hesitate for fear his pass might be intercepted. Then, with opposing linemen bearing down on him, he would begin scrambling in all directions before finally being tackled for a huge loss. When he got up from the tackle, always with an agonizing slowness, he would glance over at Evans, as if awaiting instruction. Evans did not want to have to call plays. He wanted his quarterbacks to be independent. But only when he began to call the team's plays did Long's performance improve.

Evans could not bench the quarterback, since Long retained a reputation as a star from the previous year. The alternative was to have a serious talk with the boy. Evans shunned this course of action for a number of games. He did not want to impose himself on the boy, for one thing, and for another, he did not particularly like Freddy Long. After one game in which Long had kicked three field goals, the boy had shaken hands with each assistant coach until he reached Evans' outstretched hand, which he avoided. Evans said nothing. Nor did Evans complain that although most quarterbacks stand beside their coach on the sidelines, it was Long's habit to sit as far away from Evans as possible. If Evans wanted him he would have to call for him two or three times before Long would move toward him.

Evans finally decided on a confrontation. He exhorted the

quarterback to take more charge of the situation on the field. Long nodded. Evans suggested he speak up in the pregame pep talks and team meetings. Long nodded again. Evans said a few more things and then allowed him to leave. The coach felt relieved to be rid of the boy but dissatisfied. It was partly his own fault, Evans thought. But he wondered just how he was supposed to deal with people he felt truly hated him.

By this very nature, Evans muted antagonisms and muffled anxieties, so that the team as a whole had no complaints against him. And because both blacks and whites accepted their coach, they learned to accept one another. But this acceptance, although amicable, was precarious at best. It boiled down to a grudging realization by both blacks and whites that if they wanted the team to be successful they had to accommodate themselves to one another's individuality. This was nothing new for blacks, who long before had learned to accommodate themselves to the white world. But it was a new and startling realization for whites. For the first time, they had to acknowledge the existence of blacks, with that existence being as equal and as deserved as their own. Whites called no one "boy" and made blacks the butt of few jokes. They made a point of avoiding criticism; when a black player dropped an easy pass nothing would be said.

This stiff sense of acceptance was mirrored in the relationships of the team's integrated cheerleading squad. (By now there were nine whites and five blacks on the squad.) The cheerleaders took their cue from the football players, many of whom were boyfriends. The girls formed friendly if not affectionate relationships in a way only girls can—smiling, breathless, squealing, polite—with members of their own sex they do not particularly like or trust.

Any difficulties the two races encountered seemed more rooted in life-styles than in race. The black girls seemed bewildered by the importance the whites attached to cheerleading. For the blacks, cheerleading was a small part of their lives, an end in itself, something to be enjoyed for the moment because it would lead to nothing else. They did not see the social relations of things, one to another, because for so long blacks had been denied the results of their acts or abilities. For example, being an intelligent black in Burlington in no way guaranteed a man a job commensurate with his abilities, as it did a white. So, for the same reason, the black cheerleaders viewed cheerleading solely as a casual endeavor, not a step forward—or upward.

The whites, on the other hand, were extremely conscious of the ties between things. Cheerleading, just like athletic talent, beauty and intelligence, could be extremely valuable to them in later years. It might lead to a successful marriage, a career and so on. For this reason the whites treated cheerleading with a reverence that seemed disproportionate to the blacks. The whites had thought the 1969 riot had been started because of the blacks' desire to become cheerleaders. If so, why were the black girls now cutting practice and not fulfilling their squad responsibilities? The answer lay not in the blacks' desire to be cheerleaders, but in their wish to have a part of anything they felt whites attached importance to, as if that thing had some mysterious and hidden value that would be revealed to them once they possessed it. They accepted its importance completely on the testimony of whites. But once they possessed it, the black girls began to wonder what was so special about this thing they now had?

The superficial acceptance black and white football players, coaches and cheerleaders shared for one another also affected the relationships of the Willams students, teachers and parents and citizens of Burlington. They accepted one another because they all accepted Jerome Evans, who had consciously presented a low profile that had made him palatable to the most hardened segregationists. Whatever else even the hardcore segregationists felt toward him, they were forced to admit he was, to use their toughest phrase, "a decent nigger." Evans achieved this by refusing to force himself on anyone. He avoided trouble. If he saw parents or teachers who wanted nothing to do with him, he did not burden them with unnecessary smiles or pleasantries. But neither was he critical of them.

The impression Jerome Evans leaves in his wake is narcotic, tranquilizing but temporary. It has no substance. Once its effect wears off, people discover they are left with nothing tangible of Jerome Evans to add to their knowledge or experience, no word or deed or thought they can grasp and make their own, and thus allow themselves to transfer to Evans their allegiance. Evans' personality is devoted not to allegiances but to safety. In the back of his mind he deals always with the thought of potential enemies, never with the thought of potential friends. His policy is defensive, to leave people with nothing they can use against him.

Henry Crawford, the president of the Williams Booster Club and a man who had a prominent role in the effort to reinstate Frye just months before, declared in midseason he had no complaints against Evans. "I got along very well with Frye," said Crawford, a gray-haired businessman. "He had a clique of rooters, and I guess I was one of them. Jerome, he doesn't have any clique. He's more aloof with everyone.

A lot of people like him for this, and I personally can't complain. So far he's handled himself wonderfully. The parents like him."

Not all the Boosters were as effusive in their praise. Lou Jones had been a friend of Frye's since 1956. For 19 years he carried the sideline chains at all home games. In 1970 he relinquished that duty to a Williams student.

"I guess Evans was the best-qualified one of the bunch if you want to look at it that way," said Jones. "Some don't like it any, but they ain't saying nothing. One father told me, 'My boys'll never play for no nigger, Lou.' Then one day in the paper Evans was quoted as saying the man's two sons would be real helpful to the club this year. Both sons are playing for Evans. When I asked the man why, he looked sheepish and said, 'Hell, Lou, that nigger's got a lot on the ball, you know.'

"Things ain't the same this year. Last season at the weekly Booster Club meetings Frye would introduce the Bulldog Player of the Week and then send the boy home and we'd all loosen up with a few jokes. Evans lets the boys hang around all night, and it makes us uncomfortable. And it seems Evans can't wait to get out of the meetings himself. If Marilyn Monroe was stripping naked on television you couldn't get Frye out of Booster Club meetings. But even when Evans is there he doesn't ever seem to loosen up. I'd like him a lot better if he did."

By late October the Williams team was assured of a winning record. The Bulldogs were 6–2 with two games left, and about the only question remaining was would they win their conference title and then go on to the state tournament? Although most white players acted as if a conference title and a

state championship were their sole reasons for being, much
of their enthusiasm seemed an effort. As one player put it
then, "I'm tired of football. If Dudley wins the title, I'll cry
like everybody else just to put on a good show, but I'll be
glad as hell. The only reason I played this year was because
Evans didn't make us cut our hair as Frye would have. Right
now, I'm sick of football."

Although most white players would not express themselves
this candidly, they seemed to share the view. They were tired
of living each day consciously, with no recourse to instinct
and habit that had marked their days before Evans' arrival.
They were tired of being aware of their every word and act,
tired of liking blacks, of liking their coach, tired in fact of
all the pressures that had been theirs since the year's first
practice session. They seemed anxious to simplify what had
been a complex year in their lives, to plant their feet once
again on solid ground with horizons that were familiar and
obstacles that were cleanly defined.

That was why, after their seventh victory of the season and
only a week before the final game, a number of white players
got together one night and drank Ripple wine and vodka into
the following morning. By noon they were drunk. Someone
suggested they drive to Gibsonville to see Frye. When they
arrived, according to some of the boys who talked about the
visit later, they waited nervously in his tiny office, not sure
just how Frye would take their call. He appeared, smiling.
There were handshakes and backslapping, and it was obvious
he was glad to see his former players. He was pleased they
still thought enough of him to make the trip to Gibsonville
and to know he still had a firm bond with these boys, one
which Evans had not broken.

A player complained offhandedly about something Evans had done in practice. Frye called him "a dumb nigger" and added that the Bulldogs should never have lost to all-black Dudley High, which they had done three Fridays before. The players agreed. There was a momentary silence in which each boy seemed to be wrestling with something that made him feel uneasy about what was happening. One of them said Frye was right, Evans was a dumb nigger. Someone else asked, "What could you expect from them? They are inferior." Other players chimed in, and there was an almost audible sigh of relief around the room as the boys relaxed and began to talk easily with their former coach. A player told Frye that the previous day there nearly had been a riot at Williams.

"What the hell you boys doing here, then?" said Frye. "I expect my boys to be in the thick of any trouble."

The players assured him they would be in the thick of such a fight. And when Frye asked if any of those niggers had made a move toward his daughter (a Williams senior) they told him that he didn't have to worry about that. They would make sure she was safe. Frye smiled and nodded.

"You know, we probably would have gone on to the state championship if you were still our coach," said one boy.

"We would not have lost a game," maintained a second.

Shortly before one p.m. the players said they had to leave. They were no longer drunk and were beginning to feel the unpleasant effects of a hangover.

"Ya all come back," said Frye as they piled into their cars. They said they would. "And watch out for my Cathy," Frye added, cementing the bond. "I need you guys."

"Don't you worry, coach," said a player, and they drove off. They felt satisfied at first and then less so, and by the time they reached Burlington they had begun to feel guilty, as if they had been a party to some unmanly act, had perpetrated some deceit, not only against Jerome Evans, whom they had befriended during the year, but also against C. A. Frye, in whom they had helped sustain an illusion of something that no longer existed. They were bewildered. Their visit to Frye had not simplified things after all. Far from it. They had returned to familiar ground only to find that ground no longer familiar, and now they were not sure where to turn.

The next Friday Williams won its final game, ending its season with an 8-2 record—the school's best performance in 10 years. Shortly after that last game Mike Pierce talked about Coach Evans: "You don't have much to say to him outside of football. I feel sorry for him now that the season is over. Who'll talk to him? I never know what to say to him. I can't get into him. Whenever I get close he gives me that little smile of his, like a spider's web tightening. The best he's got from whites in Burlington is a kind of acceptance and indifference. If he got fired tomorrow, people'd say, 'That's too bad. The nigger was a pretty good coach, wasn't he? I wonder who'll get his job. Maybe we'll get Frye back.'"

Dr. Proffitt substantially agreed. "I doubt if whites will ever feel emotionally committed to Jerome Evans as they were to Frye," he said. "But that's his strength. I wanted a pragmatist at Williams, not a flag-waver. Evans would need to be a wonderfully sophisticated organism to perform the type of job he's done and still attract people emotionally. His job wasn't to deal with people on a personal level but as a representative of the blacks. What annoyed me was that everyone talked all year about how much more appealing Frye was than Evans. But damn it, style isn't as important as substance. A person's charisma is frequently irrelevant to his ability to get a job done. So Frye was charismatic. Did people think this would get us safely through the year in this town? Shoot, I removed Frye not because he cussed a little but because I was afraid he would use his ability to get people emotionally committed to him in a cold and ruthless way—just as he tried to get his players to leave school for him without any thought to the boys' futures."

*Epilogue:*

Jerome Evans and I are driving along Highway 85 toward Durham. It is a stiflingly hot Saturday, but in his new station wagon, with its humming air conditioner, it is chilly. Evans reaches over and pushes a button on the car radio. A man's voice is saying: "If you're 6 foot 8 and black, you don't have to play basketball in order to go to college anymore. You can obtain a student loan from North Carolina Mutual. . . ." Evans looks at me with a sly grin. "This is a black car," he says. "You ever ride in a black car before?"

"No, what makes it black?"

"All the radio buttons are set to black stations. That's all I listen to," and he punches another button. An announcer is giving the starting lineups for the North Carolina Central vs. Charlotte-Smith football game. Both are black schools. "We're late," says Evans, and he presses down on the accelerator.

This is the first time Jerome Evans and I have gone out socially. Although we have gotten along as well as, if not better than, we expected in the weeks I have been in town, he has repeatedly declined suggestions that he and his family go out to dinner with me. "It isn't necessary," he would say. When I had first come to Burlington, with Evans' approval, to write a book, he avoided me constantly. He was often an hour late for scheduled interviews, and sometimes failed to show up entirely. Finally, in exasperation, I asked him why he consented to have the book written when obviously he had no stomach for the project. "It's my insurance policy," he said, and then went on to explain that if it were written down, plain to see, that he had not made one single mistake, one error of judgment, it would be impossible for him to be fired.

As we approached Durham we passed cars filled with well-dressed whites waving University of North Carolina banners. "My assistant coaches wanted me to go to the UNC game," Evans says. "I told them I'd promised to take you to see NCC play. You were a good excuse to get out of their invitations."

"Thanks a lot."

"What's there for me, anyway?" he says. "Nothing. They'll all be white, and I won't be able to relax. And when they go to those postgame parties, what am I gonna do, start talking to some white girl? Wouldn't that be beautiful? Everyone in Burlington would be saying Jerome Evans wants a white girl. They'd love that. No sir, I'd rather go to NCC. I know everyone there. I feel comfortable. I'm no black separatist or anything like that. But it's too late for me, I'll never mix. I've got a lot of hate buried in me and I want to keep it buried. If I mix too much it might come out.

"I'm satisfied with the way things are. More than satisfied. I've reached my goal in life. I don't want to go any higher. I'll let other blacks become leaders of my people. I'd lived in the black world for so long, I had no desire to leave it. Then they closed Sellers, and I had to. Everything that happened this year was new to me. But now that I'm dealing with whites, I don't care if they like me or not. I don't even want them to like me. I'd be content if they just acknowledged me as a good coach and a man."

The NCC campus consists of modern brick buildings spread over rolling hills. In a valley sits the football stadium. It really is not a stadium but wooden stands on either side of a field that has a number of brown patches on it. The buildings, the field and the campus remind me of the few black homes I have visited in Burlington. They are new, plain and functional, without any signs of a tradition or culture of their own.

We walk through the gate, admitted on Evans' coach's pass, and someone calls out "Little Willie, how's my man?" Evans smiles at a heavyset black and then says to me, "My nickname in college. Would you believe he was a teammate of mine? He's gotten fat."

Evans excuses himself for a minute and goes to the men's room. I am standing in an open space between the field and the entrance gate. To the right is a tent where black women are barbecuing spareribs. The smell of sweet sauce and burning pork is all about me. The game is in progress, the two teams huddled over the ball near the 50-yard line. They are all black. The referees, tall, raw-boned men in spotless white pants and black-and-white-striped shirts, are black. Patrolling the sidelines, just as at every football game in the country, are over-age, paunchy policemen. They, too, are black. Behind what must have been the NCC goal a group of black women are watching a mass of children playing in the leaves. On a rise overlooking the field a group of black men are standing, talking and arguing and laughing and passing paper cups of rum back and forth. The stands are filled with 10,000 people:

older men—alumni—in suits with hair that is slicked and gleaming; their women, plump, pants-suited, with straight hair upturned at the ends; younger men—students—with Afros, goatees, berets, sunglasses and sullen faces; young women in dungaree bell-bottoms and tight sweaters, with bushy Afros and that pouty Angela Davis look that has become popular.

Suddenly I am aware that my face is the only white one among these thousands of blacks. Evans has not returned. There is a fluttery feeling in my stomach, the kind actors must get before they go onstage before a vast audience. My head feels light, airy, as it must be with pot, and for the first time in my life I am acutely conscious of myself, of my presence, of existing somehow differently from those around me. I feel everyone must notice this difference, and that is why they stare. A girl walks by on the arm of her boyfriend. They do not even cast a curious glance in my direction. Was that deliberate? Three more girls pass, one looking quickly over her shoulder and then whispering to her friends, who begin to giggle among themselves.

When Evans reappears I relax slightly, but as we walk toward the stands I feel a tightening in my facial muscles and realize that for some insane reason I am smiling at his every word. When we reach the edge of the stands I am momentarily terrified. Is he going to lead me past all those black faces until he finds a seat on the 50-yard line? I can see them turning, an entire bleacher of black faces riveted to me as I walk past. But, mercifully, Evans sees a seat just above and begins climbing between people, motioning for me to follow. I step onto the first plank; a black man slides away without looking up at me. Was he angry that my foot almost touched

his coat, annoyed, indifferent? I move between people who
make room for my feet until halfway up, there is no opening.
I am standing idiotically in front of a girl who does, really
does, resemble Angela Davis. She makes believe she does not
notice me. "Excuse me," I say. Again that uncontrollable
smile. "Excuse me," I say louder, maybe too loud, I think.
She looks up, unsmiling, and moves over. "Thank you," I
say, and step quickly to the top of the bleachers where Evans
has made a place for me a little apart from the other fans. I
sit down, sweating, mentally exhausted from that climb.

I do not recall much of the game. It is a blur. I remember
only being so conscious of my presence among those black
faces that I did not say one word or raise a hand to scratch an
itch or cross a leg without first replaying the word or act over
and over in my mind until I was sure that it was an acceptable word or act and that certainly no one about me could
take exception to it. I do remember Evans talking a lot and
getting so engrossed in the game that he began yelling, "You
stupid, boy, you just plain stupid" every time one of the
NCC players fumbled or dropped a pass. I remember also the
NCC band coming on the field at halftime, twisting and singing, and Evans telling me that once the school's bandleader
had tried to get the group to perform like a white band and
they were booed loudly by the fans. When the majorettes appeared in shimmering tights, the crowd began cheering and
clapping. The girls began to twist, and a man a few seats
down from us looked through his binoculars and started hol-
lering, "Lorda mercy, Lorda mercy, I was born 20 years too
soon."

"Hey, man, let me at those things," said Evans. The man
handed him the glasses. Evans looked down at the girls and

said to no one in particular, "Now, that's one helluva game. Yes sir, one helluva game down there." The man who owned the glasses laughed.

We left before the game was over. I followed Evans down the bleachers, making sure to move directly into the cleared spaces people made for him. He led me past the middle-aged men who had stood throughout the game on the rise at one end of the field. They waved and called to him.

"I usually stand over there at the games," Evans told me, "although lately they've been kidding me because I won't drink much with them. They say that since I got the job at Williams I've gone white. I try to remind them that I never drank that much at our games. But they'll never believe me now that I have showed up with a white man. You know, you gonna get me in trouble. Ruin my name in the community," and he started laughing.

Was he kidding, I wondered. Or was he really ashamed to stand with his friends because of me?

When we arrived back in Burlington it was still light. I got out of the car, thanking Evans for taking me along. He said it was nothing and drove off. Across the street I could see William, the colored boy who served as the bellhop for the Alamance Motel. William, who is over 70, was helping a white man take the luggage out of his car. As I crossed the street, I realized that I had relaxed considerably. I was on familiar ground again.

DAN JENKINS

# The Disciples of Saint Darrell

ON A BRIGHT, warm Friday morning one fine October down
in Texas, a man named Elbert Joseph Coffman woke up with
a squirrel in his stomach. In his good life as an outrageous
football fan there had never been a weekend quite like the
one coming up. In the next fifty-five hours or so he was going
to see three big college games and one pro grame, and the
excitement of it all, the importance of the games, made him
nervous. Nervous but delighted. Football to Joe Coffman,
and thousands of other Texans, had always been as essential
as air conditioning. It was what a Texan grew up with, fed
on, worshipped, followed, played, and, very often, died with.
So it was that Joe Coffman, thirtyish, married, father, businessman, University of Texas graduate, football incurable,
was either going to live a lot this weekend—or die a little.

The first game, SMU against Navy, would be played that
evening in the Cotton Bowl in Dallas, just thirty-five miles
away from Joe Coffman's home in Forth Worth. The next
day he would go back to the same stadium to see the biggest
one of them all, Oklahoma, ranked first in the country,
against Texas, ranked second. He would drive to Waco

(ninety miles south) Saturday night to watch Baylor against Arkansas. And on Sunday he would return to the Cotton Bowl to see the NFL's Dallas Cowboys play the Detroit Lions.

If Joe Coffman's schedule seemed arduous, it was little more so than that of many others in the state. Thousands less fortunate than Coffman in getting tickets to the big games would settle for a game or two on television and radio and perhaps see a couple of high schools play. But Joe Coffman also knew that there would be more to his weekend than football. He knew that it was going to cost him at least $200, that he would be running into old friends, that there would be as many parties as kickoffs and that he would probably consume as much beer as might have been served in a London pub on V-E day. But Joe Coffman had been waiting months for this weekend and, as he prepared to leave home for his office at the business he owned near downtown Fort Worth, the only thing that concerned him was whether everybody was as ready as he was. Everybody included Joe's wife, Mary Sue, another couple, Pat and Cecil A. Morgan Jr. (he was a stockbroker and a former University of Texas basketball star), and the Coffmans' baby-sitter. "I'll tell you one thing, Mary Sue," said Joe. "We got to be suited up and ready to go by five o'clock. We're gonna be in Dallas by six or I'm gonna raise more hell than the alligators did when the pond went dry."

Joe Coffman was a modern Texan. This meant that Mary Sue was a pretty, loving and understanding wife, that his sons Bobby, six, and Larry, four, were healthy and happy, that his business was successful (four other branches in Austin, San Antonio, Lubbock and Amarillo), that his ranch-type home was comfortable, with all of the built-ins manufacturers sell these days, that he had an Oldsmobile Starfire and an Impala (both convertibles), that his close friends were mostly the ones he grew up with or knew in high school and college. Being a modern Texan also meant that Joe Coffman might not recognize a cow pony if it were tied on a leash in his backyard, that he despised Stetson hats, that he liked cashmere sports coats, pin-collar shirts, Las Vegas, playing golf at Colonial Country Club, Barbra Streisand ("Think she can't sing?"), good food, good booze, Barry Goldwater and, more than anything else, the Texas Longhorns. And did he like those Longhorns?

"They got too much character to lose that game," Joe said about Texas as he browsed through the mail on his desk at the office, drank some coffee and talked on the phone. Like any loyal Longhorn, his preoccupation with the OU game was all-consuming. The other games, they were good ones, Joe Coffman felt, but his good health, he said, his well-being and welfare would be riding with the Longhorns. It was not a very good day for work.

"I got to think a Bloody Mary's the answer," he said, heading out to Colonial Country Club. There would be friends there, talking football, "getting down" (making bets), and the time would pass more quickly through the endless football arguments that take place in Colonial's nineteenth hole the day before the games.

"Hey, Coffman," someone called as Joe entered Colonial and headed toward a table. "What are the Sooners gonna do to those T-sippers?" Joe Coffman removed his sunglasses, postured with his fist raised like Mussolini and said, "We're gonna send them sumitches back across the Red River, boys." He greeted a table of friends, ordered drinks and replied to every argument about the strength of Oklahoma's team with his message of the week: "Have to win, boys. Too much character. We got too much character to lose that game." Several Bloody Marys later, Joe Coffman had got through the day. Now the long, exhausting—and utterly perfect—weekend began.

It is roughly thirty-five miles, or twenty-five minutes, by way of the toll road from Fort Worth to Dallas. The first stop on Friday night for Mary Sue and Joe Coffman and Pat and Cecil Morgan was Gordo's. Gordo's was to Dallas what the Cafe Select was to *The Sun Also Rises*. It was a tiny beer–pizza–steak-sandwich parlor across from the SMU campus. Through its portals strolled many of Dallas's prettiest girls, its brawniest athletes, its newspaper columnists, flacks, poets, politicians and everyone, in fact, who was in enough to know about the place or who liked the world's best pizza or steak sandwich or who wanted Gordon West, the owner, to cash a personal check.

The dilemma of the visitor to Gordo's was what to eat. "I got to have a steak sandwich and a cheeseburger between two pizzas," said Joe. "It's all so good, I can't stand it."

Mary Sue, a small blonde who went two years to SMU and then graduated from Texas, suggested that whatever they were to have they have it quickly, because the traffic to the Cotton Bowl for the SMU–Navy game was going to be pretty brutal.

"I hope SMU does good," she said. "Do they have a chance to beat Navy, Joe?"

"Flattop Fry, boys," said Joe in his sepulchral voice, as if he had been asked to answer the entire room.

"Old Flattop," said Cecil Morgan. It was Joe and Cecil's

private way of making fun of SMU's crew-cut coach Hayden Fry, who somehow acquired that nickname from them. Coffman and Morgan, given time, can make fun of every coach in the country—except Texas's Darrell Royal.

"Can they, Joe?" Mary Sue asked.

"Hell, yes," said Joe. "They haven't got any athletes, but they'll get after 'em. Like to see it. Be the start of an upset weekend, boys. The one we gotta have is tomorrow, though. Got to send 'em back across the Red River." Joe ordered another beer. And another. And one more.

"We better move out," Cecil Morgan said presently. "They're gonna hang us up in that state fair traffic."

"Yawl want paper cups?" Gordo asked, thoughtfully.

"I 'magine," said Joe. "Take that pizza with you, Mary Sue. Grab that beer, Cecil. We got to go see the Red Helmets play the Navys."

"Old Flattop," said Cecil.

There is no easy way to reach the Cotton Bowl in Dallas except to be dropped into it by helicopter. The stadium sits squarely in the middle of the Texas State Fairgrounds, and all roads lead in confusion from downtown Dallas about two miles away. That week the fair was in full swing. Indeed, that was the reason for three games in three days. It was almost as though somebody said, "There's no use bringin' 'em in from halfway 'cross the state for one li'l ol' extravaganza." Complaining about the traffic and the parking at the Cotton Bowl has always been one of Dallas's favorite pastimes. It is not so amusing when one wants to make a kickoff.

Behind the wheel of his Starfire, Joe Coffman sighed, "Man, man. Only stadium in the whole world where you have to get here on Wednesday to make a Friday night game."

Mary Sue said, "I can't believe all these cars are going to the SMU game."

"They aren't," said Cecil. "They're goin' to buy balloons. I'll guarantee you, there's seven million people out here tonight to buy balloons."

"Main thing they're doing," said Joe, "is driving in front of me."

By the time they had reached a parking place inside the state fairgrounds and trudged through the dust of the carnival midway, with only one beer stop, and then reached their seats, the game was five minutes old.

"Look at that!" Joe said, pointing at the SMU bench. "Flattop Fry don't know how many players he can send in or take out. He just sends in ten men every time."

"Saint Darrell knows the rules," said Cecil.

"I 'magine," said Joe.

As the SMU-Navy game wore on, it became clear that SMU was in no mood to lose as easily as the odds (thirteen points) had suggested. In fact, by the start of the fourth quarter Joe and Cecil had become enraptured with SMU's blazing-fast sophomore, tailback John Roderick, whose running was exciting them more than the passing of Navy's Roger Staubach. Although there merely as impartial observers, saving their enthusiasm for the Longhorns, Joe and Cecil could not resist blending themselves into the madness of the occasion as SMU won rather miraculously 32–28. The wives, Mary Sue and Pat, might have enjoyed it more if they had not been so fascinated by the conversation of an elderly Dallas lady in front of them, who kept talking to a friend about the "common people from Fort Worth."

Once Mary Sue giggled to Joe, "You can't believe what this woman is saying. She's saying that no saleswoman in Dallas will wait on Fort Worth people because they come over here without hats or gloves on. Just common as can be, she said." Joe roared. He leaned down the aisle and repeated it to Cecil. Cecil roared. It gave them a theme for the weekend, and some exit lines from the stadium.

"Naw," said Cecil, "We jest gonna git our common little ol' wives and go git drunked up on thet ol' beer."

"Good Lord, Cecil," said Pat. "You sound country enough without talking that way."

"Hell, we jest common," Joe laughed. He looked at Cecil. "You 'bout half country, ain't you, boy?"

They were badly in need of a beer.

"It'd be gooder'n snuff," said Cecil as Pat frowned, and they walked to the parking lot.

The Friday night before the annual Texas–OU game is a night that Dallas must brace for all year long.

Even without another football game to further overcrowd the city, which considers itself a cultural oasis in a vast wilderness of oil workers' helmets and Levis, the downtown area is declared off limits by every sane person, cultured or not. Throngs of students and fans gather in the streets, whisky bottles sail out of hotel windows, automobiles jam and collide and the sound of sirens furnishes eerie background music to the unstill night. Joe Coffman skillfully managed to commit his group to a post-SMU-game party (or pre-Texas-OU-game party) in the cultural suburbs, where the status symbols are a lawn of St. Augustine grass and a full-growing mimosa tree.

"Joe, are all of those funny people really going to be

there?" Mary Sue asked as they drove out the Central Expressway.

"Honey, I got no idea. All I know is, they said come on out and they'd give a man a drink. And I know a man who really wants one."

"What's the name of the apartments?" Pat asked.

"I got the address," said Joe. "That's all. It's one of those Miami-Las Vegas names. Every apartment in Dallas, I'll guarantee you, sounds like a Polynesian drink. The Sand and Sea, or the Ski-Sky-You, or something."

"I think it's The Antigua," said Cecil.

"Well," said Joe, "that figures."

Through the night the party was both visible and audible before Joe parked the car. People were standing on the lawn, sitting on the steps of other apartment units or gathered around a clump of trees. The door was open. A Ray Charles record poured out. Inside there was a curious mixture of "stewardi," as Joe described the girls, along with SMU fans, Texas fans, Oklahoma fans, Dallas Cowboy fans, Dallas Cowboys, bartenders, musicians, entertainers from the city's private clubs, models and artists.

Joe observed the crowd and turned to Cecil and said, "Go any*whur,* do any*thang.*" And they inched toward the bar. Joe saw a man he had been with in the Army. Mary Sue saw a girl friend she was supposed to have met at the game. Cecil calmly studied the wall. On it were a Columbia pennant, a bizarre unidentified animal's head with a sign hanging around it that read, "Joe Don Looney," a bullfight poster and a drawn sign that proclaimed, "If the Lord Didn't Want Man to Drink, He Wouldn't Have Give Him a Mouth." In the bathroom hung a replica of the Mona Lisa. Joe saw an old fraternity buddy from Austin, an SAE. "Sex Above Everything," said Joe, shaking hands. Somebody said Henny Youngman had been there but left because nobody wanted to talk to him. Somebody said strippers were coming over from the Carousel club. A man who kept introducing himself as "Sandy Winfield" and "Troy Donahue" said it had not turned out to be a bad party, considering he had not called anyone. No one ever found out who lived in the apartment.

Joe Coffman was making coffee at home by seven o'clock Saturday morning on four hours' sleep. He stared blankly at the Fort Worth morning *Star-Telegram,* which had the starting lineups for the Texas–OU game, and said, half to his sons and half to the western world, "They outweigh us, but we got too much character." By nine o'clock he was dressed and ready, except for his lucky cuff links. "Tell you one thing, honey," he said. "If I can't find my cuff links, there's gonna be more hell raised than there are Chinamen." Mary Sue went to a drawer and got them. "You just won the game," said Joe.

Everything moved briskly now. Joe took one son, Bobby, to a party, and arranged for him to get home. Cecil called and said he was on the way with the car already gassed up and the beer iced down. Joe told him the sitter was due about the same time. It was Eva Mae, he said. "All I know is, she's the head pie lady at Paschal High. Bakes twenty to thirty a day." They hung up, laughing. The two couples were on the road at 10:00 A.M.

Cecil was plugging along nicely on the toll road when Pat

reminded him that he was going eighty mph. The speed limit was seventy.

"Can't get there too soon," said Joe. "Got to hear Hank Thompson. He's always singing on the fairgrounds at noon."

"Yeah," said Cecil. "That's about like you common people from Fort Worth. You *lack* them hillbilly *sangers.*"

Said Joe, "Can't beat it. Drink beer, listen to old Hank and then warp the Okies. Perfect day. I had to have about fifty dollars worth of that five and a half points."

"Did you bet, Joe?" said Mary Sue in a concerned voice.

"I 'magine."

Mary Sue looked out of the window.

"We're gonna warp 'em," said Joe. "Guarantee you Saint Darrell's gonna drown 'em. Too much character. I don't care who they got. Joe Don Looney. Jimmy Jack Drunk. Anybody. They don't have Scott Appleton. They don't have Tommy Nobis or Mr. Duke Carlisle," he said, referring to Texas's finest players: Appleton, the brilliant tackle; Nobis, the tough, dedicated linebacker; and Carlisle, the resourceful quarterback who preferred to run rather than pass.

Mary Sue and Pat opened the beer, and Joe and Cecil sang a parody on a hillbilly tune: "I don't care 'bout my gas and oil,/Long as I got my Dare-e-ull Royal,/Mounted on the dashboard o' my car."

They sang it several dozen times until the Cotton Bowl traffic slowed Cecil to a creep along Grand Avenue, one of the main entrance streets. "Joe, baby," Cecil said, "we're gonna have to sell the car, 'cause we got no place to park it."

"Keep goin'. We're gonna get in a lot right up here."

"No chance," said Cecil, observing maybe five thousand parked cars.

"Go on," Joe said. "I'm gonna show you how to ease right on in. Keep goin'. Keep goin'."

Joe said. "Right there! That lot right on the corner, just across from the main entrance. Right there, Cecil, where it says, 'Full House.' "

Cecil turned in amid the frenzied waving and shouting of parking-lot attendants, but Joe leaned out of the window and hollered, "I got a five and a cold beer, podna, if you'll let us in."

Parking was no problem.

The Texas State Fairgrounds on the day of the Oklahoma game are no more crowded than the recreation deck of any ordinary troopship. The ground seems to sag from the weight of hundreds having picnics. "Fried chicken, boys," said Joe, pushing along a walkway and observing the people sprawled on the lawn. "Two necks and a back and a piece of cold bread."

"And some black French fries," added Cecil. "Best meal they ever had. Boy, it's fun."

They stopped and bought six beers, two extra, and finally the voice of Hank Thompson greeted them as they came near Big Tex, the giant cowboy statue that is emblematic of the fair and would make fine kindling wood. Hank Thompson was singing a familiar hillbilly ballad that went, "We got time for one more drink and a . . . six-pack to go." Joe and Cecil whooped.

By prearrangement, the Coffmans and Morgans had planned to meet Joe's sister, Shirley, and his brother-in-law, David Alter, to straighten out the ticket situation. Joe had decided that Mary Sue and Shirley would sit in the end zone while he and David would take the two seats on the 50-yard line. Joe thought that seemed fair enough, and no back talk. Cecil and Pat had their own tickets. The Alters arrived, and Joe acknowledged them with, "Too much character, boys. We got too much character to lose that game." Several beers and Hank Thompson songs later, they were moving into the Cotton Bowl, again singing, "I don't care 'bout my gas and oil,/Long as I got my Dare-e-ull Royal,/Mounted on the dashboard o' my car."

The Texas–Oklahoma game is one of the maddest spectacles of sport. This was the eighteenth consecutive sellout of the series, with 75,504 seats of the stadium crammed with the throatiest, most enthusiastic partisans in football, evenly divided between Texans and Oklahomans. Regardless of the team records, the excitement is there each year; the game matches state against state, school against school, fraternity against fraternity, oil derrick against oil derrick. Some rooters become so emotional that they can see only black on the other side of the field. One who did this year was fullback Harold Philipp of Texas. Before the game, talking about the Texas boys playing on the Oklahoma team, he said: "Why that's just like somebody from the United States playing for Nazi Germany." During the game an immense roar wafts up from the stadium on every play, and the two large bands play "Boomer Sooner," the Oklahoma fight song, and "Texas Fight," the Longhorns' song, an innumerable number of times, always to the accompaniment of a cheering, jeering mob of singers. Occasionally fights break out in the stands.

The game did not provide any opportunities for Joe Coffman to fight, or even to officiate or complain. Texas was better than even he had expected, and simply swept Oklahoma away, winning 28–7. Joe still managed several excuses for leaping cries of, "Hook 'em Horns," but mainly he occupied himself with pointing out to David Alter some of the more subtle, polished tactics of Darrell Royal's second- and third-teamers. Every time Oklahoma's Jim Grisham, a superb full-back from Olney, Texas, carried the ball, Joe hollered, "Get that turncoat!" And when an OU fan near him would yell encouragement to the Sooners, Joe would quietly remark to his brother-in-law, "Jimmy Jack Drunk back there thinks he's still got a chance to win."

Later, in the usual postgame playing of "The Eyes of Texas" by the Longhorn band down on the field, Joe stood silently proud, pleased and even touched that his team had been so great on the big day. "That song chokes me up every time," he said, forcing a grin. "Man, Dare-e-ull had 'em hot today. You know what Joe Don Looney got? Mr. Scott Appleton gave him zip. Shut him out."

Joyful cries of "Hook 'em Horns" were billowing out of the apartment in north Dallas, the good side of town, or rather, the only side, when the Coffmans, Morgans and Alters got there. Unlike the party the night before, this one was strictly for Longhorns. Platters of ham and turkey were laid out on a table. A bartender in the kitchen was mixing drinks and opening beers as fast as possible. Wives and girl friends congregated on the sofas. The men pushed into the kitchen and spilled out onto a balcony, drinks lifted, in a continuous toast to Dare-e-ull Royal and Scott Appleton and Duke Carlisle and Tommy Ford and to the memory of college days at Austin. "Hey, Cecil," called Joe. "Just got the score. Florida beat Alabama!"

Cecil slumped back in a chair, laughed heartily, and said,

"All I know is, Texas is number one, two, three and four."

After a while, Mary Sue quietly asked Joe if, in the light of the Texas victory, he still intended to drive to Waco for the Baylor–Arkansas game.

"They're still playin', aren't they?" said Joe.

"Well, we'd better do something about dinner," said Mary Sue.

"Get after that turkey and ham," Joe nodded. "Tell you what. Make up some sandwiches and grab six or eight beers out of the icebox and we're gone."

Waco, Texas is noted for only two things. One is that it is the home of Baylor University. The other is that Waco, from time to time, has tornadoes. From Dallas it is about one hour and twenty minutes across the flat north central Texas farmland and, since the Baylor–Arkansas game was mercifully scheduled for 8:00 P.M., the Coffmans and Morgans should have had plenty of time to make the kickoff. But they overstayed the Texas celebration party, and Cecil was moving along too briskly on Highway 77 when the flashing red spotlight on a Texas highway patrol car encouraged him to pull over.

"It's the fuzz," Joe said. "No bad mouth now, Cecil. Don't give him any lip. Just 'Yes sir, Officer, don't hit me no more,' or he'll take us to the Waxahachie jail and nobody'll ever hear from us again."

Cecil Morgan put up a strong argument, but the patrolman decided that he probably ought to have a speeding ticket for $20.50, payable by mail. Cecil had, after all, been driving seventy-five mph in a fifty-five-mph zone.

Joe Coffman writhed in the backseat.

"Don't mind the money, just hate to miss the kickoff," he said.

They missed the whole first quarter, as it turned out. It was just as well. Although Baylor's passing wizard, Don Trull, and its excellent receiver, Lawrence Elkins, staged a wonderful exhibition, the Coffmans and Morgans could not have cared less. They were rooting for Baylor to upset the Razorbacks, which it did 14–10, but the Texas-OU game had drained them of all enthusiasm. "I'd feel okay," said Joe, "if I didn't have dust in my hair, dirt in my nose and sores in my mouth."

The group laughed faintly. Mary Sue and Pat yawned as Don Trull completed a fifty-three-yard pass to Elkins that brought 40,000 other people to their feet. Cecil and Joe pondered quietly the ability of Arkansas to defeat Texas. "No way," Joe decided, sleepily.

"Baylor's sure a swell place." Cecil said, sarcastically. "I saw one of their biggest and oldest fans a while ago, and he's sitting on the goal line. Can you imagine that? No wonder they can't win a championship."

They all yawned again, and soon the game ended. Cecil said he "might could manage" to drive home. Joe said he would pay a hundred dollars if Baylor would let him sleep all night in the parking lot.

"Shame to be this close to Austin and not go," Joe said. "Cecil, what would you give for some crispy, chewy tacos at El Rancho right now? You think El Rancho's chili con queso sounds good? Good Lord!"

The ritual of a football fan, the *real* football fan, in Dallas on Sunday was to attend the Cowboy Club, both before and after the NFL games in the Cotton Bowl. Texas being a dry state (many blame the Baptists and some Texans therefore blame Baylor), the owners of the Cowboys long ago took the precaution of seeing to it that their loyal fans (those who buy memberships) can get a "mixed" drink and something to eat at the club on the state fairgrounds. During the fair and the big football weekend, however, so many people were in town that the club had to move from air-conditioned indoor quarters to a tent just outside of the Cotton Bowl. It was still the place to be on a lazy Sunday that dawned as clear and warm and calm as Friday and Saturday had been. The Cowboys had not won a game and had lost four, but Joe Coffman kept telling people that they were a cinch to beat the Lions. "It's a sure thing," he said to Bedford Wynne, part owner, along with Clint Murchison, Jr., of the Cowboys. "It's an upset weekend, boys. It just figures."

"Hell, I'm startin' to get nervous, now that you told me that," said Bedford.

When a college game has been played in Dallas the day before, the Cowboy Club serves another purpose. It is sort of a hangover haven. Bloody Marys or Bull Shots outsell any other drink, 20–1, and frequently spectators bring their own Bloody Marys in giant thermoses. Since Bedford Wynne, like Joe and Cecil, was one of the most ardent Texas fans in captivity, the Cowboy Club was also a haven for University of Texas fans.

From table to table, the talk was all about the "Horns and that terrific thing they did to Oklahoma Saturday." Mary Sue and Pat sat with a long table of women, discussing the other women across the tent, Joe and Cecil stood, table-hopped, drank, laughed and finally ate two barbecue sandwiches.

"You think the eyeballing ain't something in this place," said Joe, looking around at the women, who even though going to the game, were dressed as fashionably as if they had just stepped out of Nieman-Marcus. "Got to be headquarters for world champion pretty," he said. "Can't wait for the game to be over so we can come back."

As Joe Coffman had said, it was the Cowboys' day to win. The game lulled along for three quarters, but finally exploded into an offensive spectacular in the fourth quarter, with the Cowboys winning a close one, 17–14.

The crowd was sparse. "Had to be a guts-up fan to make this one on top of all the others," said Joe moodily. "I got to think the crowd's bigger in the Cowboy Club—if they're still serving booze."

Mostly at the insistence of the wives, Mary Sue and Pat, there was yet to be one more stop for them all before the weekend would stagger to a halt. Mary Sue and Pat noted, without an excess of enthusiasm, that they had not eaten a hot meal in two days. The Beefeater Inn would be nice, said Mary Sue, and it was seldom crowded on a Sunday evening.

"Got to have it," Joe said pleasantly. "Steak, asparagus, coffee and cognac. Got to have it right now." They were there in twenty minutes.

It was a quiet evening, spent mostly in reflection on the four games, and all the people they had seen and in forgetting how much each had drunk. "Guarantee you," Joe said, "we saw everybody but Nasty Jack Kilpatrick."

"Who?" Pat Morgan asked.

"Nasty Jack Kilpatrick," Coffman laughed. "Toughest man I ever knew. Hitchhiked all the way from Miami to Austin one time with nothing but an old toothbrush and a Johnnie Ray record of 'Cry.' Think he wasn't tough?"

In the fatigued after-dinner silence Mary Sue thought it would be a good idea if Joe called Fort Worth long distance to check up on the children.

"Why don't you call, Honey?" Joe asked.

"Please call, Joe," she said.

"Go on, Honey," said Joe.

"You can do it quicker, Joe," Mary Sue said, pleadingly.

Joe Coffman frowned, shoved himself away from the cognac and coffee with a groan.

Walking off, he turned and said, "I'll tell you one thing, Mary Sue. You just lost yourself a fistful of dimes." A little less than two hours later, tired but full, aching but pleased, oversmoked, overlaughed, dusty-weary but all-victorious, they were home. All four teams had won, all four people had survived.

"Don't forget," said Joe, as he left Cecil and Pat, "we got to get away from here early Friday."

Pat said, "Are we really going to Little Rock for Texas–Arkansas?"

Joe Coffman looked offended.

"They're playin', aren't they?"

ARTHUR DALEY

# The Silent Mr. Stengel

ST. PETERSBURG, FLA.—"I ain' talkin'," said Charles Dillon
Stengel. The Yankee manager folded his arms across his
manly bosom and stared stonily across Miller Huggins Field,
just like a sphinx. But soon his vocal chords began to simmer
and seethe in the fashion of a volcano that has been sup-
pressed too long. An eruption was inevitable.

"I'm kinder dead this year," was his feeble explanation.
"I can't talk."

So the tourist merely sat in the dugout with him, waiting
patiently for the hot, molten lava to come cascading forth. It
was to be the Last Days of Pompeii, total engulfment.

"Now you can take Cerv," began Stengel for no particular
reason at all. It wasn't surprising, though, because Ol' Case
frequently starts his conversations in the middle.

"Like I wuz sayin', you can take Cerv and I'll explain it
to you. At one time or another we had the three most valuable players in the American Association. One wuz Cerv, one
wuz Skowron and one wuz Power, which I got rid of, and
none of them did nuthin' the followin' season. But he can
hit left-handed pitchin' and he can hit right-handed pitchin'

and he can pinch-hit, a very handy feller to have on your ball club I don't mind sayin'."

There now will be a slight pause for station identification.

The last chap he was discussing was not Cerv or Skowron or Power but Enos Slaughter. How did Enos get into the discussion? Who knows?

"Now just look at that kid, Carter, on third," said the virtually mute manager. "He's gotta good arm. You can tell by the way he throws."

A tourist is bound to learn something if he listens long enough to the Ol' Perfessor. If a man throws well, he has a good arm. Betcha never knew that before.

"For the first time and I'd better knock wood on this," Stengel droned on, "Mantle comes to spring trainin' in good health and he's a first class man in so many ways which he did like he got power, speed and an arm but strikes out too much. What's wrong with Bauer and it seems a lotta clubs desire him which you know and Noren had a very good year although I don't like to have a left-handed thrower in left field. Hey, Mantle, thatsa way to bunt you might hit .400 and beat Berra out."

The last sentence was shouted to Master Mickey after the erstwhile boy wonder had deftly dragged a bunt down the first base line.

Stengel's roving eyes stopped at sight of a mob of ball players clustered near first base, all candidates for the job there. The leading candidate, at the moment, is Bill (Moose) Skowron, a reformed football player from Purdue and a powerful right-handed hitter.

"The reason Skowron stayed in the outfield his second year," said Casey, picking up a conversational thread from the tangle, "is that I delayed him. You can look it up but I think he led the American Association two years in hittin' although I may be wrong. Yankee success at first has been with lefty hitters but when you mention Gehrig you take in a lot of time.

"Mr. Kryhoski played on our ball club part of the year and he lives in New Jersey where a lotta writers and ball players live. He once hit sixteen home runs in the American League which ain't the American Association but the big leagues although he only hit one homer last year with Baltimore which is a bad ball park.

"He's thrilled to be back with the Yankees and one of the things which annoys the management is the salaries of all the first basemen we've got which is more than the rest of the league combined. We have the most first basemen, the largest and they eat the most which you should see their hotel bills.

"And now we come to Collins which may be an outfielder. He played center field in Newark and also played right field for me in the world series. You can look it up but he had Novikoff on one side of him and some one else whose name I've forgotten on the other but you can look it up. That should prove he's a great outfielder in order to be able to do it with them guys on either side of him.

"There's a kid infielder named Richardson who wuz in our rookie camp which he don't look like he can play because he's stiff as a stick but—whoost!—and the ball's there and he does it so fast it would take some of them Sunshine Park race track handicappers with the field glasses to see him do it so fast does he do it. He never misses. As soon as he misses a ball we'll send him home.

"We start out to get us a shortstop and now we got eight

of them. We don't fool we don't. I ain't yet found a way to play more than one man in each position although we can shift them around and maybe make outfielders outa them or put 'em at ketch like we done with Howard but if some of the second division teams don't start beatin' Cleveland we may be in trouble.

"Like I said, though, I wanna see some of these guys before I start passin' comment and that's why I ain't talkin'."

Sorry, folks. That's why it's impossible to offer any quotes today from Charles Dillon Stengel, the sphinx of St. Pete.

GRANTLAND RICE

# The Big Fellow, Babe Ruth

THE FIRST TIME I saw Babe Ruth was in April 1919. Ruth was taking his turn in batting practice at Tampa, Florida, the springtraining camp of the champion Boston Red Sox. Since covering my first World Series in 1905, I'd seen a lot of swingers. But never a swinger like this!

Babe blasted one pitch clear out of the park into a ploughed field. I gauged that trip as about 500 feet—not bad, even without a publicity man around to check the distance with a tape measure. While Ruth hit, I watched, and Ed Barrow, the Red Sox manager, talked.

"Ruth was our main holdout," said Barrow. "He's been signed to a three-year contract. At twenty-four, this fellow can become the greatest thing that's happened to baseball. He's a fine southpaw pitcher—he can become a great one. But the day I can use him in the outfield and take advantage of his bat every day—well, they'll have to build the parks bigger, just for Ruth."

After bombing about ten shots, Ruth circled the bases, mincing along with short, pigeon-toed steps—a base-circling trot destined to become as celebrated as Man O'War's gallop.

When Ruth came over to mop his face in a towel, Barrow introduced us.

"You sound like you got a cold," said Ruth.

"I have, sort of," I replied.

Taking an enormous red onion out of his hip pocket, Ruth thrust it into my hand. "Here, gnaw on this," he said. "Raw onions are cold-killers." While Ruth talked I gnawed, with tears streaming from my eyes.

From the start, Ruth and I hit it off. Absolutely honest, the Babe from first to last said exactly what he thought. The Chicago White Sox, he felt, had a smart, hustling club, and Boston would need the breaks to stick close.

"Babe," I said, "I was watching your swing. You swing like no pitcher I ever saw."

"I may be a pitcher, but first off I'm a hitter," said Babe. "I copied my swing after Joe Jackson's. His is the perfectest. Joe aims his right shoulder square at the pitcher, with his feet about twenty inches apart. But I close my stance to about eight and a half inches or less. I find I pivot better with it closed. Once committed . . . once my swing starts, though, I can't change it or pull up. It's all or nothing at all."

Throughout a career that spanned 20 years, Ruth never changed the basic fundamentals of that gorgeous, gargantuan arc—a swing that captured the imagination of the crowd nearly as much as the man behind it. To watch Ruth go down, swinging from the heels, often sprawling from the sheer violence of his cut, was almost as exciting as seeing him blast one out of the park.

Of all the sluggers that the advent of the lively ball has spawned, Babe was the only one I ever knew who never shortened or choked his grip when the count reached two strikes.

He gripped his bat with the knob of the handle "palmed" in his right hand. So perfect was his wrist snap—and the other reflexes that go into the perfectly timed swing—that he could wait on the pitch until the last split second and "pick" the ball practically out of the catcher's mitt. Ted Williams is about the only other long ball hitter I know who has this amazing faculty.

The Babe liked plenty of lumber in his war clubs. Many of his bludgeons weighed 42 ounces—about a half-pound more than the average bat.

That spring the Red Sox and McGraw's Giants played a four-out-of-seven exhibition series at Tampa. In '18 the Giants had finished second, behind Chicago, and in '19 John J. felt he had a hustling club that was really going places. A Giant rookie that spring was Jim Thorpe, the big, amiable Carlisle Indian. McGraw said Thorpe couldn't hit a curve ball, but I still feel the main reason he got rid of Jim was that Thorpe was turning his team inside out—in friendly wrestling matches.

I hung around for several games to watch Ruth hit and play left field. The New York writers were pop-eyed; the Boston boys had already oiled up their best adjectives for him. In the first game he hit the longest ball I ever saw—some six miles over the right center-field fence and into the infield of an adjacent race track.

Bill McGeehan, of the New York *Tribune*, who didn't impress easily, wrote: *The ball sailed so high that when it came down it was coated with ice . . . a drive that would have rattled off the clubhouse roof at the Polo Grounds.*

My own notes includes this gem: *No less than 134 automobiles chugged through the gate and surrounded the play-*

*ing field in a gleaming cordon. This gave Ruth a shining target to shoot at, but the Babe still prefers the old-fashioned fence—over which today's winning smash traveled like a runaway comet.*

That Giants series put the exclamation mark on Ruth, the home-run hitter, and practically wrote his finis as a pitcher. That was O.K. with Babe. Ruth, the outfielder, no longer would have to muscle his way in.

"It was sorta rough at that," he commented years later. "I came up as a southpaw pitcher—and pitchers aren't supposed to hit—or to clutter up the batter's box *trying* to hit during practice. I saw no reason why I shouldn't take my licks. I'd get them, usually, but there were times I'd go to my locker next day and find my bats sawed in half."

That '19 season was one week old when I opened my column with this verse:

### Son of Swat—Babe Ruth

When you can lean upon the ball
    And lay the seasoned ash against it,
The ball park is a trifle small,
    No matter how far out they've fenced it.
Past master of the four-base clout,
    You stand and take your wallop proudly—
A pretty handy bloke about,
    I'll say you are . . . and say it loudly.

I've seen a few I thought could hit,
    Who fed the crowd on four-base rations;
But you, Babe, are the Only It—
    The rest are merely imitations.
I've seen them swing with all they've got

And tear into it for a mop-up;
But what they deem a lusty swat
To you is but a futile pop-up.

Somewhere amid another throng,
    Where Fate at times became unrully,
I've heard Big Bertha sing her song
    Without an encore from yours truly.
Yes, she had something—so to speak—
    A range you couldn't get away with,
But when you nail one on the beak
    They need another ball to play with.

Boston finished in sixth place as Chicago's brilliant team roared in, despite the fact that Ruth hit 29 homers. In January 1920, when owner Harry Frazee of the Red Sox was heavily in debt, he sold Ruth to Jake Ruppert's third-place New York Yankees for 125,000 dollars outright, plus a 350,000 dollar loan. The transaction remains baseball's all-time bargain.

A word anent baseball's only scandal, the '19 World Series between Cincinnati and the Chicago White Sox, who overnight became known as the Black Sox. Installed as heavy Series favorites for the best of nine games—a short-lived concession to postwar fervor—eight Chicago players sold out to the gamblers. I covered that Series with Ring Lardner, Jack Wheeler, Runyon and the rest of the New York crowd.

Chicago was at least 5 to 3 to win it all and could easily have been an even more lopsided favorite. Their pitching staff featured Ed (Knuckles) Cicotte, who had won 29 games that year; Claude (Lefty) Williams, 23 and 11; and Dickie Kerr, practically an also-ran with a 13–8 record.

"Champ" Pickens, organizer of the Blue and Grey football game at Montgomery, Alabama, years later, was in our party. The eve of the first game in Cincinnati, "Champ" walked into my room and said, "I've just been offered five to four on Cincinnati by a professional gambler."

"How much of it did you take?" I asked.

"Take, hell! This Series is fixed," replied Pickens, tossing his ticket on the bed. "You can have it—I'm going to the race track."

Cicotte was knocked out of the box in the first game, the Reds winning 9 to 1.

Williams opened the second game against the Reds' "Slim" Salee, and it was a pitching duel for three innings. Williams "blew" in the fourth, giving three bases on balls and three runs, the Reds winning that one 4 to 2.

I was sitting next to Lardner when Ring started pounding his typewriter furiously. He kept humming, "I'm Forever Blowing Bubbles." His bitter parody of that song, dedicated to Williams, opened with, "I'm forever blowing ball games. . . ."

Kerr, never implicated in the "fix," won two games, his first a 3-hit shutout, but there just weren't enough Kerrs to go around. I felt as though I'd been kicked in the stomach. The investigation lasted through the '20 season, the guilty ones being banned from organized ball for life.

And so it remained for this great, overgrown kid, Ruth, to lead baseball out of the wilderness and back into the aura of respectability. It was at the Princess Martha Hotel in St. Petersburg in 1930, after Ruth had signed a contract calling for 80,000 dollars a year for two years, that Colonel Ruppert commented, "Who are we kidding? I could pay 'Root' two hundred thousand dollars a year and he wouldn't be over-paid."

In 1920, the year following the Black Sox scandal, baseball needed a Superman, a man who could capture the imagination of the public—who could restore America's faith in baseball. Babe fit the bill. The public wanted to see the ball smashed out of the park—where there couldn't be any question of inside baseball—and the game's leaders moved to help. The ball was given a shot of rabbit juice, and in '20 Babe's big bat boomed for 54 homers. He alone realigned the game on the order of the long hit—the big inning. Lifting the Yankees aboard his shoulders, Ruth immediately became the heartwood of what was to become "Murderers' Row." In '20 the Yanks, again third, outdrew the Giants—in the Polo Grounds, to McGraw's chagrin. In '21, '22 and '23 the Giants and Yanks tangled in the World Series —'23 being the year Ruppert's team moved from the Polo Grounds into their own million-dollar home across the Harlem River, "The House That Ruth Built."

Concerning Ruth "the kid"—he seldom mentioned his childhood. Actually Babe recalled little about it himself. He was in St. Mary's Industrial Home at Baltimore from the time he was seven or eight until he was seventeen, when Jack Dunn, the old Orioles manager, took him from Brother Gilbert and signed him to a contract calling for 600 dollars for the 1914 season.

Johnny Evers, keystone of Chicago's immortal Tinkers-to-Evers-to-Chance combine, once told me an anecdote that Ruth told him.

When Babe was about seven, it seems he tapped the family till. "I took one dollar," said Babe, "and bought ice cream cones for all the kids on the block. When my old man asked me what I'd done I told him. He dragged me down cellar and beat me with a horsewhip. I tapped that till again—just to show him he couldn't break me. Then I landed in the Home, thank God!"

Some years ago, Tom Meany, writing a book on Babe's life, ran into a tout who sold his daily tips, in printed form, at the New York tracks, and who had spent his childhood with Babe at "The Home."

"You know," he said, "either Babe's gone soft or I've gone nuts. But I hafta laugh when I hear that place mentioned as 'The Home.' All I know is that there was guys with guns on the walls. . . ."

Small wonder, then, that for a youngster who had known only the roughest kind of treatment, life as a baseball hero was a case of Christmas every day.

Down the years I've always had a fondness for the horses— the kind that run. And in my wanderings I've come across a lot of tracks in many climes. But I've never been burned as badly as Babe was during the winter of 1925—the year of his giant bellyache—when he visited Charles Stoneham's Oriental Park at Havana and tried beating the ponies. John McGraw was also down there that winter having a go at 'em. In less than two weeks Ruth blew between 30 and 50 thousand dollars. That cured him. College football also intrigued him— but for only one game as a betting medium.

"I bet five thousand on them Harvards," he told me. "But the Yales win it. I'm off that football business, too."

In March of 1933—my third year with the Bell Syndicate— I headed South for spring training, stopping en route at Bob Woodruff's shooting preserve in south Georgia. When it came time for me to pull out, Woodruff gave me his car, chauffeur and a luggage compartment loaded with game.

"I'll throw a Florida dinner in your honor," I said. "We'll feast on Woodruff's eighteen-carat birds, basted with Coca Cola."

"If you do," replied Woodruff, "I wish you'd invite Walter Lippmann and his wife. They're down near Bradenton, and they're good friends of mine."

The dinner—to which Babe was also invited—was a huge success, until the dignified Mrs. Lippmann asked Babe to describe the homerun he "called" in the '32 Series against the Cubs, a four-straight rout for the Yankees.

"It's like this," boomed Babe, bigger than a freshly laundered barn in white gabardine and puffing on a huge cigar. "The Cubs had (censored) my old teammate Mark Koenig by cutting him for only a measly, (censored) half share of the Series money.

"Well, I'm riding the (censored) out of the Cubs, telling 'em they're the cheapest pack of (censored) crumbums in the world. We've won the first two and now we're in Chicago for the third game. Root is the Cub's pitcher. I pack one into the stands in the first inning off him, but in the fifth it's tied four to four when I'm up with a man on base. The Chicago fans are giving me hell.

"Root's still in there. He breezes the first two pitches by—both strikes! The mob's tearing down Wrigley Field. I shake my fist after that first strike. After the second, I point my bat at these bellerin' bleachers—right where I aim to park the ball. Root throws it, and I hit that (censored) ball on the nose —right over the (censored) fence for two (censored) runs.

" 'How do you like those apples, you (censored, censored,

censored),' I yell at Root as I head towards first. By the time I reach home I'm almost fallin' down I'm laughin' so (censored) hard—and that's how it happened."

The Babe's baccalaureate finished, a battered Mrs. Lippmann mumbled that they'd have to be leaving. A minute later the Walter Lippmanns were history.

"Why did you use that language?" I asked Babe.

"What the hell, Grant," snorted Babe. "You heard her ask me what happened. So I told her!"

As a golfer, Ruth was a long but not a terrific hitter. I was with him at Clearwater, Florida, when he bet Babe Didrikson 50 dollars a tee shot. She outdrove Ruth by at least 20 yards—for 200 dollars—before he was convinced. But nobody ever enjoyed the game—or cussed it and himself—more than Ruth. His special meat was match play, man-to-man competition.

One morning in '33, Babe and I had a date to play with Dizzy Dean at Belleair, in Clearwater. Having recently started the game, Diz was pretty wild with his woods and long irons.

"I got a bushel of bets riding with Dean today," bellowed Babe. "I'm giving him strokes on ten different bets—from one to ten shots—and I expect to collect on 'em all."

"Diz may be wild, but not that wild," I warned.

As we reached the club, Babe spotted Pat Dean, Dizzy's handsome bride.

"Pat," said Babe, "come on out with us this morning. The walk will do you good."

Puzzled, but appreciative of Babe's invitation, Pat accepted. Diz said nothing. He hit a good drive, then smothered two shots. After another sloppy shot by Diz on the second hole, Pat commented, "Dear, you're ducking!"

"Ducking, hell!" exploded Dean. "Who asked you on this rabbit shoot anyhow?"

Followed the fireworks. Ruth howled. Pat stalked off. Dean couldn't hit a shot the rest of the round. The Babe never collected an easier hatful.

McCarthy's Yanks were headed north in 1934, Babe's last year aboard. At Atlanta, always an important exhibition stop, Ruth suddenly developed a huge hankering for chicken Georgia style. I called Bob Woodruff and in the course of our conversation mentioned Babe's fresh craving for chicken.

"I'll send my car over," said Bob. "Take it and look over these spots." He named a number of attractive places, and Bob Jones added a few more. Clare Ruth, Babe and I covered the list and ultimately chose a small hideaway several miles from town. The proprietor promised he'd prepare four of Georgia's finest hens for Babe's dinner. As we were leaving, Babe admired the front lawn, swarming with spring flowers. He plucked one and handed it to Clare.

"They're pretty daisies," he remarked.

"No, dear, they're daffodils," commented Mrs. R.

"They're still daisies to me," replied Babe. Any flower, from a dandelion to a white orchid, was simply a "daisy" to Babe.

Ruth showered after the sixth inning. Returning to our little hacienda, we were greeted by the beaming proprietor, flanked by a retinue of darky waiters, shining and popeyed.

"The chickens—they are prepared," said our host proudly.

"Chickens hell!" exclaimed Ruth. "I want beef steak!"

He got it.

The following day Babe visited his friend Bob Jones. Bob III, now manager of the Coca Cola plant in Pittsfield, Massachusetts, was then a youngster. We were fanning a highball in Bobby's living room when young Bob roared in with the neighborhood kids in his wake.

"That's him!" cried Bobby III. Babe grabbed an old bat

from one of the youngsters, found it was cracked and tore it apart.

"Bobby," said Babe, "I want your old man to buy you a *good* bat. Make him promise."

Had Santa Claus visited 32–50 Northside Drive that day, he would have had to wait his turn.

Babe's love of kids was sincere. In many ways he was a big kid himself. I was in his room for dinner on the eve of the World Series in Chicago in 1932. (He always ate in his room before games because he would have been mobbed by fans and autograph hustlers in the hotel dining room.)

"I've got to go for a short trip, Grant," he said.

"Where are you going on the night before a World Series?" I asked.

"I'll tell you, but if you print it I'll shoot you. I'm going to take a baseball to a sick kid on the other side of town. I promised his mother and father I'd come. He's pretty sick."

The place was 20 or 30 miles away—over an hour to get there and another to get back. No publicity.

Babe was known by more motorcycle cops than any athlete who ever lived. They enjoyed giving Ruth an escort to the Stadium or helping him to get away after a game. They were usually there, like the Travelers' Aid, whenever the Babe needed a lift home to Riverside Drive after a late party.

One morning Babe asked me to pick him up for our golf game at Leewood, in Tuckahoe. "Sure," I replied, "but what happened to your car?"

"I lost it," said Babe.

"Lost it?" I said. "You had it last night."

"That was last night," replied Babe. "I wrecked it somewhere in Westchester and left it."

So he had. The cops had driven him home.

Another time, when Babe was roaring along by dawn's early light, the law stopped him, checked on his condition and suggested he be driven home.

"Why you (censored)!" roared Babe, and punched the cop on the nose.

"Now I *know* you're drunk," said the cop. "Move over! I'm drivin' you home."

I was with Babe one evening when he turned down a one-way street—the wrong way. "This is a one-way street," said the cop.

"I'm only drivin' one way!" yelled Ruth.

"Oh, hello, Babe! I didn't know it was you," replied the cop. "Go anywhere you please—but take it easy!"

And so it went.

I once had Babe on a national radio hookup, with Graham McNamee in charge. A short script had been prepared for Ruth to read—pretty much on split-second timing. He worked it over and was practically letter-perfect. Came the big break, with orchestra lending background music. At the last minute, Babe's carefully rehearsed script became scrambled. Before I could throw a halter on him, he was off and running. McNamee was frantic; the orchestra leader was frantic; the producer was frantic—as Ruth rambled on.

At one point the Babe was supposed to refer to the Duke of Wellington's historic remark that the Battle of Waterloo had been won on the playing fields of Eton. Babe managed to come out with this gem:

"As Duke Ellington once said, the Battle of Waterloo was won on the playing fields of Elkton."

Later I asked Babe how he could louse up one short statement so completely.

"About that Wellington guy I wouldn't know," he replied. "Ellington, yes. As for that Eton business—well, I married my first wife in Elkton (Maryland), and I always hated the goddamn place. It musta stuck."

The network got a load of Ruth at his purest that night. But it certainly wasn't NBC's conception of a tight program.

One evening Babe and I were having a few drinks in the grill room of the Chatham Hotel. Suddenly he looked at his watch. "Jesus!" he cried. "I gotta run!" In a flash he'd grabbed his cap and coat and was flagging a cab. Alarmed, I asked what the trouble was.

"Trouble?" yelled Ruth. "Why, 'Gangbusters' is on!"

Moe Berg, the eminent linguist, Princetonian and major-league catcher, once said: "Ruth isn't a man; he's an institution." Ruth was a man who loved crowds. And the crowds always swarmed to see Babe hit. The Yankees from 1926 to '34 were a terrific aggregation, each man big in his own right. But it was Babe the crowds came to see. Each Yankee exhibition-game contract carried this clause in heavy type: "It is understood and agreed that Babe Ruth will play." He seldom missed a curtain call.

I've seen the great ones, from Cobb through Williams, but Ruth was the only ball player I have known who could turn out capacity crowds every time. He did this in every city the Yankees played. When the Yankee Stadium was dedicated in April 1923, more than 74,000 people turned up—to see the Yankees, sure, but more important, to see Ruth cavort around "The House That Babe Built."

He was the greatest single magnet sport has ever known. Jack Dempsey was top man in his game. But Jack fought in defense of his title only six times in seven years. Babe played each day, six months a year, for nearly 15 years. He lured packed stands in the big cities and he drew them out in the bush. I know, for I followed him from 1919 to his final game in 1935. Big league, bush league, the great cities, small hamlets—at the ball park or train depot—always capacity.

I've ridden in cars with Babe in cities all over the map. Everywhere, the mobs would wave or call his name, and Babe would answer, "How're you, Mom!" . . . "Hello, Pop!" "How can they miss this silly mug?" he used to ask.

Whether it was playing baseball or golf, hunting, fishing or sitting around a room drinking and punching the bag, I can recall no one who got as much joy out of sheer living as the Babe.

Friendship—pure, warm, unadulterated friendship with no holds barred, ever—is the key to the Babe Ruth I most treasure. For the 30 years I knew Babe—until cancer killed him in 1948—I never saw Ruth really sore at anybody. Oh, I've seen him lose his temper—at himself—on a golf course, when he'd bury his club in a bunker after missing a shot or lash his putter after a missed putt. (Once he wrapped the clubhead around his leg so hard he thought he'd broken his ankle and roared like a hopped-up elephant.) But Ruth, the man—boy, was the complete embodiment of everything uninhibited. He couldn't possibly fail—that was Ruth's credo. And when he found that baseball, particularly the Yankees, had no managerial berth for him, he was deeply hurt. But in remarks or actions, the Babe was kindly—so kindly.

Ruth established many records, most of them Homeric, and no pun intended. It will be a long time before any slugger breaks his all-time homerun mark of 714. And, at the risk of sounding disloyal to the game, I hope it's an eternity before some youngster, teeing off on today's jet ball, smashes Babe's mark of 60 homers in one season: This I hope for Babe, wherever he is, kicking his heels around on some king-size cloud.

WILLIAM BARRY FURLONG

# Where the Action Is

JUST INSIDE THE BLEACHER ENTRANCE to Wrigley Field in Chicago is a sign that warns: "No gambling." At the top of the ramp, patrolling the aisle of the mezzanine, is a cop whose presence warns: "No gambling." In the right-center-field bleachers are Stace and Sambo, Jonesy and Zsa-Zsa, Dynamite and The Preacher—all there to sit in the sun and enjoy the National Pastime: gambling on baseball.

"Sollie! Hey, where's Sollie?"

"Where's-a Duke? Somebody see-a Duke?"

"Wha'd'ya gimme, I take-a Cubs?" ask a man with a nervous tic.

"Six ta five." This is a man called Groundhog.

"Six to five!" screeches Nervous Tic. "Them Cardinals are gonna start Gibson!"

"I don't care they start Samson," growls Groundhog. "It's still six ta five."

Nervous Tic sits down petulantly. "Why-a Cubs?" he complains. "Why you always gotta take-a Cubs? The Cubs, they're the same bunch-a crumbs as always."

Groundhog remains silent, above interrogation. Around

him, some of the Faithful are becoming annoyed at the gau-
cheries of a noninvestor who wonders aloud why the Cubs
never have put lights into the ball park and let the fans come
out in the cool of night. Two bare-chested men, elaborately
preparing to be parboiled in oil—suntan oil—glare at him.
"Baseball sup*posed* to be played inna daytime," one says
scathingly. "This ain't no drive-in movin' pitcher place."

Wrigley Field in Chicago is the last surviving temple of
baseball in the sun. As the only major-league ball park with
no night baseball, it is the last tie to those more languid days
when the baseball was less an industry than a sport. For many
fans, it is still a neighborhood gathering place, one they can
walk to after lunch to sit and gossip and watch the Cubs lose.
For others, it is a place to come and get a suntan while im-
mersing themselves in the pleasant brouhaha of the bleachers.
For still others, it is the place to come to engage in that ancient if fast-fading tribal ritual, ball park betting.

Nobody knows quite how much money is bet on baseball
every year. A vague idea came out of an investigation made
seven years ago by the New York State Commission of Investi-
gations. It found that one bookmaker handling bets on baseball from upper New York State gamblers alone made a profit
of $500,000 in eight weeks. Given the normal illicit profit
margin of bookmaking on baseball, that particular entrepre-
neur had to have handled more than $20 million in baseball
bets in that eight-week period or the equivalent of $60
million for the entire season, a cash flow that shows booking
bets on baseball is a more prosperous business than merely
running baseball or playing it.

Most of the money bet on baseball engages the leisurely
judgment of the bettors, who have all day to survey the odds

or the records of the starting pitchers, or to apply their systems. Theirs is a Gothic approach, one that relies less on wit or nimbleness of mind than on a religious dedication to records or a "system." One very popular system, for instance, is to bet on "streaks," to bet a team to win if it has won two or more consecutive games or to bet it to lose if it has lost two or more consecutive games. The first half of the 1961 baseball season is reckoned the wildest bull market in streak-betting history. The Cincinnati Reds lost eight straight games, then turned around and won nine straight. The Minnesota Twins had a 13-game losing streak, the Chicago White Sox won 19 of 20 games in one stretch, and the Philadelphia Phillies had one 10-game losing streak and three more seven-game losing streaks. Altogether, there were 93 streaks of four or more games in the period, streaks in which the bettor stood to win at least two bets and thus come out ahead. (He is certain to lose one bet on each streak—the one in which the streak ends.) The season was climaxed a little later when the Philadelphia Phillies lost 23 consecutive games, a sort of *ne plus ultra* for streak bettors.

For many years, a more sporting approach to baseball was to bet while the game was in progress. This involved the investor's pride as well as his purse, for such bets demanded a willingness to make bets, and mistakes, in public. The bettor called out his bid—"Three to one the double play, gimme three to one the double play"—in a gambling parlor called an "open room," a shop where he could listen to the game over the radio or follow it by wire, and make a bet just as investors now visit the "public" rooms of securities houses to play the stock market. Or he might go to the ball park where he could gather with others of like mind to carry on a loud, incessant conversation about the game and its environment. ("Here comes a-rain. Wha'd'ya gimme the rain?" "Three ta two the rain. Give ya three ta two the rain comes!") In those days, the select part of such ball parks combined the speculative flavor of Lloyds of London and Big Julie's floating crap game. Over the year, the owners of various major-league teams labored hard to eliminate the "open room" aspect of their operations and they have, by and large, succeeded.

The most viable remaining gambling outpost is the right-centerfield bleachers of Wrigley Field. In these years of the Long Drought, when the Cubs set a league record by finishing in the second division 19 consecutive times, the bettors are the only bleacherites to show up day in and day out—the Cubs' solitary sentinels against dullness and deficits. Long years of watching the Cubs, and betting on them, have left them sour of mien and little leavened by grace of human spirit, something like a drama critic whose only exposure to the theater is an Edward Albee festival. If the bettors are ever disturbed by the thought that what they are doing is slightly illegal, they are fortified by the conviction that what the Cubs are doing on the field is downright criminal. Their activities, to be sure, are not endorsed by the management. Indeed, in the last few years, undercover agents for the police have infiltrated the bleachers, implausibly disguised as baseball fans, and carried out mass arrests of the investors.

At their best, the bettors in the bleachers give the game a flavor beyond the Cubs' poor power to add or detract. They exchange information and bets not only verbally but through a system of finger signals as abstruse as the bidding at Sotheby's. The bidding has a pace and rhythm that is almost contrapuntal, as in a game when the Cubs threatened to break a 3–3 tie with the St. Louis Cardinals by putting two men on base with one out in the eighth inning.

"Wha'd'ya gimme the ball game? Wha'd'ya gimme the game?" chanted a man in a peaked cap.

"Two-an'-a-half the ball game. Two-an'-a-half the game," said a bespectacled man with a rain check folded over his nose as a sunshade.

"Wha'd'ya gimme the run scores? Wha'd'ya gimme the run?"

"Seven ta five the run scores. Seven ta five the run," said Sunshade.

A drunk stood up and, with a rich, winy sense of grandeur, announced, "I'll take twenny thousand dollars on whatever happens next!" He lurched down a step or so and swayed ominously in the dead calm. "Eight to five the drunk falls! Eight to five the drunk!" cried out an investor.

A ripple of laughter drifted through the bleachers. Next to me, a bookish man in his 60's watched the performance with satisfaction. He had been kind enough, as the game progressed, to explain some of the investing situations, which are as formalized as a sonnet: With Willie Mays of the San Francisco Giants at bat in the late innings of a close game, the odds are customarily seven to five not simply that he'll get on base, but that he'll score. Though he was not betting on this game, it became clear that my neighbor had an extraordinary insight into baseball and betting.

Shortly I was to learn why: He was long regarded by many as the most knowledgeable bettor on baseball—indeed, on most sports—in the country. Because of his singular gifts he was much sought after as a shill by the operators of the open rooms that once flourished in Chicago. He would assay the situation in a game, as reported by radio or wire, and make a bet for the house; the other bettors would then bet against him, increasing the volume—and the profits—of the management. It sounded like a taxing job, one that required great speed in appraising a situation and developing within seconds a set of odds that would attract business and still leave an edge for the house. He said he had the ideal education for the job: a degree in economics and experience as a securities analyst in a bank. The latter experience was during the depths of the Depression—and "If that didn't teach you to play the angles, nothing would." His banking career came to an end when, indulging his hobby, he made bets with other employees on how long the various executives would hold their jobs in the bank. When the bank president learned that the odds on his tenure had shortened to three to one, he fired the securities analyst.

"At the time," he says laconically, "I had eight to one on myself."

Through the years he had nevertheless managed to prosper enough—by gambling in the stock market and the ball park—to acquire an interest in several small businesses, retire by and large from the labor of betting, and establish a reputation in the community.

Most bettors, he explained to me, lack that very quick wit—the ability to sift swiftly through a maze of mathematical possibilities—to enjoy long-term success at the game. This is so common a failing that an enterprising man named A. C. Lowther drew up a chart, certified by a CPA, that many bettors have found indispensable for betting baseball parleys, a form of self-immolation in which the winnings from one game are bet on another and the accumulation on a third game and so on and on until eventually everything is lost. A dreamer—and betting is filled with them—might want to know the return on a $100 investment on a four-team parlay at odds of five to seven, one to two, two to three, and four to five. A glance at the Lowther chart would provide the answer: $685. My companion in the bleachers could perform much more complex problems in his head. "When I was five years old," he said, "I was making up calendars in my head for three years in advance."

On occasion, his astonishing gift for mathematics allowed him to penetrate the obscurities of oddsmaking and so to place a sure-thing bet. About a month before the end of the 1961 baseball season, he consulted a bookmaker about the prospects in the National League pennant race. The book-maker reeled off some odds that were, as is usual, designed to lure bettors to bet on their favorite team to win. As he listened to the odds, The Analyst translated them into another dimension—"Los Angeles 17 to 10 to lose the pennant, Cincinnati $4\frac{1}{2}$ to one to lose the pennant, Milwaukee 10 to 13 to lose the pennant"—and came up with a remarkable conclusion: He was a sure winner if he bet on everybody to lose! By betting $1,700 on Los Angeles, $2,250 on Cincinnati, and $1,300 on Milwaukee—all to lose the pennant—he'd be sure to come out with a profit ranging from $200 (if Milwaukee won the pennant) to $490 (if Los Angeles won). (Customarily he bet on baseball in large multiples of these figures, but he chose them to illustrate the technique.) Moreover San Francisco had been coming up hard, and if it won the pennant The Analyst would win all three bets. "A San Francisco win means $3,190," he said, "and I don't even have to bet on them!" Ultimately, Cincinnati won the pennant—San Francisco finished third—and The Analyst netted $440.

Nearby, one of the Faithful began talking about a friend in a voice as cheerless as death. "The G's picked up Abe at the trots the other night," he said. There had been a raid by Federal agents at a harness-racing track. "They caught him without a tax stamp," he said. He leaned back on his elbows and thrust his face upward, as if by this act of martyrdom—letting the sun burn into his ample eyeballs—he could mitigate the manifold injustice of it all. "He's got no chance," he lamented. "The G's, how you gonna beat the G's?"

It was a question that also bothered The Analyst. Several years ago, Congress passed a law making it a felony to communicate gambling information, or bets, across state lines. As a political and economic conservative ("I'm the last of what Roosevelt called the 'economic royalists' "), he considers this an encroachment of the Federal Government on individual enterprise. It also interferes with his "public service," the judgment he offers—like a high court—on some of the plaguier problems of betting. In July, 1960, for instance, he handed down a landmark decision over how a starting pitcher is designated. For most baseball bettors, the choice of a starting pitcher is the most influential factor in their bet. It is so important that some New York newspapers print the odds with the names of the starting pitchers, just as they print the odds on the horses at the track. (The difference, of course, is that betting on pitchers is illegal in New York, while betting on horses is legal, at least at the tracks.) In the particular dispute that The Analyst came to adjudicate, Don Newcombe was listed as the starting pitcher for the Cincinnati Reds in a game against the Pittsburgh Pirates in Pittsburgh. After the Reds batted in the first inning, Newcombe took his place on the pitcher's mound for his warm-up pitches. On the pitching arm of his sweat shirt he was wearing a long, loose sleeve that flapped mightily as he threw the ball. Dusty Boggess, the umpire at home plate, was fearful that the flapping sleeve would distract and thus endanger the batter. He ordered Newcombe either to change his sweat shirt or to bind up the sleeve so that it would no longer flap. Newcombe objected. Heated words followed and Newcombe was thrown out of the game, before he'd even faced the first batter. Cal McLish warmed up hurriedly and replaced Newcombe on the mound for the Reds. Pittsburgh eventually won the game, 5–0.

Now a subterranean argument swept the nation. Was Newcombe really the starting pitcher—for betting purposes—or was it McLish? If Newcombe was the starting pitcher, then bettors backing Pittsburgh, who based their bets on the published list of starting pitchers, won their bets. If McLish was, then all bets were off and Cincinnati backers would get a refund. The argument raged back and forth until a good many bookmakers, in desperation, asked The Analyst to hand down a decision. He could be dispassionate; he had no bets on the game and, at the time, no great interest in betting on baseball. He also had an intellectual's approach to the question, weighing the abstractions as well as the realities. On the one hand, Newcombe was listed on the lineup card given to the umpires by the team manager just before the game (which made him, by the official rule, the starting pitcher); he was listed in the box score as the starting pitcher; and a half-inning of the game *had* been played before he was dismissed. On the other hand, Newcombe appeared *only* in the box score and on the lineup card; he never appeared in the game. It was McLish who had thrown the first, or starting, pitch for the Reds.

The man in Chicago, handling the dispute with all the probity of a Supreme Court justice, ruled that a man must throw at least one pitch in a game to be considered the starting pitcher. Therefore, McLish was the starting pitcher in this game and all bets had to be called off. That decision now transcends baseball's own rule on the matter, at least among the backers of the National Pastime who have a lot more invested in it than baseball's owners.

Behind us we could hear that chant of a bookmaker hustling bets on the game. My companion commented on the risks he was taking. "Bookmakers go to jail," he said. "Bettors do *not* go to jail." Bookies have to hustle because they make their money—as do chain stores—on a high volume with a low markup. On an even-money bet, called a "105 pick-it," their commission is 2.4 percent. It's figured this way: The bookmaker collects $105 from each of two bettors on a game or a total of $210. To the winning bettor, he'll pay $100 in winnings plus the original $105, or a total of $205. That leaves him a profit of $5 on his original handle of $210 or 2.4 percent. Bookmakers tend to liken themselves to stockbrokers as the middlemen on the bet. "In betting, as in handling securities, you need a buyer as well as a seller," said the defrocked securities analyst.

It's true that the bookmaker expects to make his money out of a commission for acting as broker for the bet (although a bookmaker who doesn't bet—even in the way he handles his books—is as rare as the stockbroker who doesn't play the market). And it is true that the bookmaker did, in the days before the aforementioned Federal law, take all long-distance calls collect from his customers, as do stockbrokers. And he must also pay his overhead—rent, lights, phone protection—out of the commission. But there the resemblance ends. For the bookmaker is supposed to pay a Federal tax of 10 percent of all moneys handled in a transaction, or $21 of the $210 in the example cited above. Since that would not only wipe out his profit but put him 7.6 percent into the hole on an even-money bet, the bookmaker rarely, if ever, pays it. Some book-makers are said to tithe scrupulously, paying 10 percent of their tax. But this seems unlikely to become widespread, since a bookmaker who is successfully evading 90 percent of his taxes is likely to figure he can as easily evade 100 percent.

In ball-park betting, the bookmaker has more leeway on odds and on handling parlays, all of which can boost his commission. "The remarkable thing," said my companion, "is the faith that the small bettor has in baseball. It's not like college basketball or pro football. They *believe* in this game." Their faith was reflected in the brisk give-and-take of the crowd at this game. In the last half of the eighth inning, Ron Santo of the Cubs came to bat with runners on second and third. The score was still tied, 3–3, and on the first pitch Santo lowered his bat as if to bunt. The man called Zsa-Zsa reeled into the aisle in mock horror and clapped a hand to his forehead. "The world's worst bunter! The world's *worst* bunter," he said, "and they send him up there to squeeze inna run." His voice trailed upward in a wild derisive giggle that ended in a singsong, "Zsa-zsa-zsa-zsa zsa-zsa-zsa!"

But Santo didn't bunt. Instead he took a full swing on the next pitch and singled to left to drive in two runs. Now the betting in the bleachers had a staccato tempo that reflected the Cubs' chances of winning the game. "Eight ta one the ball game! Who'll gimme eight ta one the ball game!" The Cubs scored again. "Twelve ta one the ball game . . . twelve ta one the ball game!" Then the Cubs got a runner on second base with one out. "Sixteen ta one the ball game . . . twenny ta one the ball game . . . who'll take twenny-two ta one the ball game?" There were no takers, and some of the older hands thought this was deplorable. A well-manicured man in a tan Eisenhower jacket stood up, elaborately fingered his plastic-tipped cigar, and announced, "I just get back from Las Vegas and wha'd I find? Everybody's dead. Dead!" The bettors sat hunched against the storm of his criticism. "We had Cincinnati out here one day, they're leadin' by eight runs in the ninth," he went on. "So wha' happens? So the Cubs up with nine runs in the ninth, and I'm a year payin' off the bets!"

The lesson was lost on the investors that day. With two out in the top half of the ninth and the Cubs leading, 6–3, they stood up—almost at an invisible command—to pay off or collect their bets all around. Suddenly the Cardinals got a runner on base and everything stopped, as in a freeze. "Thirteen ta one the ball game," said a thin reedy voice. It was a feeble effort and there were no takers. A moment later the game was over and the Faithful were shuffling toward the exits and past the "No gambling" signs. "What I shudda done," said Zsa-Zsa, "I shudda taken that pick-it and then I ony lose five."

He shrugged, "If lose, I lose—so what. I'm gonna take the gas pipe?"

Next to me, my companion got up, expressed some pleasure at the mental calisthenics the game had afforded, said, "Six to five you never write about it." Then he disappeared into the crowd.

REX LARDNER

# The Assault and Battery
# of Lacrosse

IT IS EASY TO GET EMOTIONAL about a hard-contested game of
lacrosse, the "stick game" that is America's fastest-growing
sport. There is the classic confrontation of the big man with
the little man in head-to-head duels—guile, stick-handling
and speed pitted against size, strength and determination.
There is the constantly flowing movement of the players in
quickly changing patterns of offense and defense. There are
the clearly observable individual performances, ranging from
the merely skillful to the uniquely brilliant—runs, catches,
interceptions, dodges, clears, ball-recoveries, stops by goalies,
checks, *hustle*. There are displays of disciplined teamwork:
rapid passes, the setting up of plays and screens. There are
occasional violent crashes and purposeful bumps (permitted
by the rules) to slow down or exhaust tricky opponents or
raise the siege of a harried goalie; obliviousness to risk of injury in pursuit of the ball; and finally the game's mystic
origin.

Lacrosse is called dry-land hockey. Queen Victoria, after
witnessing a match between a team of Mohawks and white
men from Canada at Windsor Castle, pronounced the game

"very pretty to watch." President Taft was an avid fan. Grant-land Rice, dean of American sportswriters, said lacrosse re-quired more elements of skill than any game he knew. Base-ball pioneer A. G. Spalding—pitcher, manager, club owner—called it the best game ever invented. It is the oldest Ameri-can contact sport, the only truly American sport.

The modern game, briefly, is played on a field 110 yards long and about 60 yards wide. Goals—six feet high and six feet wide—are near the end boundaries of the field, 80 yards apart, allowing players to maneuver behind the goal area, as in ice hockey. A circle 18 feet in diameter, called a "crease," is marked around the center of each goal line. No player ex-cept the goal-keeper or a defense man not carrying the ball is allowed to enter it. There are ten players on a side—three defensemen, three midfielders and three attackmen besides the goalie. At the beginning of play the defensemen are posi-tioned near their goal, the midfielders spread near the center of the field and the attackmen in the area of the opponents' goal.

Play is started with a face-off between two midfielders in the center of the field. As soon as play starts, players may move from their assigned positions, except that a team must keep at least four men in its defensive half of the field and at least three men in its offensive half of the field. When a team is on the attack, the men in the defensive portion are generally three defensemen and the goalie; when it is defend-ing, the three attackmen generally stay downfield. Midfield-ers, who run like hell, have license to play both attack and defense and do so. Former Cleveland Browns fullback Jim Brown, an All-America at Syracuse in both lacrosse and football, says playing midfield in lacrosse requires more stamina than playing any position in any other game.

Using their sticks, players are allowed to carry the ball, throw it or bat it; they may also kick it. Only the goalie, however, may touch it with his hand and he is not allowed to catch it. The object of the game is for a team to ram or bounce or loft a five-ounce white or orange India rubber ball about eight inches in circumference into the opposing goal; and keep the opponents from doing the same thing.

A goal counts one point. Sticks (also called crosses) are made of hickory or ash and range from 40 inches in length (for attackmen) to six feet (for the goalie). The lengths of sticks for midfielders and defensemen run between these extremes.

So complex are the requirements for an acceptable stick—according to the rules and player preferences—that 97 percent of the world's supply comes from a factory on an island near Ontario operated by Mohawk Indians. It takes a year of careful preparation to make a stick. The stringing is done by squaws.

A game lasts an hour among collegians—four fifteen-minute quarters with a ten-minute break at the half. High schools and prep schools play shorter quarters. Ties being anathema to lacrosse players, if the score is even at game's end, two five-minute periods (one minute rest between them) are played. If the score is still tied, it stays a tie.

As with the prizefights of Joe Louis and Rocky Marciano, violence is not always present in lacrosse, but the threat of it is. "Doc" Blanchard, an All-America fullback on the great Army teams of the mid-40s, was reluctant to play the game.

"When you give football players sticks and turn them loose on the field," he said, "you're inviting mayhem." Some years ago in a game between Rutgers and Lehigh, the ball was sent flying under the grandstand bordering the field. There being no side boundaries at the time, a Rutgers player and a Lehigh player dashed after it and disappeared. A few seconds later the Rutgers man emerged with the ball. About twenty minutes after that the Lehigh man emerged, clutching his head. A few years later side boundaries were instituted to allow spectators to see all the action and prevent the clandestine bludgeonings of one player by another.

Glenn "Pop" Warner, coach of the Carlisle Indians, had his football squad play lacrosse in the spring. If they could survive that, he felt, they would have no problem with football in the fall. An international game between Australians and Canadians got so rough—fisticuffs, use of the stick to batter the heads and crack the ribs of opponents—that mounted police repeatedly had to invade the field to calm down the players.

Some protection is given the players by the rules: You are not allowed to crash into an opponent unless he is within five yards of the ball or in possession of it; and then not from the rear or below the knees. You may not hack at your opponent's stick in a vicious manner (even missing him calls for a penalty) or trip an opponent. For these—called personal fouls —a player is suspended from the game for from one to three minutes, his team playing short-handed during that time. If a player commits five personal fouls he is out of the game for good.

The combative nature of lacrosse stems from its Indian

origin—some 48 Indian tribes played lacrosse. The Winne-bagos played on a prairie near what is now La Crosse, Wisconsin. Among most of them the game was more a mystic ceremony than a sport, preceded by complex pagan rites. There is no denying, though, that it was a splendid substitute for a battle or massacre. Every tribe was conscious that the players were watched by a critical audience of godlings in the sky.

The Cherokees called the game "the little brother of war" and acknowledged that one of its main purposes was to toughen up braves for hand-to-hand struggles. Goals were miles apart and there were no side boundaries, time-outs or substitutions. Games lasted from early morning to sunset. Some took three days. A team could be made up of as many as a thousand warriors. The usual strategy was to whittle down the opponents with blows of the sticks, and then concentrate on scoring goals.

Betting—generally undertaken by squaws—was extremely heavy, and woe to any brave who slowed down after a couple of hours' play because of exhaustion or a bloody nose! Squaws would take after him and lash him with switches to remind him of his duties on the field. In Oklahoma, squaws encouraged their team's zeal by brandishing shotguns. After the Oklahoma Indians' game, the chiefs of the winning side slept for three nights with the wives of the chiefs of the losing side.

In Pontiac's War against the English (called Pontiac's Conspiracy, since the English won it), lacrosse figured in as neat a piece of chicane as you will find in all North American history. In 1763, as chief of the combined Chippewa, Potawatamie and Ottawa tribes, Pontiac arranged a game between the Chippewas and Sacs to be played outside Fort Michilimackinac, Michigan. The purpose, ostensibly, was to celebrate the birthday of George III.

Squaws huddled on the sidelines in blankets—to ward off the June heat, apparently—as the game got under way. Soon dust rose, players began bloodying each other and the game got so exciting that soldiers, officers and white trappers in the fort came outside to watch. In their preoccupation they left the gate open. Then Whoops! The ball sailed over the wall into the fort and the players surged after it, not forgetting to snatch tomahawks and war clubs from under the blankets of the squaws before entering. At the game's end the score was: One English officer, 24 enlisted men and one trader killed. Those left were carried off as captives.

Preoccupied with baseball in its embryo form, the United States only slowly took to lacrosse. In Troy, N.Y., a team of Canadian Indians played a team of American baseball players and won without breaking a sweat. (In the early days of white man's lacrosse, the team scoring the first three goals won; many games lasted only a short while. A time limit for games was set in 1881.)

Clubs began to spring up in the latter part of the century in Troy, New York and Brooklyn, with Indian teams taking part in tournaments, and then Eastern colleges got interested. N.Y.U., Harvard, Princeton, Columbia and Yale fielded teams. A Canadian attending the university founded the Johns Hopkins lacrosse club, and a collegiate dynasty was begun.

As far back as 1900 institutions like Baltimore City College and Baltimore Polytechnic, as well as Hopkins and local lacrosse clubs, encouraged youngsters in and near the city to take up the game, partly for its own sake and partly to furnish a future supply for college ranks. Many of them naturally attended, and attend, Hopkins and other nearby colleges.

The result of this foresight is that while lacrosse is the national game of Canada, it is, out of pride and tradition, the national game of Baltimore—as much a part of the social scene as crabcakes, the Preakness and terrapin stew. The world's largest supplier of lacrosse equipment is in downtown Baltimore.

When spring shows its face in the Monument City, parked cars develop fender dents from getting hit by errant lacrosse balls flung by the young of Baltimore practicing on their way to and from school. Before Hopkins home games they come early with their sticks to Homewood Field to chase balls that get past the varsity. Great care is lavished on their sticks; some sleep with their sticks by their sides. Backboards in Baltimore parks are not used for paddleball, handball or practicing tennis strokes but to hurl lacrosse balls against.

Lacrosse is to Johns Hopkins what football is to Notre Dame, and the Blue Jay record is more impressive. No great shakes at baseball, basketball or, till lately, football, the school has won or shared in 26 intercollegiate championships —more than any other college. It usually places more players on the All-America than any other college.

Johns Hopkins represented the U. S. in the Olympics of 1928 and 1932 in lacrosse, winning both times. Over 400 undergraduates in a student body of 2,000 play lacrosse on intramural teams. In his drive to build up Yale lacrosse and tear down that of Johns Hopkins, Burt L. Standish, in one of his *Frank Merriwell* books, had the Hopkins captain try to get Frank drunk and smoke a cigarette and then attempt to steal Frank's girl. All these ploys failed, however, and Yale won the big game. But that is only Merriwell's side of it, you understand.

The growth of the game in the past ten years has been phenomenal. The number of member colleges in the Intercollegiate Lacrosse Association has doubled. The total number of colleges fielding teams has jumped from 54 to 112. Types of lacrosse currently played, besides ten-man field lacrosse, include: boxla (box lacrosse), contested indoors with seven on a side, usually on iceless hockey rinks; seven-man field lacrosse; and women's lacrosse, less violent than men's, with its main centers Philadelphia, Virginia, Delaware, Boston and Long Island. Night-time "fireball" lacrosse was tried in Ottawa quite a few years back. The ball was soaked in turpentine and set alight. It soon came apart but not before it had set several crosses on fire. So the game was abandoned for a time.

Will lacrosse someday replace baseball in high schools and colleges as the major spring sport? Many athletic authorities think so.

Lacrosse is an ideal game for the football player as a substitute for spring practice or a supplement to it. It appeals to the sturdy young man who is not big enough for football but likes contact, and for the small, fast, brainy man who delights in outfoxing larger opponents. While baseball on the professional level is a gigantic industry, has glorious traditions going for it and is a staple of American entertainment, it is too slow a game, many believe, for a number of today's young athletes and sports spectators. In Eastern high schools and colleges, lacrosse regularly outdraws baseball as an attraction. Sometimes it dramatically outdraws professional baseball: One afternoon in 1956 the Navy–Maryland game drew 11,500 paying customers. The Baltimore Orioles played to 3,800. Traditional rivalries—Maryland–Navy, Johns Hopkins–Maryland, Johns Hopkins–Navy—sometimes attract 13,000 and 14,000 fans.

"In baseball," asserts Phil Kneip, a second-team All-America from Johns Hopkins, "there's too much waiting around for something to happen. And there's no contact." Other criticisms of the national game by lacrosse players are: A single player, the pitcher, dominates baseball; in lacrosse every player has a vital function. Many plays in baseball, like catching a pop fly, are routine; in lacrosse, because each player is hounded by an opponent, every move is made under a certain amount of pressure. In baseball, many plays are automatic—throwing to first on a ground ball, for instance; the lacrosse player, with the ball or without it, constantly makes decisions about where to go and what to do, depending on a combination of a half-dozen variable factors.

For many ex-football players it is a more enjoyable game than football because the player has a chance to perform as an individual rather than a pawn rigidly following lines in a coach's diagram. "Just throw a bunch of lacrose sticks on the ground during gym class," says "Dutch" Hess, athletic director of Great Neck South High School in Great Neck, L.I., "and they go wild. Lacrosse is the greatest release in the world for the healthy teen-ager."

Release for the healthy adult, too.

PETE AXTHELM

# The Fallen Idol: The Harlem
# Tragedy of Earl Manigault

IN THE LITANY of quiet misfortunes that have claimed so
many young athletes in the ghetto, it may seem almost impossible to select one man and give him special importance.
Yet in the stories and traditions that are recounted in the
Harlem parks, one figure does emerge above the rest. Asked
about the finest athletes they have seen, scores of ballplayers
in a dozen parks mention Connie Hawkins and Lew Alcindor
and similar celebrities. But almost without exception, they
speak first of one star who didn't go on: Earl Manigault.

No official scorers tabulate the results of pickup games;
there are no composite box scores to prove that Manigault
ranked highest among playground athletes. But in its own
way, a reputation in the parks is as definable as a scoring
average in the NBA. Cut off from more formal channels of
media and exposure, street ballplayers develop their own
elaborate word-of-mouth system. One spectacular performance or one backward, twisting stuff shot may be the seed
of an athlete's reputation. If he can repeat it a few times in
a park where the competition is tough, the word goes out
that he may be something special. Then there will be chal-

lenges from more established players, and a man who can withstand them may earn a "neighborhood rep." The process continues in an expanding series of confrontations, until the best athletes have emerged. Perhaps a dozen men at a given time may enjoy "citywide reps," guaranteeing them attention and respect in any playground they may visit. And of those, one or two will stand alone.

A few years ago, Earl Manigault stood among the loftiest. But his reign was brief, and in order to capture some feeling of what his stature meant in the playground world, one must turn to two athletes who enjoy similar positions today. Herman "Helicopter" Knowings, now in his late twenties, is among the most remarkable playground phenomena; he was a demigod before Manigault, and he remains one after Earl's departure. Uneducated and unable to break into pro ball, the Helicopter has managed to retain the spring in his legs and the will power to remain at the summit after many of his contemporaries have faded from the basketball scene. Joe Hammond, not yet twenty, is generally recognized as the best of the young crop. Neither finished school and vaulted into the public spotlight, but both pick up money playing in a minor league, the Eastern League—and both return home between games to continue their domination of the parks.

The Helicopter got his name for obvious reasons: when he goes up to block a shot, he seems to hover endlessly in midair above his prey, daring him to shoot—and then blocking whatever shot his hapless foe attempts. Like most memorable playground moves, it is not only effective but magnetic. As Knowings goes up, the crowd shouts, "Fly, 'copter, fly," and seems to share his heady trip. When he shoves a ball down the throat of a visiting NBA star—as he often does in the Rucker Tournament—the Helicopter inflates the pride of a whole neighborhood.

Like Connie Hawkins, Knowings can send waves of electricity through a park with his mere presence. Standing by a court, watching a game in progress with intent eyes, the Helicopter doesn't have to ask to play. People quickly spot his dark, chiseled, ageless face and six-foot-four-inch frame, and they make room for him. Joe Hammond is less imposing. A shade over six feet, he is a skinny, sleepy-eyed kid who looks slow and tired, the way backcourt star Clinton Robinson appeared during his reign. But like Robinson, Hammond has proved himself, and now he stands as the descendant of Pablo Robertson and James Barlow and the other backcourt heroes of the streets.

The kings of playground ball are not expected to defend their titles every weekend, proving themselves again and again the way less exalted players must. But when a new athlete begins winning a large following, when the rumors spread that he is truly someone special, the call goes out: If he is a forward, get the Helicopter; if he's a guard, let's try him against Joe Hammond. A crowd will gather before the star arrives. It is time for a supreme test.

Jay Vaughn has been in such confrontations several times. He saw the Helicopter defend his reign, and he watched Joe Hammond win his own way to the top. He described the rituals:

"When I first met the Helicopter, I was only about seventeen, and I was playing with a lot of kids my age at Wagner

Center. I was better than the guys I was playing with and I knew it, so I didn't feel I had anything to prove. I was playing lazy, lackadaisical. And one of the youth workers saw how cocky I was and decided to show me just how good I really was. He sent for the Helicopter.

"One day I was just shooting baskets, trying all kinds of wild shots, not thinking about fundamentals, and I saw this older dude come in. He had sneakers and shorts on and he was ready to play. I said, 'Who's this guy? He's too old for our games. Is he supposed to be good?'

" 'The coach sent for him,' somebody told me. 'He's gonna play you.'

"I said to myself, 'Well, fine, I'll try him,' and I went out there one-on-one with Herman Knowings. Well, it was a disastrous thing. I tried lay-ups, jump shots, hooks. And everything I threw up, he blocked. The word had gone out that Herman was there, and a crowd was gathering, and I said to myself, 'You got to do something. You're getting humiliated.' But the harder I tried, the more he shoved the ball down into my face. I went home and thought about that game for a long time. Like a lot of other young athletes, I had been put in my place.

"I worked out like crazy after that. I was determined to get back. After about a month, I challenged him again. I found myself jumping higher, feeling stronger, and playing better than ever before. I wasn't humiliated again. But I was beaten. Since that time, I've played against Herman many times. He took an interest in me and gave me a lot of good advice. And now, when I see he's going to block a shot, I may be able to fake and go around him and score, and people will yell, 'The pupil showed the master.'

"Then, of course, he'll usually come back and stuff one on me. . . ."

"Joe Hammond was playing in the junior division games in the youth centers when I was in the senior games," Vaughn continued. "He was three years younger than me, and sometimes after I'd played, I'd stay and watch his game. He wasn't that exceptional. Just another young boy who was gonna play ball. In fact, at that time, I didn't even know his last name.

"Then I came home from school in the summer of 1969, and one name was on everyone's lips: Joe Hammond. I thought it must have been somebody new from out of town, but people said, no, he'd been around Harlem all the time. They described him and it sounded like the young kid I'd watched around the centers, but I couldn't believe it was the same guy. Then I saw him, and it was the same Joe, and he was killing a bunch of guys his own age. He was much improved, but I still said to myself, 'He's young. He won't do much against the older brothers. They've been in business too long.'

"But then I heard, 'Joe's up at 135th Street beating the pros. . . . Joe's doing everything to those guys.' I still didn't take it too seriously. In fact, when Joe came out to Mount Morris Park for a game against a good team I was on, I said, 'Now we'll see how you do. You won't do anything today.'

"Now I believe in him. Joe Hammond left that game with seven minutes to go. He had 40 points. Like everybody had said, Joe was the one."

Many reputations have risen and fallen in the decade between the arrival of the Helicopter and of Joe Hammond. Most have now been forgotten, but a few "reps" outlive the men who earn them. Two years ago Connie Hawkins did not show up for a single game during the Rucker Tournament. When it was time to vote for the Rucker All-Star team, the coaches voted for Hawkins. "If you're going to have an all-star game in Harlem," said Bob McCullough, the tournament director, "you vote for Connie or you don't vote." (Having been elected, The Hawk did appear for the All-Star game—and won the Most Valuable Player award.) One other reputation has endured on a similar scale. Countless kids in Harlem repeat the statement: "You want to talk about basketball in this city, you've got to talk about Earl Manigault."

Manigault played at Benjamin Franklin High School in 1962 and 1963, then spent a season at Laurinburg Institute. Earl never reached college, but when he returned to Harlem he continued to dominate the playgrounds. He was the king of his own generation of ballplayers, the idol for the generation that followed. He was a six-foot-two-inch forward who could outleap men eight inches taller, and his moves had a boldness and fluidity that transfixed opponents and spectators alike. Freewheeling, unbelievably high-jumping, and innovative, he was the image of the classic playground athlete.

But he was also a very human ghetto youth, with weaknesses and doubts that left him vulnerable. Lacking education and motivation, looking toward an empty future, he found that basketball could take him only so far. Then he veered into the escape route of the streets, and became the image of the hellish side of ghetto existence. Earl is now in his mid-twenties, a dope addict, in prison.

Earl's is more than a personal story. On the playgrounds, he was a powerful magnetic figure who carried the dreams and ideals of every kid around him as he spun and twisted and sailed over all obstacles. When he fell, he carried those aspirations down with him. Call him a wasted talent, a pathetic victim, even a tragic hero: he had symbolized all that was sublime and terrible about this city game.

"You think of him on the court and you think of so many incredible things that it's hard to sort them out," said Bob Spivey, who played briefly with Earl at Franklin. "But I particularly recall one all-star game in the gym at PS 113, in about 1964. Most of the best high school players in the city were there: Charlie Scott, who went on to North Carolina; Vaughn Harper, who went to Syracuse, and a lot more. But the people who were there will hardly remember the others. Earl was the whole show.

"For a few minutes, Earl seemed to move slowly, feeling his way, getting himself ready. Then he got the ball on a fast break. Harper, who was six feet six, and Val Reed, who was six feet eight, got back quickly to defend. You wouldn't have given Earl a chance to score. Then he accelerated, changing his step suddenly. And at the foul line he went into the air. Harper and Reed went up, too, and between them, the two big men completely surrounded the rim. But Earl just kept going higher, and finally he two-hand-dunked the ball over both of them. For a split second there was complete silence, and then the crowd exploded. They were cheering so loud that they stopped the game for five minutes. Five minutes. That was Earl Manigault."

Faces light up as Harlem veterans reminisce about Manigault. Many street players won reputations with elaborate innovations and tricks. Jackie Jackson was among the first to warm up for games by picking quarters off the top of the backboard. Willie Hall, the former St. John's leader, apparently originated the custom of jumping to the top of the board and, instead of merely blocking a shot, slamming a hand with tremendous force against the board; the fixture would vibrate for several seconds after the blow, causing an easy lay-up to bounce crazily off the rim. Other noted leapers were famous for "pinning"—blocking a lay-up, then simply holding it momentarily against the backboard in a gesture of triumph. Some players seemed to hold it for seconds, suspended in air, multiplying the humiliation of the man who had tried the futile shot. Then they could slam the ball back down at the shooter or, for special emphasis, flip it into the crowd.

Earl Manigault did all of those things and more, borrowing, innovating, and forming one of the most exciting styles Harlem crowds ever watched. Occasionally, he would drive past a few defenders, dunk the ball with one hand, catch it with the other—and raise it and stuff it through the hoop a second time before returning to earth.

"I was in the eighth grade when Earl was in the eleventh," said Charley Yelverton, now a star at Fordham. "I was just another young kid at the time. Like everybody else on the streets, I played some ball. But I just did it for something to do. I wasn't that excited about it. Then there happened to be a game around my block, down at 112th Street, and a lot of the top players were in it—and Earl came down to play. Well, I had never believed things like that could go on. I had never known what basketball could be like. Everybody in the game was doing something, stuffing or blocking shots or making great passes. There's only one game I've ever seen in my life to compare to it—the Knicks' last game against the Lakers.

"But among all the stars, there was no doubt who was the greatest. Passing, shooting, going up in the air, Earl just left everybody behind. No one could turn it on like he could."

Keith Edwards, who lived with Earl during the great days of the Young Life team, agreed. "I guess he had about the most natural ability that I've ever seen. Talent for talent, inch for inch, you'd have to put him on a par with Alcindor and the other superstars. To watch him was like poetry. To play with him or against him—just to be on the same court with him—was a deep experience.

"You can't really project him against an Alcindor, though, because you could never picture Earl going to UCLA or anyplace like that. He was never the type to really face his responsibilities and his future. He didn't want to think ahead. There was very little discipline about the man. . . ."

And so the decline began. "I lived with the man for about two or three years," said Edwards, "from his predrug period into the beginning of his drug period. There were six of us there, and maybe some of us would have liked to help him out. But we were all just young guys finding themselves, and when Earl and another cat named Onion started to get into the drug thing, nobody really had a right, or was in a position, to say much about it. And even as he got into the drugs, he remained a beautiful person. He just had nowhere to go. . . ."

"The athlete in Harlem," said Pat Smith, "naturally becomes a big man in the neighborhood. And if he goes on to college and makes his way out of the ghetto, he can keep being a big man, a respected figure. But if he doesn't make it, if he begins to realize that he isn't going to get out, then he looks around, and maybe he isn't so big anymore. The pusher and the pimp have more clothes than they can ever get around to wearing; when they walk down the street they get respect. But the ballplayer is broke, and he knows that in a certain number of years he won't even have his reputation left. And unless he is an unusually strong person, he may be tempted to go another way. . . ."

"You like to think of the black athlete as a leader of the community," said Jay Vaughn, "but sometimes the idea of leadership can get twisted. A lot of the young dudes on the streets will encourage a big-time ballplayer to be big-time in other ways. They expect you to know all the big pushers, where to buy drugs, how to handle street life. And if they're fooling with small-time drugs, maybe they'll expect you to mess with big-time drugs. It may sound ridiculous at first, but when you're confronted with these attitudes a lot, and you're not strong enough, well, you find yourself hooked."

It didn't happen suddenly. On the weekends, people would still find Earl Manigault at the parks, and flashes of the magnetic ability were there. Young athletes would ask his advice, and he would still be helpful; even among the ones who knew he was sinking deeper into his drug habit, he remained respected and popular. But by early 1968, he seldom came to the parks, and his old friends would find him on the street corners along Eighth Avenue, nodding. "He was such a fine person," said Jay Vaughn, "you saw him and you wished you could see some hope, some bright spot in his existence. But there was no good part of his life, of course. Because drugs do ruin you."

In the summer of 1968, Bob Hunter was working on a drug rehabilitation program. He looked up Earl. They became close, building a friendship that went deeper than their mutual respect on a basketball court. "Earl was an unusual type of addict," said Hunter. "He understood that he was a hard addict, and he faced it very honestly. He wanted to help me in the drug program, and he gave me a lot of hints on how to handle younger addicts. He knew different tricks that would appeal to them and win their trust. And he also knew all the tricks they would use, to deceive me into thinking they were getting cured. Earl had used the tricks himself, and he helped me see through them, and maybe we managed to save a few young kids who might have got hooked much worse.

"But it's the most frustrating thing in the world, working with addicts. It's hard to accept the fact that a man who has been burned will go back and touch fire. But they do it. I have countless friends on drugs, and I had many more who have died from drugs. And somehow it's hard to just give up on them and forget that they ever existed. Maybe you would think that only the less talented types would let themselves get hooked—but then you'd see a guy like Earl and you couldn't understand. . . ."

Some people hoped that Earl would be cured that summer. He did so much to help Hunter work with others that people felt he could help himself. Hunter was not as optimistic. "The truth is that nobody is ever going to cure Earl," he said. "The only way he'll be cured is by himself. A lot of people come off drugs only after they've been faced with an extreme crisis. For example, if they come very close to dying and somehow escape, then they might be able to stay away from the fire. But it takes something like that, most of the time."

Earl was not cured, and as the months went on the habit grew more expensive. And then he had to steal. "Earl is such a warm person," said Vaughn, "you know that he'd never go around and mug people or anything. But let's face it: most addicts, sooner or later, have to rob in order to survive." Earl broke into a store. He is now in prison. "Maybe that will be the crisis he needs," said Hunter. "Maybe, just possibly . . . But when you're talking about addicts, it's very hard to get your hopes too high."

Harold "Funny" Kitt went to Franklin three years behind Earl Manigault. When Funny finished in 1967, he was rated the best high school player in the city—largely because he had modeled himself so closely after Earl. "We all idolized Earl in those days," Kitt said. "And when you idolize somebody, you think of the good things, not the bad. As we watched Earl play ball, we had visions of him going on to different places, visiting the whole world, becoming a great star and then maybe coming back here to see us and talk to us about it all.

"But he didn't do any of those things. He just went into his own strange world, a world I hope I'll never see. I guess there were reasons. I guess there were frustrations that only Earl knew about, and I feel sorry for what happened. But when Earl went into that world, it had an effect on all of us, all the young ballplayers. I idolized the man. And he hurt me."

* * *

Beyond the hurt, though, Earl left something more. If his career was a small dramatization of the world of Harlem basketball, then he was a fitting protagonist, in his magnitude and his frailty, a hero for his time. "Earl was quiet, he was honest," said Jay Vaughn, "and he handled the pressures of being the star very well. When you're on top, everybody is out to challenge you, to make their own reps by doing something against you. One guy after another wants to take a shot, and some stars react to all that by bragging, or by being aloof from the crowd.

"Earl was different. The game I'll never forget was in the G-Dub [George Washington High] tournament one summer, when the team that Earl's group was scheduled to play didn't show. The game was forfeited, and some guys were just looking for some kind of pickup game, when one fellow on the team that forfeited came in and said, 'Where's Manigault? I want to play Manigault.'

"Well, this guy was an unknown and he really had no right to talk like that. If he really wanted to challenge a guy like Earl, he should have been out in the parks, building up a rep of his own. But he kept yelling and bragging, and Earl quietly agreed to play him one-on-one. The word went out within minutes, and immediately there was a big crowd gathered for the drama.

"Then they started playing. Earl went over the guy and dunked. Then he blocked the guy's first shot. It was obvious that the man had nothing to offer against Earl. But he was really determined to win himself a rep. So he started pushing and shoving and fouling. Earl didn't say a word. He just kept making his moves and beating the guy, and the guy kept grabbing and jostling him to try to stop him. It got to the point where it wasn't really basketball. And suddenly Earl put down the ball and said, 'I don't need this. You're the best.' Then he just walked away.

"Well, if Earl had gone on and whipped the guy 30 to 0, he couldn't have proved any more than he did. The other cat just stood there, not knowing what to say. The crowd surrounded Earl, and some of us said things about the fouling and the shoving. But he didn't say anything about it. He didn't feel any need to argue or complain. He had everyone's respect and he knew it. The role he played that day never left anyone who saw it. This was a beautiful man."

# HERMAN HICKMAN

# Rasslin' Was My Act

MY FIRST KNOWLEDGE of Dan Parker, the distinguished sports columnist of the *New York Daily Mirror,* was in 1932. I had just arrived in New York City to embark on a career as a professional wrestler, and his column in those days was "must reading" for the fraternity, just as *Variety* is for other branches of the entertainment field. He must have had a pipeline into our booking office, because his column kept picking the wrestling winners on the nose. He even got so brazen as to name the particular hold that would end a match, and the time of the fall.

It became a guessing game for the powers that be to try and cross him up on the results. Sometimes his information was so late that it was impossible to switch the outcome. The average wrestler didn't have to go by the office in Times Square to get the script for the evening's show. He could read it in Dan Parker's column. I can tell you that it was very demoralizing for a young and ambitious professional.

I remember one night when we fooled him. It was during the famous Jim Londos–Ray Steele series at Madison Square Garden, which, I understand, drew gates of around $70,000 for each match. Dan Parker came out with the prediction that Londos would win this particular match with his famous "airplane spin" in 50 minutes, and thus retain the heavyweight wrestling championship (Jack Curley Division). But did Dan miss it! Londos won, but not until 57 minutes and 30 seconds, and then not with an airplane spin at all but with a series of flying tackles.

I'll say this for Dan. He was a gentleman. The next day his column came out all draped in black, and with the heading, AN APOLOGY TO THE PUBLIC. He said that he was deeply humiliated to have been off on the time of a professional wrestling match by as much as seven minutes and 30 seconds. As for his not getting the winning hold right, there was just no excuse for that.

I felt pretty good about it all until I read his column a few days later. It was a question-and-answer affair. Question: What becomes of old broken-down wrestlers? Answer: They are still wrestling.

The wrestling bug bit me while I was a student at the University of Tennessee. Every Friday night I would go to the Lyric Theater in Knoxville and watch the matches. Soon the promoter, Sam Seigel, started giving me complimentary tickets. It wasn't long before he began taking me backstage to meet the wrestlers.

To a big-eyed East Tennessean, it was wonderful to hear their talk of faraway places—St. Louis, New Orleans, Memphis, Houston. They certainly were glamorous figures to me. I even began to like the "villains," who used such dirty tactics in the ring. I could not understand how these men, perfect gentlemen in their dressing rooms, could be such bullies when they wrestled. None of the wrestlers ever showed any nervousness about their coming matches, although I knew that they must be really on edge, the way I was before a football game.

I met them all during the next few years. The big names were all on the "gasoline circuit," as the Southern territory was called, because the cities were so far apart that the wrestlers had to jump into their cars after a match and head for the next engagement. They could not make connections by train, and airplane travel then was just a name. When I became established on the circuit myself, driving from one city to another after a hurried alcohol bath—usually there weren't any showers in the dressing rooms—and three or four silver-dollar-sized hamburgers, I would think about how I once dreamed of the excitement of new cities and new faces every night.

Here's a sample itinerary. Slip quietly out of Griffith Park in Washington, where the matches have been held outdoors. Grab something quick to eat at the nearest lunch wagon. Walk four blocks to an appointed rendezvous, where two of the boys are waiting in an automobile. Drive a couple more blocks and pick up your opponent. He was disqualified for choking you just an hour ago. Now he is busily engaged with ham sandwiches and a quart of milk as he flops alongside you on the back seat.

It is midnight Thursday, and our next match is in Knoxville, Tennessee, over 500 miles away, on Friday. We head out toward Charlottesville, then Waynesboro. We'll pick up old U.S. 11 between Staunton and Lexington. Then we will be on the beam heading due south.

We play three-handed poker for hours by the flickering overhead car light. The driver is ruled out, but we each take turns at the wheel. We play a spelling game, which I usually introduce. If a word of over three letters ends on an individual, it costs him a dime, and he has to start a new word. If we get a neophyte into the game with old hands who know the "lock" words, it can be an expensive spelling lesson.

We sing. We sleep a little. We stop at our regular all-night filling station after we hit Route 11, have soft drinks and more cold, slightly stale sandwiches, and are off again. We arrive in Knoxville at noon, separate before we get downtown, and go to our hotels. By driving all night we have saved a one-night hotel bill. We will spend this night in Knoxville, then drive all the following night en route to the next town.

The same "villain" who strangled me in Washington does the same thing to me in Knoxville, and is disqualified again. It is more serious here because this is my home territory. It takes three deputy sheriffs and two members of the fire department to get him safely to his dressing room.

After the matches, this is a night for rest and relaxation. I go by Weaver's Restaurant and order "the works." A crowd gathers to talk to me, and among them are some of the Tennessee football players. They look at me enviously as I talk of the places and people I've seen.

"How does it feel to be in the big time, Herman?" they ask.

"There's nothing like it, nothing like it," I tell them expansively, as I push the remains of a two-pound porterhouse away from me. It's the first real meal I have had in two days.

Saturday afternoon we meet again. I have my friend, French Harris, drive me ten miles out on the highway, because I'm well known around here and must not be seen fraternizing with my opponents. They pick me up, and we're off to New Orleans for a Monday-night match. Then comes Birmingham on Tuesday, Atlanta on Wednesday, Nashville on Thursday, and back to Knoxville on Friday. Meanwhile I keep asking myself why I didn't get a job coaching some small-town high-school football team or try to work my way through law school, as I had planned.

But in 1932 money was a scarce item, and there weren't many jobs floating around even if you did weigh 230 pounds, had made the All-American football team, and could recite a conglomerate collection of verse. So, when Rudy Dusek, the oldest and the mastermind of the Dusek brothers, undertook to sell me on the idea of becoming a professional wrestler, he did not find it difficult. He mentioned something about the possibility of making $1,000 a week and becoming champion of the world. He could have got me for less than half of that, and he did.

Up to then, I knew nothing about the inner workings of the wrestling game. I was worried about my lack of experience, but when I started asking about that, they passed it off with, "You're big and you're strong, and you're an All-American football player. We'll teach you everything you oughta know." That was all I knew until I arrived in New York City.

I was really scared when I got off the train at Pennsylvania Station. I decided to take a taxi to the Greystone Hotel at Ninety-first and Broadway, where I was to meet Toots Mondt, who would take charge of my training. I pictured a big gymnasium with a lot of tough guys hanging around. I had read about how there were gangsters all up and down Broadway. This might be their hangout.

It was about 11 A.M. when I arrived at the Greystone. I

asked at the desk for Mr. Mondt. They said he was expecting me. I was getting more nervous all the time as I stepped off the elevator. I had read hundreds of pages about Joe (Toots) Mondt. He was Mr. Big in wrestling. I rang the bell to his apartment.

A big voice boomed, "Come in!" I walked falteringly into the living room, and I could see him through the open bedroom door. Was I disillusioned! There he was in a big oversize bed, having breakfast, and wearing pink silk pajamas. His pleasantly round face was bordered with a big smile, and his baby complexion matched his pajamas.

"How are you, kid?" was his greeting. "Rudy Dusek and Sam Seigel have told me a lot about you. You should be ready for your first match in a couple of weeks. We've got a room all fitted out with a wrestling mat on the next floor. That's your gym. I'll have two or three of the boys work out with you each day, and you'll be ready to go in no time."

He ordered a big breakfast sent up for me and asked, "How's your cash, son?" I told him that I had some money, but he pulled a fat roll of bills out of a pair of trousers hanging across a chair. He flipped off five $100 bills and said, "Well, you might need a little more to tide you over until you get going good. You can pay me back then."

I want to digress for just one moment here and say that I've been mixed up in many kinds of enterprises since my wrestling days and have met many kinds of people, but none can compare with the wrestlers for generosity, friendliness, and real straight shooting. This term may sound a little incongruous when applied to participants in a "sport" that was fixed every night. But they never thought of it that way. They considered themselves performers attempting to please a crowd every night, just as a tumbling act might do on the vaudeville circuit. There have never been any gambling scandals in wrestling, because there has never been any betting mixed up in it. The athletic commissions in the different states consider the matches exhibitions, and in most places the referee gets in on the act with the wrestlers.

My training period progressed to the satisfaction of my mentors, Toots Mondt and Rudy Dusek. I worked out in the gymnasium room three or four hours each day. Men like Jim McMillen, who was an All-American guard during the Red Grange era at Illinois; Earl McCready, the Canadian who was intercollegiate heavyweight wrestling champion at Oklahoma A & M; Tiny Roebuck, the great Indian football star at Kaskell Institute, and Ernie Dusek, a younger brother of Rudy, would work with me every day, after they had wrestled the night before in Albany, Boston, or Baltimore.

They taught me how to "work," which means putting on a performance, instead of "shooting," which means straight wrestling. They showed me how to take a fall without getting hurt, how to "go" with a wristlock without getting a dislocated shoulder, how to slam an opponent without injuring him. This latter is done by making his feet hit the mat first with a resounding thud, and not his head. They taught me to work "loose." Some of the best, like McMillen and the Duseks, could appear to be tearing a man's head off with a headlock, all their muscles straining, and yet their opponents could not even feel the pressure of their arms.

To get the proper dramatic effect, usually one wrestler in each match was "clean" and the other was a villain. Ordinarily you were typed in one role or the other, although some of the wrestlers would play the villain in one town and the hero in the next. I was presented as the clean-cut-college-boy type and because of my football background, the flying tackle was my key hold. Whenever I used that offense, it was usually curtains for my opponent.

Later I became noted for my "belly bounce." I would beat my opponent into submission by bouncing up and down on him—always remembering to break the bounce with my hands hitting the mat first, so as not to start an epidemic of internal hemorrhages—after I had weakened him with the flying tackles.

But I get ahead of my story. My debut was one to remember. I opened in Syracuse at the cavalry armory. My opponent had been selected with care. In fact, I had worked with him in many places under many names. Bill Nelson was quite a character. He must have had 3,000 matches. He was semi-retired from active duty, being engaged in the office with the bookings. Toots and Rudy figured that I couldn't go wrong with him.

I remember that Ed (Strangler) Lewis, one of the great "shooters" of all times and an equally outstanding "worker," was in the main event that first night at Syracuse. I was in the second preliminary with Bill Nelson—Wild Bill in that town. I don't think that Lewis or Hickman either was much of a draw in Syracuse. The crowd was thin, and the odor of the horses was thick. Andy Kerr, the Colgate football coach, who had coached me in the East–West game, brought John Orsi, his great All-American end, and some other members of the squad to see my debut. I was a little embarrassed when they started inquiring about my strategy for the match, and asked me if I weren't nervous. Sure, I was nervous—even though I knew how it was coming out—but I had learned my lessons well.

Wild Bill refused to shake hands with me in the center of the ring before the match. The crowd booed. He complained about the oil on my ears and hair. The crowd booed. He had an argument with the referee about what constituted a fall in the state of New York, and threatened to leave the ring. The crowd hated him already.

The bell rang. I put out my hands to start wrestling, and he hit me with a left to the jaw. I staggered. He hit me with a right to the body which sounded like a pistol shot. I reeled. He started kneeing me in the groin and pulling my hair at the same time. The referee broke his illegal hold and warned him. He came right back and knocked me down with another left hook to the jaw. He put a "punishing" Japanese toe hold on me.

I suffered and suffered, but I would not give up, because I had so much courage. I would not even try to crawl to refuge outside the ropes, because I was a clean-cut college boy and would not resort to anything in the least dishonorable.

Then it happened, and it wasn't in the script. For some reason, the referee broke the hold and had Wild Bill over in a corner of the ring, lecturing him about his dirty tactics. I didn't see them, because I was too busy suffering. I must have lain there on my stomach for a full minute with my feet bent over my back, not realizing that Bill was not still there. Then I happened to glance back over my shoulder and saw both of them.

I wanted to crawl under the ring and die, but instead I recovered my composure and started launching my flying tackles. He ran from me. He cried to the referee. He got outside the ring and asked for mercy. But I was riled up now, and nothing could stop me. The crowd was going wild.

The referee started counting him out. Wild Bill protestingly came back in the ring. I hit him with one tackle, then another. Each time he would sail into the air and hit the mat with a thud—the back of his heels. He couldn't get away from my terrific onslaught. He was a helpless mass in the middle of the ring, so I rushed over and pinned his shoulders to the canvas.

"Nice going, you old mountaineer hillbilly; you made it look good," Bill whispered to me. These were pleasant words from an old trouper to a neophyte during an out-of-town tryout. I had busted one line, but the master had forgiven me. I was ready for the big time.

The job of booking wrestlers in 20 or 30 cities all over the United States each night of the week is a complex operation. The Curley office in New York, which was really run in the early '30's by Toots Mondt, Jack Pfeffer, and Ed White, Jim Londos' manager, was the center of all activities. From here went the instructions to the hinterlands as to the lineup and outcome of the week's matches.

All the wrestlers had code names. For instance, Jim Londos was Chris, Ray Steele was Glendale—his hometown; George Zaharias was Subway—his first trip to New York, he got mixed up and rode all day from one end of the line to the other, so the story goes. Jim McMillen was Football, Rudy Dusek was Mitch. I was Cannonball.

In those days the Postal Telegraph Company was still in existence, in addition to Western Union. The New York office would send out the instructions on one wire service and have them confirmed on the other. This is a sample message: "Cannonball moon Subway around thirty-five confirm." It meant that I was to lose—look up to the moon—to George Zaharias in about 35 minutes.

To be a good attraction for a promoter, you had to be

either greatly liked or greatly hated. A mere scientific exhibit of clean wrestling skill won't draw at the gate. There must be a hero and a villain. The hero doesn't always win, but when he loses, the villain must always beat him by foul means.

I think that amateur wrestling, as conducted in high schools and colleges, is a wonderful sport. I have coached college wrestling, and I enjoyed it. The contestants must be in top physical condition to go all out for nine minutes—the length of a regular college match. It would be physically impossible to wrestle like this for an hour or more, the way the professionals sometimes do.

But amateur wrestling has never been a big spectator sport and never will be, because it is impossible to inject the thrills and pathos in a shooting match that the professionals create in their exhibitions. I have seen many shooting matches by top professionals in the gymnasium, and they are just as dull and uninteresting to the average spectator as the college matches.

So wrestling, in order to draw crowds, must of necessity be "rasslin'." It always has been and always will be an exhibition. Taken in this light, I can see nothing harmful in it. As entertainment it is usually better than a lot of movies, and it should not have a bad influence on any member of the family, because virtue is always supreme.

I get quite a kick out of some of the old-time sports fans who say, "Wrestling today is just a hoax and a vaudeville act, but I remember back in the days of Hackenschmidt and Gotch and the Zbyszkos when it was really wrestling. Why, I've seen them stay in one hold for 50 minutes, and wrestle many a night for two hours, and none of this rough stuff either. They were scientific."

They were scientific, all right, and maybe excellent shooters, although myths can flourish with the passage of time. I can tell you one thing, and that is that their so-called scientific wrestling matches were exhibitions, and not very exciting ones, either. I saw many of those early matches, which were for the most part put on by foreign wrestlers, and I later worked with some of them, such as Stanislaus and Wladek Zbyszko.

The style of that time was a carry-over from the old German beer gardens, where the longer the performers wrestled, the more beer they could sell the customers. Some of them told me that they would "wrestle" five or six hours during the course of the evening in the Graeco-Roman style, in which no holds are allowed below the waist, and when anyone is thrown to the mat, it constitutes a fall. They would lock in each other's arms and stay in one position for an hour or so. Then one would straighten up his arm slowly, flexing his muscles mightily, and the customers sitting around the tables would go wild and more beer would flow. Finally, when the wrestlers got thirsty, one would be thrown to the mat with a mighty thud, and they would rest for 30 minutes. And so on through the night.

The only public shooting match I ever saw took place in Madison Square Garden in 1933 between Strangler Lewis and Ray Steele. Ed Lewis was representing what was then the Paul Bowser branch of the industry, and Ray Steele was the standard-bearer for the Curley wheel. They were both excellent wrestlers. Lewis may have been the best of all time— on the basis of my personal observations in the gymnasium. Both were popular with their fellow wrestlers.

This match was supposed to decide the "real" championship. I don't know yet how the powers that be ever let the match happen, but I do know that I have never seen such tension around the Times Square office as there was the week before the match. I was booked in the Broadway Arena in Brooklyn for the same night, along with seven other unfortunates. Ordinarily a wrestler never goes to a wrestling match, but this was different. We made our plans. We knew that in order to reach the Garden in time for the Lewis–Steele event, we would have to get four matches over with by 9:30. Never did the old Broadway Arena see such fast and short matches.

The match had already begun when we got to our seats. Lewis was fat, 50, and balding, with a big chest, big belly, and small legs. He was built like the great Babe Ruth. Steele, approaching 40, had the body beautiful. He weighed around 220 pounds to the Strangler's 250.

From the very start it was no contest. Steele could do nothing with the Strangler. Lewis was a big cat, darting in, going behind, making Steele look like a boy on a man's mission. The fans yawned and started stamping their feet for action. The wrestlers, on the other hand, sat with their eyes glued on the ring. They watched every movement intensely. They were thrilled with the skill of Lewis. They were seeing the master give a pupil the lesson of his life.

Lewis and Steele were personal friends. I have no doubt that the Strangler could have pinned him at any time. Steele had courage, but realized that he was hopelessly outmatched. Some whispering probably occurred, and Steele started punching Lewis with his closed fists. So it ended with the referee disqualifying him after the match had gone about 20 minutes.

We saw Ed next morning at Grand Central Station on his way to another match in Buffalo.

"How was Ray?" we asked.

"Good little man, good little man," he replied, between puffs of his cigar.

My first match for the heavyweight championship of the world was held in the baseball park at Memphis in 1932. I had not been defeated in about 50 matches, so a bout with Jim Londos, the perennial champion, was a natural in my home state of Tennessee. I was drawing big crowds everywhere in the South, so the authorities did not want to see me beaten, even by the champion, except under extraordinary circumstances. I was told to go about 50 minutes, and then, after Londos had narrowly escaped defeat, to take a dive from the elevated ring platform out into the infield and be counted out.

There is a mistaken idea that wrestlers rehearse every move of their matches. Usually, the only orders you receive are as to who is to "moon." Only if there is to be an unusual finish is it discussed. A good match must be extemporaneous. The wrestlers must feel the reaction of the crowd. They must attain the moment of the highest excitement, and then have the finish come with dramatic suddenness.

Most wrestling fans know that the matches are pure exhibitions, but they forget everything they know when an exciting bout is in progress. I have seen more violent reactions from fans at a wrestling match than I ever saw or heard during a football game. Men and women alike wildly cheer and boo—the two reactions that the performers like to hear.

Jim Londos looked and acted the part of a champion. He trained hard, had no bad habits, and when he walked into the ring he carried himself like the king. I understand that he was an excellent shooter, and I know that he was a great showman and worker. He had the lightest touch in the ring of anyone I ever met.

His strategy against me was to keep away. He had decided to be the "villain," or at least the cautious type who was slightly afraid of me. The partisan crowd in Memphis was overjoyed when I broke his wristlock with pure brute strength. When he failed to get me above his head for his famous finishing hold, the airplane spin, he looked at me with amazement. Then, when I hit him with two flying tackles, he crawled outside the ropes for a rest as the crowd booed. Twice I had him pinned for a count of two—a count of three with both shoulder blades touching the mat consti- tutes a fall—but he managed to get away from me before I could finish him.

After 40 minutes the crowd excitement had reached its crescendo. The moment had arrived. I hit him with a flying tackle and knocked him all the way into the ropes with such force that he bounced back, and I hit him again on the re- bound. He went down, and as he staggered to his feet I let him have another shoulder block in his midsection. He sailed high into the air.

This was the end of a champion. The crowd could sense that just one more flying tackle and he would be done. I felt the elation of the crowd myself—once a ham, always a ham— as I prepared for the kill. I backed into the ropes to get more spring for my final assault. As I dove through the air, Londos fell flat to the mat. I sailed out of the ring, which was six feet above the ground, going between the second and third ropes.

I was aiming for some soft laps in the second row of the ringside seats, but either my aim was poor or the soft laps saw me coming, because I missed completely and landed flat on my back in the infield on a lighted cigar butt. I was to lie there unconscious while a count of 20 was being tolled over my inert form. I have been through some tough moments, but it took all my fortitude to withstand that burning cigar butt. I thought of Barrymore, of the theater, of "the show must go on," as the slow count of 20 was intoned.

When I heard the magic number of "twenty," I rolled over on my face just as someone dumped a whole bucket of ice water on me. Then three or four people dragged me off by the heels as they would a dead bull. I had failed at my first championship attempt, but had fought the good fight, and I still have a big scar to show for it where that cigar burned a hole in my back.

Many years have passed since my rasslin' days, and I look back on them with pleasant memories. I know that there have been few legitimate professional matches since Milo of Croton was six times champion of Greece and Theseus laid down the wrestling rules in 900 B.C. I even have my doubts about whether that historic match between Ulysses and Ajax was a shoot. I do know that I met a lot of good guys who were the straightest shooters I've ever known, and that I got to see a lot of "faraway places." I still don't think you can get a better night's entertainment than you will seeing your favorite "hero" tangle with a "villain." This plot has had the longest run in show business, so it must have something.

PAUL GALLICO

# *Farewell to the Babe*

IT IS NOW CLOSE to twenty-five years since I first laid eyes on
Babe Didrikson in the lobby of the Chapman Park Hotel in
Los Angeles upon the occasion of the 1932 Olympic Games.
She was then a rawhide kid of 18 with short-cut, sand-colored
hair, a well-defined Adam's apple and a faint down on her
upper lip. I watched her "up" to a big girl who was wearing
the jacket of an Olympic competitor, pin her with her gray-
green eyes and announce levelly—"Ah'm gonna whup yo' tomorrow."

We sportswriters thought that this was cockiness. There
was no way for us to know at the time that it was just a simple declarative sentence spoken by a simple declarative person. It took all of us some time to find out that this lithe girl
from Port Arthur, Texas who was apparently not made like
other girls of sugar and spice, but instead, of whipcord, steel
springs and Monel metal, enclosing the heart of a lioness,
had also the makings of an extraordinary woman.

None of us who watched this unknown and unheralded
youngster foresaw that she would become the greatest woman
golfer that ever lived, a champion of champions, and then

thrill a nation with the courage and gallantry of her battle against cancer.

There were many sports in which the Babe excelled super-latively—*all* track and field events, basketball and golf—but there was hardly any game at which she could not perform creditably, or at which she could not have become a champion, and these included swimming, diving, billiards, lacrosse, bowling and tennis. But she also invaded the men's fields. Her record for throwing a baseball still stands. She could pitch, hit and cover a bag. She could peg a football and kick left-footed. Once she even thought of boxing. Nothing came of it, but it is recorded that when she threw a punch it wasn't a roundhouse or a fly-swatter like a woman, but straight down the old trolley wire a la Ruby Goldstein, a sharpshooter of our era.

While it is true that none of the Babe's track and field or Olympic records, with the exception of the baseball throw, are still on the books today, no girl before or since has matched her record of events won in a diversity of sports. Nor had any other woman even approached her in the number and caliber of golf championships captured, some of them played while suffering from pain, illness and physical handicaps that would have seen most grown men laid up in the hospital.

Competitively, the record she brought to Los Angeles in 1932 has never been equaled. I refer to her performance on July 16, 1932 at the National Women's AAU Track and Field Championships and Olympic tryouts at Evanston, Illinois, in which she was entered by herself as a one-woman team representing the Employers Casualty Company, of Dallas, Texas.

Singlehanded the Babe won the *team title* with an aggregate of 30 points. In second place was the famous Illinois Woman's AC, with 22 points, collected by a full complement of girls.

Now consider that in such comprehensive competitions as pentathlons or decathlons, the entrants usually excel in one or two events, are good in several more and do the best they can in the others. Thus there is a balance and the battle tends to even out. But in this incomparable performance, the girl, barely turned 18, was pitted against the best *specialists* in the entire country in *each* event, never less than half a dozen of them and sometimes two and three from one team.

On that day the Babe staged and won a private octathlon. She entered eight of the 10 events scheduled. Five of these, the 80-meter hurdles, the baseball throw, the shotput, the broad jump and the javelin toss she won outright; and in the high jump, although she equaled the world record jump of winner Jean Shiley, she was just nosed out of a tie. She placed fourth in the discus throw, picking up another point. During the course of the afternoon she set three world's records and was shut out only in the 100-meter dash, when she was just nipped in the semifinal heat.

I cannot think of any male athlete with the possible exception of old Jim Thorpe who has come even close to spread-eagling a track meet all by himself in this manner.

Two weeks later the Babe went to the Olympics in Los Angeles. Allowed to participate in only three events, against the best women of every nation, she won two of them, setting world's records in each, the aejvlin throw and the 80-meter hurdles. She was languaged out of the third, the high jump. After she tied with Jean Shiley for first place, at a world-record height, Babe cleared the bar in the jump-off but was ruled to have dived over. Thus she lost the record and the event. The roll that she used, incidentally, is legal today.

But prior to these events this wonderful little girl, the sixth child born to a poor Norwegian cabinetmaker and his wife who emigrated to Port Arthur, Texas, later moving to Beaumont, had already been a star basketball player named three times on the women's All-America team, a high scorer who in one game is recorded to have tanked the ball for an individual total of 106 points. And she was likewise a home run hitting star in soft ball, a crackerjack at pool and billiards and good enough at swimming and high diving to appear in exhibitions.

All this, however, was only the beginning of a career that was to take her to an alltime record as a golf champion, including the distinction of becoming the first American girl to break the jinx and win the British Women's Amateur championship.

Much has been made of Mrs. Zaharias' natural aptitude and talent for sports, as well as her competitive spirit and indomitable will to win, with both of which she was endowed in full measure. But not nearly enough has been said or written about the patience and strength of character expressed in her willingness to practice for endless hours, and her recognition even as a child that with all her natural ability she could reach the top and stay there only by means of incessant drill and hard work.

The hours of practice the Babe devoted in her life to various games ought to be made compulsory reading for every fresh kid who can swim, skate, run, ski a little or is handy at sports and thinks that all he or she needs to do is get out there and the opposition will swoon away. When the Babe leveled on a sister athlete and husked, "Ah'm gonna whup yo' " it wasn't brag (though an element of games-womanship and psychological attack was involved). She had put in the necessary hours of slavery to perfect her form and to be able to deliver the goods; and she just knew she could.

At 16, preparing for her first track and field meet, she would work two hours in the afternoon with her teammates and then go out alone after supper and practice from two to three hours more until darkness enveloped her, working on her step-timing for the jumps, her balance in the weight events and her starts in the sprints.

She learned golf the same way. The first full game she ever played followed the 1932 Olympics when she paired with Grantland Rice against Olin Dutra and the writer at Brentwood. She had a fine natural swing and could paste the ball as far as a man, but that isn't golf and the Babe knew it. When she decided to go in for the game seriously, she took lessons, drilled and practiced for hours on end until her hands were a mass of blisters. She taped and bandaged them and kept on, stopping only when the bandages became soaked with blood.

In the spring of 1935 while she was working for her old friends, the Employers Casualty Company in Dallas, this was her schedule:

Up at 5 in the morning and practice from 5:30 to 8:30. Report at the office at 9. During the lunch hour, putt on the carpet in the boss's office and chip balls into his leather chair. After work, back to the golf course hitting balls until dark. Thus it went, until the pain in her hands made another shot impossible. At night she would go to bed with the rule book.

It was the same story when in 1940 Babe took up tennis

during the probationary period in which she was regaining her amateur golf status. Married by then to George Zaharias and living in California, she took lessons, played matches and practiced against a backboard from morning until night, for a year and a half. Had she continued, nothing could have kept her from the national championships.

But entangled as she was in the flypaper of the most ridiculous set of amateur rules ever devised, Babe quit tennis when the sportsmen running the game advised her that because she had been ruled a pro in golf she was likewise a pro in tennis. So she devoted the same long hours to bowling and became good enough to bowl major league teams in California.

Golf, however, was where Babe Didrikson reached her greatest heights. Who will ever duplicate her most impossible feat of winning 17 major golf tournaments in a row, including the National Women's Amateur, Tam O'Shanter All-American, North and South, Augusta Titleholder tourney, Broadmoor, Texas Women's Open, and finishing the sweep by capturing the British Women's Amateur championship? Only a golfer who has known the agonizing treachery of which his nerves and body are capable in letting him down in tight corners can appreciate the accumulative tension of extending a winning string of tournaments of match play against the best girl and woman golfers culled from a nation of over 143 million people and crowning this achievement by winning the one that had defied American girls for close to half a century.

Nor must it be forgotten that when the Babe had finished this grueling struggle, she was the darling of the Scots and Britons in the gallery, as well as the pet of the whole village of Gullane. She not only beat the best they had; she made them love her.

And this is perhaps the clue as to why it may be another 50 or 75 years before such a performer as Mildred Didrikson Zaharias again enters the lists. For even if some yet unborn games queen matches her talent, versatility, skill, patience and will to practice, along with her flaming competitive spirit, and manages, let us say, to run an unbroken string of tournament victories in her specialty to 20, there still remains the little matter of courage and character, and in these departments the Babe must be listed with the champions of all times.

Indeed her unique quality has been noted, for in addition to being chosen Woman Athlete of the Year by the Associated Press poll of sportswriters and broadcasters for the years 1932, 1945, 1946, 1947 and 1950, she was named the woman athlete of the half century.

In 1953 Mildred Zaharias was stricken with cancer and suffered one of the most dangerous and excruciating of all operations, a colostomy. Yet just three and half months after the operation, this incredibly brave and unquenchable girl was back on a golf course again in competition in the Tam O'Shanter All-American championship in killing midsummer heat in Chicago.

She did not win it. The miracle was that she fought her way back that far. Her presence on that first tee was an act of heroism that should have been rewarded with the Congressional Medal of Honor. The value of her example in inspiration to others, and the magnificence of the banner she waved aloft to those of less courage and steadfastness, cannot be overestimated.

Ten months after her operation, the Babe won the Serbin Tournament in Florida, and that same year, 1954, took the National Women's Open and this time, the Tam O'Shanter "All-American" too.

The following year all of her splendid courage was called upon again. The trouble was that she had too much of it. No longer the wiry rawhide tomboy of 18 who could practice and compete all day and dance all night, Babe was now a mature woman of 41 who had never spared herself. On a car trip vacation with two girl friends on the Texas coast she ruptured a disk in her spinal column getting the car out of sand when it got stuck. In agony with the pain in her back, she played in three more tournaments, winning one at Spartanburg, South Carolina before she was finally forced into the hospital for an operation on the ruptured disk.

Hospitalized again late in 1955 for a recurrence of cancer, her fiery fighting spirit remained undimmed and the golf clubs still accompanied her. During her first operation and again for her second they stood in the corner of her room where she could see them, play mentally over old courses, plan to correct old mistakes. They were her beloved tools, and they will forever be with her. Without them she would surely be remembered, but with them she carved herself an imperishable niche in the great American world of sports, and likewise in the hearts of all who loved her for what she was, a splendid woman.

# TED GREEN with AL HIRSHBERG

# from *High Stick*

DECEMBER 2, 1970. As I skated out to my right defense position for the Boston Bruins in Chicago Stadium, I was thinking: I wonder if this game will be better? Here we are, halfway through the season, halfway through another game, and I still don't want to be here. I don't like the nervous feeling I get when I go on the ice. I don't like thinking the way I'm thinking or the way my hands sweat and my knees shake. I don't like not being able to do the job as I want to do it. My doctors and teammates tell me to forget these things— just think about playing hockey. It's so easy for them to say, so hard for me to do. I can't forget that easily.

I look over at my defense partner, Don Awrey. We have gone out to relieve Dallas Smith and Bobby Orr, a tough act to follow. Who can do the things Orr can do? I couldn't have done them even before Wayne Maki of the St. Louis Blues nearly killed me in September 1969. And now—

Now? So many nows. Every game a question mark. I could imagine what the hockey crowds were thinking: he makes mistakes he never made before. He won't fight. He wears a helmet. Whoever thought Terrible Teddy Green would need protection on his head—or anywhere else? Or want it? Terrible Teddy Green. The tough guy of the National Hockey League. That was the reputation I had before Maki bashed in my skull with his stick during an exhibition game in Ottawa. I didn't like the name or the reputation. I played hockey hard and I hit because it was my job to hit. In my younger days maybe I went out of my way to find a fight, but not later. Two, three years before Maki hit me I had stopped being Terrible Teddy Green. I held my ground, I battled for puck control, I hit back when I got hit. But that was to protect my part of the ice, my goalie, my partner and myself.

And when I had the puck, I bulled my way down the ice with it, passing and taking passes, fighting across the blue line and through opposing defensemen. And I was respected. Leave Ted Green alone and you'll be O.K. Just don't start anything with him, not unless you want trouble.

That's the way it had been, but not now. Physically, I was in as good shape as ever, maybe a little better. But an awful feeling of inadequacy had possessed me. I wasn't afraid, just unsure of myself. That doubt was killing me, killing my game, making me wonder what I was doing out on the ice.

I remembered a game we lost to Oakland a few weeks before. I lost that game. It was tied 1–1 in the third period when one of the Seals dumped the puck in on my side. Ordinarily this would have been no problem. I might have started up ice with it. Or, if a man were right on me and Awrey was free, I might have passed it across to Don. Or, if I got really tangled up with my opponent, I might have battled him to the boards to freeze the puck and force a face-off.

I didn't do any of these things. In fact, I'm not sure what I did. All I know is that one minute I had control of the puck and the next minute I didn't. One of the Seals just swooped down, stole it right from under me, and with nobody in front of the net but our goalie, Gerry Cheevers, slammed it home for a 2–1 win for them. Cheevers didn't have a chance.

If I were the coach, I would have yanked me out right away. But Tom Johnson, a former defense partner of mine on the Bruins, kept me in for a few more minutes to save further embarrassment. Johnson, who treated me with understanding and consideration almost all year, didn't fool me or the crowd, either. My mistake was obvious to everyone at Boston Garden. I was all alone out there, holding the puck on my stick and obviously in control of it. When I lost control, a spectator had ot be blind or looking the other way to miss it.

Maybe I was imagining things, but I could hear the crowd murmuring that night, too: Teddy Green hasn't got it anymore.

As I skated out on the ice in Chicago, memories of that Oakland loss and of all those early games flashed through my mind. Obvious mistakes, not always as costly but just as obvious: passing the puck to an opponent, letting it slip away when it was right on my stick, losing it on the boards after I had beaten my man to it, not freezing it solidly enough for a face-off, getting in the way of the goalie instead of protecting him, failing to carry the puck because I didn't trust myself to keep it.

And not fighting. Despite my reputation, I hadn't been looking for fights even before I was hurt; I just never ran away from them. Now I was avoiding them, backtracking if one seemed to be coming my way. If I was lucky, I could divert a man into the corner, but I didn't fight him, didn't battle, didn't try to crash him into the boards, didn't swing at him, grab him or do anything to get the puck away from him. The word was getting around the league: go down Green's side. He won't hit and he can't hurt.

Worse were those other words going through the league: don't go after Green. Don't try to hurt him. He's been hurt enough. Pity. Compassion. Sympathy. I didn't want that. I wanted to earn my way back.

The brain damage had all been on the right side of my head, which controls nerves on the left side—and I'm left-handed. While recovering I could skate, handle a stick and carry a puck before I could write my name. When I was Terrible Teddy Green and even after that they all tried to stay away from my left side. I hit with my left hip or my left shoulder, I punched with my left hand. My left side was my strong side. And now, as guys came down the ice, they knew I couldn't—or wouldn't—use it.

I could not understand why. The doctor had assured me my left side was as strong as ever, the plastic coating over the hole in my head sturdier than the bone it had replaced. And yet I was gunshy. Before every game I gave myself fight talks: Hit, hit with your left. Fight, punch with your left. Check, check on your left. Then I got into games, and I flinched. It bothered the hell out of me. And it was bothering me when I moved that night in Chicago into the spot Orr had played.

There was another problem, an odd one. The Bruins were so much the class of the league that they often ran away with a game, sometimes winning by three or four goals. That made it doubly hard for me to get fired up. The close games were the kind I needed. But because we were so strong I got more ice time than I would have on a losing club. And by using me as much as he did, Tom Johnson was giving me the time I so badly needed to regain my form.

Since Tom and I understood each other, there were rarely any problems between us. We had a lot in common. While we were defense mates, Tom, who for 15 years was an NHL stickout, first with the Montreal Canadiens and then with us, was knocked out of hockey by Wayne Maki's brother, Chico, who has been with the Hawks all through his career. It was entirely accidental but when Chico snicked Tom in the back of the legs with his skates and severed a nerve, that was the end of Tom's career.

My own feeling about Wayne Maki was zero. He was with Vancouver last season, and every time we played the Canucks people wondered what would happen if Maki and I collided. We didn't. If he hadn't stayed away from me, I'd have stayed away from him. I wanted—and want—no part of that guy. He's apparently a little reckless with his stick, because even after he cooled me with it he couldn't control his urge to use it on people.

Don't get me wrong—I'm not afraid of Maki. I just don't want to have anything to do with him. Maybe he feels the same way. The few times we were on the ice together we hardly ever went near each other. Frankly, if I saw him coming at me, I'd go the other way. Maybe I'm afraid of myself, of what I might do to the guy.

In all those early games I was thinking too much. The moves used to be natural, a part of me. I didn't have to think *I'm going to hit this guy*. I just hit him. I didn't have to think *I'm going to block the puck*. I just blocked it. Now everything was mental. It was a problem I had to lick. If I didn't, it would lick me. After enduring all I had gone through to get into shape to return to the NHL, I couldn't let overthinking get the better of me. Something had to happen to get all the gremlins out and make me the Teddy Green I wanted to be again.

Suddenly in Chicago I was in the middle of a rough game, with a lot of pushing and elbowing and scrambling—one of those games you know will blow sky-high sooner or later. We were about halfway through the second period when Don Awrey got into a fight with one of the Black Hawk players. I skated over to give him a hand. I definitely wasn't looking for a fight—all I wanted to do was break up this one. As I approached the two guys battling near the boards on the left side of our defensive zone, Dan Maloney, a 20-year-old Chicago rookie who stand 6'2" and weighs about 200 pounds, grabbed Awrey from behind and started punching him.

That Don had been covering for me all year, probably doing more for me than anyone else on the ice because he was my partner, was not nearly as important to me as the fact he was a teammate in trouble. He needed help, and you help a teammate any time you can. That's the code of our business.

My original reason for going over to where Awrey was fighting was to help him, and maybe Maloney's reason for hitting him was to help a Chicago player. When I got there Maloney had already hit Awrey and was trying to hold him from behind. By then all I wanted to do was get Maloney— get the kid off Awrey's backs so Don could keep swinging or at least protect himself. I dropped my stick and gloves and started hauling Maloney off Awrey. As I pinned his arms and pulled him away, Maloney said, "Let go, I'm not going to hit you."

I wasn't going to fall for that without being ready to protect myself—in fact, I didn't want to fight at all because I still wasn't sure of myself. But since he was now clear of Awrey, I let him go—and he threw a punch at me. I ducked, and his punch went over my shoulder and by my head. My Helmet slipped down over my face, scratching my nose, and I blew up. While I yanked at the helmet, Maloney tried to punch me again, and again he missed. By the time I was rid of that damn helmet instinct took over and I could swing freely. I did it naturally—left-handed. I nailed him with four good lefts in a row, hitting him so hard that he started sliding down the boards onto the ice. Somebody had to pull me off before I stopped swinging. The way I was hitting the kid, I'd have knocked him cold. As it was, I dazed him, and he had to go to the dressing room when most of us drew penalties.

I guess I wasn't even thinking as I picked up my gloves and stick and skated over to the penalty box. But I know I felt a sudden warmth, the comfort that comes when something very good happens. I was grinning, almost laughing, as I served my time in the penalty box. And I grinned still more after getting out and going over to our bench, where the guys were yelling and laughing and throwing friendly punches at me.

Not until then did I realize the little finger on my left hand hurt like hell. This was curious, because one of the effects of my skull fracture had been paralysis of my left side, including my arm and, with it, numbness in my hand and fingers. Actually, even that long after the injury, I couldn't write easily or clearly, and—as is still the case—I had no feeling in the tips of the fingers of my left hand. I looked down and saw the little finger was crooked. I tried to move it and almost yelled with pain.

Then I smiled—smiled like a crazy man. I thought *God, I broke my finger throwing punches! Imagine, I belted him so hard I broke my finger—and on my left hand!* I studied my hand again. Except for the little finger, it was fine. I found Frosty Foristall, our assistant trainer, and eased over to him.

"My finger's sore," I said. "I've got to keep playing tonight, so fix it up."

"It looks broken," Frosty said.

"It probably is," I said. "Do something."

Frosty quickly made a little mold for a temporary splint, while I thought *I can use my left! I can use my left! I can use my left!* The words rang in my mind as Frosty worked fast; I don't think I missed a turn on the ice. When Tom Johnson gave the word, I jumped the boards with Awrey, ready for anything.

I played the rest of the game with that broken finger, and not only did I not worry about what might happen, I played exceptionally well. Nothing much did happen, really. The Hawks had learned something, too, and they left me alone. When the puck came into my zone, nobody came barreling hard after it the way everyone had before. Nobody wanted to tangle with me or start a fight or try to belt me around. I thought *They're not afraid of hurting me anymore. They're afraid of me hurting them.*

We lost the game, which didn't make me happy, but my heart was singing when it was over. They could call me Terrible Teddy Green all they wanted to now. It was just an incident, but what an incident! It taught me to feel what everyone, including the doctors who checked me from time to time, had been telling me right along: my left side was strong; I could expose it to anything I had ever exposed it to before, and it would hold up.

In the locker room later Frosty and Dan Canney, our head trainer, made a removable metal splint, while guys came in and out, joking and patting my back and saying things like, "what the hell's a broken finger?" Despite the loss, they were happy for me. They knew I had found something I'd been looking for all year—myself, the old Teddy Green.

September 21, 1969. Ottawa, clean and beautiful, glistened beneath a warm sun that Sunday morning. It was a lovely day, a lovely town, a lovely place to be. It was good to be alive, to go to Mass and give thanks to God for my wife and children and parents, and for the talent to play hockey which He had blessed me with.

I strolled with Turk Sanderson past the Chateau Laurier Hotel and through the greenery of Parliament Park, its old, impressive government buildings towering over acres of grass extending the seven or eight blocks between the Chateau and the Ottawa General Hospital. The grounds looked like a huge, flat, marvelously well-kept golf course that was all fairway and no greens. Although this was my eighth season with the Bruins and my 11th in professional hockey, I had never seen Ottawa, which is slightly off the beaten paths between NHL cities and is almost 300 miles from our training camp in London, Ontario.

I don't remember much of the conversation with Turk, except that I remarked how foolish it was to go all-out in training or any of the preseason exhibition games we played, and that I didn't intend to do so. We were in Ottawa for a game that night with the St. Louis Blues, who trained there. The preceding night we had played an exhibition with the Canadiens in Montreal. I never liked exhibition games because of the chances of getting hurt before the regular season. What with injuries or contract disputes, I doubt if I had played more than half a dozen exhibition games the previous five years. I kept myself in condition during the off season at my home in St. Boniface, just outside Winnipeg. The only reason I cared about training at all after I made the club was to get into skating shape, which never took more than a few weeks.

I had played in the Montreal game and was to play again that night against the Blues. I wasn't happy about it and told Sanderson so, but I needed the work; I had reported late to training camp. I remember being very pleased because, after a summer of doubt and some hassling over my contract, everything had just been settled. Only a few days before, Charlie Mulcahy, the Bruins' lawyer, and I had reached an agreement. I'd had a great year the season before—I made the second NHL All-Star team and now I was getting a new three-year contract at a nice raise. The only reason I hadn't actually signed was that a few clauses were being changed on paper in Boston. All I had was a handshake, but with the Bruins that was all I needed. The signing would come in due time.

After meandering through the park for an hour or so, Turk and I went back to the hotel. I loafed around with the guys, ate and slept a little before going with the team to the arena in the city's new Civic Center. We arrived a couple of hours before the game, our usual procedure, and horsed around in the locker room before changing into uniform. There is this thing on the club about me looking Jewish, and every once in a while the guys call me "Abie." This is one of the ways we all loosen up—yelling foolish names at each other. Anyway, somebody said this was a Jewish holiday and asked me if I was going to play that night. If Sandy Koufax could take a Jewish holiday off, why couldn't I? While the guys were kidding me, Milt Schmidt, our general manager walked into the dressing room. When I saw him, I handed him my skates and said, "I can't play tonight."

"What the hell's wrong with you?" he said.

"It's a Jewish holiday."

It broke up the locker room. The guys were still laughing when we went out for our pregame workout. The place was full. I didn't pay much attention to the Blues. They had players I knew, and a lot I didn't. As on most expansion clubs, there was a flock of rookies. Those kids are usually the ones to watch because they play harder than veterans in exhibition games. Fighting for jobs, they have to make an impression or they get lost in the shuffle.

The first 12 minutes of the game went by without much happening. There was no checking, no scoring, no fighting, no nothing. Around the 12th or 13th minute, while I was guarding the right side of our defensive zone, somebody shot the puck over our blue line and followed it in. I didn't even notice who it was—to me it was just a blue uniform. Later I discovered it was Wayne Maki, a left wing, but I didn't know that then. He had been with the Black Hawks and he was one of the kids fighting for a regular job with the Blues. The only time I had ever played against him had been when he took one turn on the ice against us while he was a Hawk. I wasn't particularly concerned about him.

As I trapped the puck behind the net the kid hit me from behind, and I got a little ticked off, as I always do when that happens. But my first obligation was to clear the puck. I kicked it with my skate up to my stick and shot it out around the boards to our right wing. Then I turned to take care of the guy who hit me. By that time we had both moved in front and a little to the left of our net. I reached out with my gloved left hand and shoved Maki in the face. He went down by the side of the net. Figuring that was the end of that, I turned away, but then Maki speared me. Spearing, which is shoving the blade of your stick into a guy, is a filthy trick, because if you get him in an unprotected spot he can be badly hurt. That and butt-ending (hitting an opponent with the butt of your stick) are dangerous.

Where at first I had just been annoyed, now I was sore as hell, and I hit Maki with my stick just below the shoulder at the biceps, knocking him off balance and, I think, down on one knee. I say "I think" because I am really not sure, and I wouldn't know at all what happened next except from pictures and from what I was told. Seeing Maki on the ice is the last clear memory I have. My last thought was *Well, I guess that'll straighten him out,* and again I turned to skate away.

The next thing I knew, I was lying on my stomach with my head turning violently. I remember trying to stop it from moving, but I couldn't because I had no control over it. It was whipping back and forth, and everything else that followed is vague in my memory—little snatches of action, dim pictures of guys around me. I didn't know what hit me, didn't remember anything hitting me, didn't feel a thing—no pain, nothing except this violent head movement that I couldn't stop.

I don't remember going down and I don't remember getting up. Everything was hazy because my eyes were full of water and things were very, very blurry. I still felt no pain, didn't see or feel any blood. I was just in a complete fog, terribly dazed and yelling something—I don't know what. And I remember that nothing came out clearly; I couldn't control my speech. I saw a haze of players, but the only one I remember was Bobby Orr, who had been on the bench and was now on the ice. Dan Canney and somebody else (I found out later it was Phil Esposito) were trying to lead me off the ice, but I tried to push them away. I don't remember how I got off, who led me, where I went, what I did. And I didn't know what had happened, where I had been hit, what I had been hit with, how badly I was hurt. It was the only time in my career I ever got hit without seeing the blow coming— the only time I turned away thinking a fight was over when it wasn't.

"I saw the two guys pushing each other around, but I didn't think anything of it," Canney said later. "That sort of thing happens all the time in a game. I turned away for a second, then turned back just in time to see Maki hit Ted with his stick. Bobby Orr, sitting in front of me, jumped the boards, saying something about going after Maki. I followed him because I knew Ted was badly hurt. He went down with his knees, buckling, and then his head kept thrashing around. Even as I was jumping the boards, I could see his eyes glazed and staring oddly. I got to him as fast as I could, but I was still 20 feet away when he stood up under his own power.

Phil was holding him by the arm and Ted was mumbling almost incoherently. The only blood I saw was from a small cut on the right side of his scalp.

" 'Canney,' he muttered thickly, 'I'm gonna get that guy.'

" 'Come on, Teddy, you're cut,' I said. 'Let's go in and get you fixed up. Bobby's taking care of Maki. You'll get a shot at him later.'

"He kept muttering, his speech so garbled I though he had broken his jaw. The head wound seemed slight, but I knew Ted was in serious trouble. When I tried to grab him, he pulled away from me, so I took him by the seat of the pants, and, with Phil holding him on the other side, we finally got him off the ice."

"My first thought was to get Maki," Orr said, "but by the time I got across the ice, he was swinging his stick while the Blues were trying to get him out of there. Then I went over to Teddy, who was stumbling around on his feet. I had no idea how badly hurt he was. I just said, 'Take it easy,' and stood and watched Dan and Phil lead him off."

"I was at the red line, right at center ice, when the fight started," Esposito recalled. "They were sparing over in the corner near the Bruins' goal when Maki went down on one knee. He got right up and hit Greenie over the head with the hardest part of his stick—at the bend where the shaft joins the blade. Greenie was down when I reached him, and he looked awful. When he got up his voice was fuzzy and he kept saying something like, 'I'm gonna get that sonofabitch. I'll kill him—I'll kill him.' His eyes were glassy, and spit or something was coming out of his mouth, which was all twisted on the left side. He looked so bad I was scared to death. I took him by the left side, and when Dan came he tried to take his right. But Greenie kept pulling away from him and telling us to leave him alone so he could get Maki. Canney was saying, 'It's all right, Teddy—it's all right,' but we both knew damn well it wasn't all right. We finally got Greenie off. I just went as far as the boards, and Dan took him from there.

"When I started back, Maki was taking wild swipes with his stick to keep us away from him. I don't blame him for being scared. I guess he thought we really would kill him. We were all trying to get at him until the Blues pulled him off the ice. Later I was thrown out for heckling the referee. I told him he was calling a lousy game and should have stopped the fight. I guess I called him a few names, and he gave me a 10-minute misconduct. I didn't give a damn. All I could think of was that funny look in Greenie's eyes, and the funny way he was talking."

"After Maki knocked Green down, I thought the whole Bruins team would go nuts," said Howard Darwin, owner of Ottawa's junior hockey team, the 67s, who saw the game. "They poured off their bench heading for Maki, but somebody hustled him into one of the rooms. He got dressed and later I saw him watching the game in street clothes from upstairs."

I don't remember leaving the ice or how I got into one of the rooms beneath the arena stands. I have a vague recollection of sitting on a table trying to get my eyes to focus properly. There were a lot of people milling around, but few I recognized. One was Frosty Foristall, who seemed very agitated about something, and I think Eddie Johnston was in the room. I don't remember seeing Canney. Still dazed, my eyes watery, my speech almost unintelligible, I wondered what all the excitement was about, because in those few minutes I really didn't think I was badly hurt. I kept grabbing Foristall's jacket and mumbling at him, but I don't know what I said. When I heard somebody mention a stretcher and an ambulance, I tried to yell, but the words didn't come out right. My tongue seemed all twisted up. A couple of doctors were there, and one told me to lie down so he could put a stitch in my scalp. When I did, it suddenly felt very, very good. The doctor worked on me for only a few seconds. Then I heard Frosty (or maybe it was Canney) screaming, apparently in an argument with somebody. I didn't know. I didn't care, I just lay there, kind of comfortable, wishing everybody would go away and leave me alone.

I remember somebody grabbing me and taking off my skates, pads and shirt, but the rest of my equipment—pants, underclothing, shoulder pads, jockstrap—all stayed on. The next thing I knew I was being moved, and I guess people thought I was unconscious, but I wasn't. My left hand felt tingly, and I remember a lot of faces, none of which I recognized.

After they lifted me into an ambulance, my hand seemed worse. The tingly feeling changed to numbness. Frosty was with me, but I don't recall if we talked or anything except being wheeled along a corridor, with walls, ceiling and people speeding by because they were wheeling me so fast. I was taken into a brightly lit room and put on a table, where nurses and guys trying to take off the rest of my clothes all seemed jumbled together.

Now my head was beginning to hurt badly, and I was getting mad at everybody for trying to strip me without damaging any of my equipment. This was ridiculous, because we rip that stuff off all the time when we have to—what's the sense of trying to save a jock? I was trying to tell the nurse to cut everything off. My head was hurting and I wanted somebody to do something about it. The nurse didn't pay any attention, but kept trying to take that junk off as if it were a ballet skirt. Maybe she couldn't make out what I was saying. Or perhaps she didn't understand English, since this was a predominantly French hospital. Anyhow, somebody else came along and finally cut off the stuff and covered me up.

I must have pased out for a few minutes, because the next thing I remember was asking for the last rites of the church, and I remember the priest coming in. It was the first time I had ever asked for last rites, and I didn't know what to say and couldn't have made myself understood if I had known. He told me not to try to talk, and he touched my forehead and said something I couldn't understand. He asked me questions, but I don't remember what they were—or maybe he asked me before he told me not to talk. It's all mixed up in my mind, except I must have finally realized that I was badly hurt.

Off and on, I remember crying. It was almost a reflex. I cried when I couldn't feel anything in my left hand and when I couldn't control the left side of my face. I cried because my head hurt, and I cried because I didn't know if I was going to die when I wanted so badly to live, and I cried when I thought of my wife Pat and my kids and my parents and my brothers.

\*   \*   \*

"I was a little surprised when Mr. Green asked for the last rites," Fr. Jean-Paul Hupé, the hospital's head chaplain, said some time afterward. "Although I have given rites to people of all faiths, they are mostly Catholics. Mr. Green was entered as a Protestant, which I thought he was, until he told me he was a Catholic. Actually, he didn't get the last rites. That is what people used to call them, but now the last rites are given only after death. The sacrament we once called the last rites is really a prayer for the sick, and that is what I gave Mr. Green."

Dr. Michael Richard, a prominent young neurosurgeon, operated. He discovered a cut on the brain and several bone fragments that had been driven into it. It took him 2½ hours to clean things up. When I awoke I felt no particular pain, but my speech was garbled and there was considerable paralysis in my left arm. In the next few days my condition improved rapidly. The paralysis dwindled to the point where it was only noticeable in the left hand. I was able to sit up in bed and walk a little.

Despite my condition, we had a few laughs that first week in the hospital. There was a note from Larry Mann, a friend who is a television character actor in Los Angeles. It wasn't a letter, just a newspaper clipping headlined, GREEN HAS 2½-HOUR OPERATION, beneath which Mann had scribbled, "Dear Ted. Sorry to hear about your accident, but I know it can't be serious because I've known you long enough to realize that you haven't got a brain in your head." My wife didn't think it at all funny, although it tickled me.

Eddie Johnston phoned Pat daily to see how I was doing. When they finally let me talk to him, I got so emotional tears came to my eyes, and my speech, confused enough anyway, got worse. Eddie pulled me out of it very quickly by saying, "Hey, Dum-Dum, how do you expect me to understand you when you talk like that?" That may sound cruel, but, as Eddie says, maybe it's a way of softening the blow. Or of making an injured guy feel better. Or of keeping our sanity.

Then one night I woke up doing one hell of a dance in bed. My whole body was shaking and my head hurt something awful. What had happened was that I had hemorrhaged and gone into convulsions. There was pressure on the brain that had to be eased at once. As I went into the operating room my left side was completely paralyzed. Dr. Richard had to reopen the scalp and drain the blood off the brain. Where before he had felt I would be able to leave the hospital in a day or two, entirely free of paralysis, now he believed I would never be able to play hockey again.

My impressions of the days following the second operation are a mad jumble. I do remember my throat being very sore, being terribly sick to my stomach, my leg dragging when I walked—although I did not remember getting in and out of bed—and crying a good deal. And I remember thinking I was going to die. Or maybe hoping I would, because I thought I might be no more than a vegetable.

For a week or so, I am told, it was touch and go. There was danger of more bleeding. There was the possibility of still another operation—one the doctors did not want to perform unless it was necessary to save my life, because without it there would be less chance of permanent disability. And then suddenly I began to improve. Once I pulled out of the critical period, I improved pretty fast. Soon I was walking up and down the corridor. My foot dragged a little, but it was getting better all the time. My arm continued to feel like a dead weight, but I refused to believe it would not come back.

My physiotherapist, Mrs. Winifred Platt, was warm and understanding. She explained that you have many brain cells controlling the same part of the body, some of which are dormant and never used. When the active cells are destroyed, you have to develop these dormant cells. And unless they, too, are damaged, they can take over for the cells you have lost. "You must concentrate on putting those cells to use," she said.

So I lay in bed and concentrated on my shoulder. As the part affected last, it should be the first to come back. I had never before gone into such deep concentration, blocking everything else out of my mind. I lay there and thought *Brain to shoulder—brain to shoulder—brain to shoulder.* About six o'clock one morning, unable to sleep, I lost myself in concentration on the shoulder. I lifted my limp left arm with my good right hand and moved it straight up over my head. When I then tried to move the left arm, the strangest feeling came over me, and I thought *It's going to work!* And, sure enough, my whole arm, propelled by my shoulder, actually moved all by itself about three inches. At that I cried like a baby. I yelled for the nurse. That afternoon I showed Pat what I could do. "If I can do that," I told her, "I can do anything."

Next my fingers came back, and even my left thumb, which had been the worst before the hemorrhage. The first time I got a flicker of movement out of it Pat was in the room; the two of us jumped around like maniacs.

After that things went pretty well. I felt better all the time. The day before Pat and I went home to Winnipeg, Clarence

Campbell, president of the National Hockey League, came to Ottawa to conduct an investigation. I didn't know it at the time, but the Crown was already preparing a case against Maki and me, charging us both with assault with attempt to injure. I guess it was an unprecedented action, because the only cases involving professional hockey games had been civil actions between players and fans. This was the first time two players were accused in a criminal action arising from something in a game. I understood very few of the ramifications, and to this day I'm not sure exactly what they were or precisely why the authorities had singled out Maki and me for prosecution. Our hassle had been a typical hockey fight. The only thing that distinguished it from many others was I had been badly hurt.

Mr. Campbell's hearing was held in the offices of Edward S. Houston, an Ottawa lawyer the Bruins had engaged to represent me. Mr. Campbell had asked that all the principals be present. The first time I saw Maki after the fight was in Houston's office. I wasn't embarrassed, but I think he was, or maybe just sorry. He saw me paralyzed and bald-headed, with a big ugly scar, my left arm in a sling, my face over to one side, and my speech still garbled. We didn't talk much. Just shook hands and exchanged "Hi's" or something.

Eventually, in separate trials, Maki and I were each acquitted. Mr. Campbell suspended both of us without pay, myself for 13 games and Maki for 30 days. Mr. Campbell said he was satisfied on two points: first, that Maki had speared me, but also that "Maki's blow ricocheted off Green's stick before it hit Green on the head, causing his injury." While I remember nothing about being hit, everything I've been told points to the certainty that Maki hit me squarely.

I doubt I would have been as severely hurt if his stick had ricocheted off mine. Anyway, I could have done very nicely without that hearing. The next day Pat and I flew home.

*Green played out the 1970-71 season as a Bruin regular. But then, having pulled abdominal muscles in an early exhibition game, saw limited service the following year on the same Boston team.—ED.*

# NORMAN MAILER

# "*King of the Hill*"

IT IS THE GREAT WORD of the 20th Century. If there is a single word our century has added to the potentiality of language, it is ego. Everything we have done in this century, from monumental feats to nightmares of human destruction, has been a function of that extraordinary state of the psyche which gives us authority to declare we are sure of ourselves when we are not.

Muhammad Ali begins with the most unsettling ego of all. Having commanded the stage, he never pretends to step back and relinquish his place to other actors—like a six-foot parrot, he keeps screaming at you that he is the center of the stage. "Come here and get me, fool," he says. "You can't, 'cause you don't know who I am. You don't know *where* I am. I'm human intelligence and you don't even know if I'm good or evil." This has been his essential message to America all these years. It is intolerable to our American mentality that the figure who is probably most prominent to us after the President is simply not comprehensible, for he could be a demon or a saint. Or both! Richard Nixon, at least, appears comprehensible. We can hate him or we can vote for him, but at least we disagree with each other about him. What kills us about a.k.a. Cassius Clay is that the disagreement is inside us. He is *fascinating*—attraction and repulsion must be in the same package. So, he is obsessive. The more we don't want to think about him, the more we are obliged to. There is a reason for it. He is America's Greatest Ego. He is also, as I am going to try to show, the swiftest embodiment of human intelligence we have had yet, he is the very spirit of the 20th Century, he is the prince of mass man and the media. Now, perhaps temporarily, he is the fallen prince. But there still may be one holocaust of an urge to understand him, or try to, for obsession is a disease. Twenty little obsessions are 20 leeches on the mind, and one big obsession can become one big operation if we refuse to live with it. If Muhammad Ali defeats Frazier in the return bout, then he'll become the national obsession and we'll elect him President yet—you may indeed have to vote for any man who could defeat a fighter as great as Joe Frazier and still be Muhammad Ali. That's a combination!

Yes, ego—that officious and sometimes efficient exercise of ignorance-as-authority—must be the central phenomenon of the 20th Century, even if patriotic Americans like to pretend it does not exist in their heroes. Which, of course, is part of the holy American horseball. The most monstrous exhibition of ego by a brave man in many a year was Alan Shepard's three whacks at a golf ball while standing on the moon. There, in a space suit, hardly able to stand, he put a club head on an omnipurpose tool shaft, and, restricted to swinging with one arm, dibbled his golf ball on the second try. On the third it went maybe half a mile—a nonphenomenal distance in the low gravitational field of the lunar sphere.

"What's so unpleasant about that?" asked a pleasant young jet-setter.

Aquarius, of the old book, loftily replied, "Would you take a golf ball into St. Patrick's and see how far you can hit it?"

The kid nodded his head. "Now that you put it that way, I guess I wouldn't, but I was excited when it happened. I said to my wife, 'Honey, we're playing golf on the moon.'"

Well, to the average fight fan, Cassius Clay has been golf on the moon. Who can comprehend the immensity of ego involved? Every fighter is in a whirligig with his ego. The fight game, for example, is filled with legends of fighters who found a girl in an elevator purposefully stalled between floors for two minutes on the afternoon of a main-event fight. Later, after he blew the fight, his irate manager blew his ears. "Were you crazy?" the manager asked. "Why did you do it?"

"Because," said the fighter, "I get these terrible headaches every afternoon, and only a chick who knows how, can relieve them."

Ego is driving a point through to a conclusion you are obliged to reach without knowing too much about the ground you cross between. You suffer for a larger point. Every good prizefighter must have a large ego, then, because he is trying to demolish a man he doesn't know too much about, he is unfeeling—which is the ground floor of ego; and he is full of techniques—which are the wings of ego. What separates the noble ego of the prizefighters from the lesser ego of authors is that the fighter goes through experiences in the ring which are occasionally immense, incommunicable except to fighters who have been as good, or to women who have gone through every minute of an anguished-filled birth, experiences which are finally mysterious. Like men who climb mountains, it is an exercise of ego which becomes something like soul—just as technology may have begun to have transcended itself when we reached to the moon. So, two great fighters in a great fight travel down subterranean rivers of exhaustion and cross mountain peaks of agony, stare at the light of their own death in the eye of the man they are fighting, travel into the crossroads of the most excruciating choice of karma as they get up from the floor against all the appeal of the sweet swooning catacombs of oblivion—it is just that we do not see them this way, because they are not primarily men of words, and this is the century of words, numbers, and symbols. Enough.

We have come to the point. There are languages other than words, languages of symbol and languages of nature. There are languages of the body. And prizefighting is one of them. There is no attempting to comprehend a prizefighter unless we are willing to recognize that he speaks with a command of the body which is as detached, subtle and comprehensive in its intelligence as any exercise of mind by such social engineers as Herman Kahn or Henry Kissinger. Of course, a man like Herman Kahn is by report gifted with a bulk of three hundred pounds. He does not move around with a light foot. So many a good average prizefighter, just a little punchy, does not speak with any particular éclat. That doesn't mean he is incapable of expressing himself with wit, style, and an esthetic flair for surprise when he boxes with his body, any more than Kahn's obesity would keep us from recognizing that his mind can work with strength. Boxing is a dialogue between bodies. Ignorant men, usually black, and usually next to illiterate, address one another in a set of *con-*

*versational* exchanges which go deep into the heart of each other's matter. It is just that they converse with their physiques. But unless you believe that you cannot receive a mortal wound from an incisive remark, you may be forced to accept the novel idea that men doing friendly boxing have a conversation on which they can often thrive. William Buckley and I in a discussion in a living room for an evening will score points on one another, but enjoy it. On television, where the stakes may be more, we may still both enjoy it. But put us in a debating hall with an argument to go on without cease for 24 hours, every encouragement present to humiliate each other, and months of preparation for such a debate, hooplas and howlers of publicity, our tongues stuck out at one another on TV, and repercussions in Vietnam depending on which one of us should win, then add the fatigue of harsh lights, and a moderator who keeps interrupting us, and we are at the beginning of a conversation in which at least one of us will be hurt, and maybe both. Even hurt seriously. The example is picayune, however, in relation to the demands of a 15-round fight—perhaps we should have to debate nonstop for weeks under those conditions before one of us was carried away comatose. Now the example becomes clearer: Boxing is a rapid debate between two sets of intelligence. It takes place rapidly because it is conducted with the body rather than the mind. If this seems extreme, let us look for a connection. Picasso could never do arithmetic when he was young because the number seven looked to him like a nose upside down. So to learn arithmetic would slow him up. He was a future painter—his intelligence resided somewhere in the coordination of the body and the mind. He was not going to cut off his body from his mind by learning numbers.

But most of us do. We have minds which work fairly well and bodies which sometimes don't. But if we are white and want to be comfortable we put our emphasis on learning to talk with the mind. Ghetto cultures, black, Puerto Rican and Chicano cultures having less expectation of comfort tend to stick with the wit their bodies provide. They speak to each other with their bodies, they signal with their clothes. They talk with many a silent telepathic intelligence. And doubtless feel the frustration of being unable to express the subtleties of their states in words, just as the average middle-class white will feel unable to carry out his dreams of glory by the uses of his body. If black people are also beginning to speak our mixture of formal English and jargon-polluted American with real force, so white corporate America is getting more sexual and more athletic. Yet to begin to talk about Ali and Frazier, their psyches, their styles, their honor, their character, their greatness and their flaws, we have to recognize that there is no way to comprehend them as men like ourselves— we can only guess at their insides by a real jump of our imagination into the science Ali invented—he was the first psychologist of the body.

Okay. There are fighters who are men's men. Rocky Marciano was one of them. Oscar Bonavena and Jerry Quarry and George Chuvalo and Gene Fullmer and Carmen Basilio, to name a few, have faces which would give a Marine sergeant pause in a bar fight. They look like they could take you out with the knob of bone they have left for a nose. They are all, incidentally, white fighters. They have a code—it is to fight until they are licked, and if they have to take a punch for every punch they give, well, they figure they can win.

Their ego and their body intelligence are both connected to the same source of juice—it is male pride. They are substances close to rock. They work on clumsy skills to hone them finer, knowing if they can obtain parity, blow for blow with any opponent, they will win. They have more guts. Up to a far-gone point, pain is their pleasure, for their character in combat is their strength to trade pain for pain, loss of faculty for loss of faculty.

One can cite black fighters like them. Henry Hank and Reuben Carter, Emile Griffith and Benny Paret. Joe Frazier would be the best of them. But black fighters tend to be complex. They have veins of unsuspected strength and streaks when they feel as spooked as wild horses. Any fight promoter in the world knew he had a good fight if Fullmer went against Basilio, it was a proposition as certain as the wages for the week. But black fighters were artists, they were relatively moody, they were full of the surprises of Patterson or Liston, the virtuosities of Archie Moore and Sugar Ray, the speed, savagery, and curious lack of substance in Jimmy Ellis, the vertiginous neuroses of giants like Buster Mathis. Even Joe Louis, recognized by a majority in the years of his own championship as the greatest heavyweight of all time, was surprisingly inconsistent with minor fighters like Buddy Baer. Part of the unpredictability of their performances was due to the fact that all but Moore and Robinson were heavyweights. Indeed, white champions in the top division were equally out of form from fight to fight. It can, in fact, be said that heavyweights are always the most lunatic of prizefighters. The closer a heavyweight comes to the championship, the more natural it is for him to be a little bit insane, secretly insane, for the heavyweight champion of the world is either the toughest man in the world or he is not, but there is a real possibility he is. It is like being the big toe of God. You have nothing to measure yourself by. Lightweights, welterweights, middleweights can all be exceptionally good, fantastically talented—they are still very much in their place. The best lightweight in the world knows that an unranked middleweight can defeat him on most nights, and the best middleweight in the world will kill him every night. He knows that the biggest strongman in a tough bar could handle him by sitting on him, since the power to punch seems to increase quickly with weight. A fighter who weighs two-forty will punch more than twice as hard as a fighter who weighs one-twenty. The figures have no real basis, of course, they are only there to indicate the law of the ring: a good big man beats a good little man. So the notion of prizefighters as hard-working craftsmen is most likely to be true in the light and middle divisions. Since they are fighters who know their limitations, they are likely to strive for excellence in their category. The better they get, the closer they have come to sanity, at least if we are ready to assume that the average fighter is a buried artist, which is to say a *body* artist with an extreme amount of violence in him. Obviously the better and more successful they get, the more they have been able to transmute violence into craft, discipline, even body art. That is human alchemy. We respect them and they deserve to be respected.

But the heavyweights never have such simple sanity. If they become champions they begin to have inner lives like Hemingway or Dostoyevsky, Tolstoy or Faulkner, Joyce or Melville or Conrad or Lawrence or Proust. Hemingway is the example above all. Because he wished to be the greatest writer in history of literature and still be a hero with all the body arts age would yet grant him, he was alone and he knew it. So are heavyweight champions alone. Dempsey was alone and Tunney could never explain himself and Sharkey could never believe himself nor Schmeling nor Braddock, and Carnera was sad and Baer an indecipherable clown; great heavyweights like Louis had the loneliness of the ages in their silence, and men like Marciano were mystified by a power which seemed to have been granted them. With the advent, however, of the great modern black heavyweights, Patterson, Liston, then Clay and Frazier, perhaps the loneliness gave way to what it had been protecting itself against—a surrealistic situation unstable beyond belief. Being a black heavyweight champion in the second half of the 20th Century (with black revolutions opening all over the world) was now not unlike being Jack Johnson, Malcolm X and Frank Costello all in one. Going down the aisle and into the ring in Chicago was conceivably more frightening for Sonny Liston than facing Patterson that night—he was raw as uncoated wire with his sense of retribution awaiting him for years of prison pleasures and underworld jobs. Pools of paranoia must have reached him like different washes of color from different sides of the area. He was a man who had barely learned to read and write—he had none of the impacted and mediocre misinformation of all the world of daily dull reading to clot the antenna of his senses—so he was keen to every hatred against him. He knew killers were waiting in that mob, they always were, he had been on speaking terms with just such subjects himself—now he dared to be king—any assassin could strike for his revenge upon acts Liston had long forgot; no wonder Liston was in fear going into the ring, and happier once within it.

And Patterson was exhausted before the fight began. Lonely

as a monk for years, his daily gym work the stuff of his meditation, he was the first of the black fighters to be considered,
then used, as a political force. He was one of the liberal elite,
an Eleanor Roosevelt darling, he was political mileage for the
NAACP. Violent, conceivably to the point of murder if he
had not been a fighter, he was a gentleman in public, more,
he was a man of the nicest, quietest, most private good manners. But monastic by inclination. Now, all but uneducated,
he was appealed to by political blacks to win the Liston fight
for the image of the Negro. Responsibility sat upon him like
a comic cutback in a silent film where we return now and
again to one poor man who has been left to hold a beam
across his shoulders. There he stands, hardly able to move. At
the end of the film he collapses. That was the weight put on
Patterson. The responsibility to beat Liston was too great to
bear. Patterson, a fighter of incorruptible honesty, was
knocked out by punches hardly anybody saw. He fell in open
air as if seized by a stroke. The age of surrealistic battles had
begun. In the second fight with Liston, Patterson, obviously
more afraid of a repetition of the first nightmare than anything else, simply charged his opponent with his hands low
and was knocked down three times and out in the first round.
The age of body psychology had begun and Clay was there
to conceive it.

A kid as wild and dapper and jaybird as the president of
a down-home college fraternity, bow-tie, brown-and-white
shoes, sweet, happy-go-lucky, *raucous,* he descended on Vegas
for the second Patterson-Liston fight. He was like a beautiful
boy surrounded by doting aunts. The classiest-looking middle-aged Negro ladies were always flanking him in Vegas as
if to set up a female field of repulsion against any evil black

magnetic forces in the offing. And from the sanctuary of his ability to move around crap tables like a kitten on the frisk, he taunted black majestic king-size Liston before the fight and after the fight. "You're so ugly," he would jeer, crap table safely between them, "that I don't know how you can get any uglier."

"Why don't you sit on my knee and I'll feed you your orange juice," Liston would rumble back.

"Don't insult me, or you'll be sorry. 'Cause you're just an ugly slow bear."

They would pretend to rush at one another. Smaller men would hold them back without effort. They were building the gate for the next fight. And Liston was secretly fond of Clay. He would chuckle when he talked about him. It was years since Liston had failed to knock out his opponent in the first round. His charisma was majestic with menace. One held one's breath when near him. He looked forward with obvious amusement to the happy seconds when he would take Clay apart and see the expression on that silly face. In Miami he trained for a three-round fight. In the famous fifth round when Clay came out with caustic in his eyes and could not see, he waved his gloves at Liston, a look of abject horror on his face, as if to say, "Your younger brother is now an old blind beggar. Do not strike him." And did it with a peculiar authority. For Clay looked like a ghost with his eyes closed, tears streaming, his extended gloves waving in front of him like a widow's entreaties. Liston drew back in doubt, in bewilderment, conceivably in concern for his new great reputation as an ex-bully; yes, Liston reacted like a gentleman, and Clay was home free. His eyes watered out the caustic, his sight came back. He cut Liston up in the sixth. He left him beaten and exhausted. Liston did not stand up for the bell to the seventh. Maybe Clay had even defeated him earlier that day at the weigh-in when he had harangued and screamed and shouted and whistled and stuck his tongue out at Liston. The Champ had been bewildered. No one had been able ever to stare him in the eyes these last four years. Now a boy was screaming at him, a boy reported to belong to Black Muslims, no, stronger than that, a boy favored by Malcolm X who was braver by reputation than the brave, for he could stop a bullet any day. Liston, afraid only, as he put it, of crazy men, was afraid of the Muslims for he could not contend with their allegiance to one another in prison, their puritanism, their discipline, their martial ranks. The combination was too complex, too unfamiliar. Now, their boy, in a pain of terror or in a mania of courage, was screaming at him at the weigh-in. Liston sat down and shook his head, and looked at the Press, now become his friend, and wound his fingers in circles around his ear, as if saying, Whitey to Whitey, "That black boy is nuts." So Clay made Liston Tom it, and when Liston missed the first jab he threw in the fight by a foot and a half, one knew the night would not be ordinary in the offing.

For their return bout in Boston, Liston trained as he had never before. Clay got a hernia. Liston trained again. Hard training as a fighter grows older seems to speak of the dull deaths of the brightest cells in all the favorite organs; old fighters react to training like beautiful women to washing floors. But Liston did it twice, once for Clay's hernia, and again for their actual fight in Maine, and the second time he trained, he aged as a fighter, for he had a sparring partner, Amos Lincoln, who was one of the better heavyweights in the country. They had wars with one another every afternoon

in the gym. By the day before the fight, Liston was as relaxed
and sleepy and dopey as a man in a steambath. He had fought
his heart out in training, had done it under constant pressure
from Clay who kept telling the world that Liston was old
and slow and could not possibly win. And their fight created
a scandal, for Liston ran into a short punch in the first round
and was counted out, unable to hear the count. The referee
and timekeeper missed signals with one another while Clay
stood over fallen Liston screaming, "Get up and fight!" It
was no night for the fight game, and a tragedy for Clay since
he had trained for a long and arduous fight. He had developed his technique for a major encounter with Liston and
was left with a horde of unanswered questions including the
one he could never admit—which was whether there had
been the magic of a real knockout in his punch or if Liston
had made—for what variety of reasons!—a conscious decision
to stay on the floor. It did him no good.

He had taken all the lessons of his curious life and the
outrageously deep comprehension he had of the motivations
of his own people—indeed, one could even approach the beginnings of a Psychology of the Blacks by studying his en-
counters with fighters who were black—and had elaborated
that into a technique for boxing which was almost without
compare. A most cultivated technique. For he was no child of
the slums. His mother was a gracious pale-skinned lady, his
father a bitter wit pride-oriented on the family name of Clay
—they were descendants of Henry Clay, the orator, on the
white side of the family, nothing less, and Cassius began boxing at 12 in a police gym, and from the beginning was a phenomenon of style and the absence of pain, for he knew how

to use his physical endowment. Tall, relatively light, with an exceptionally long reach even for his size, he developed defensive skills which made the best use of his body. Working apparently on the premise that there was something obscene about being hit, he boxed with his head back and drew it further back when attacked, like a kid who is shy of punches in a street fight, but because he had a waist which was more supple than the average fighter's neck, he was able to box with his arms low, surveying the fighter in front of him, avoiding punches by the speed of his feet, the reflexes of his waist, the long spoiling deployment of his arms which were always tipping other fighters off-balance. Added to this was his psychological comprehension of the vanity and confusion of other fighters. A man in the ring is a performer as well as a gladiator. Elaborating his technique from the age of 12, Clay knew how to work on the vanity of other performers, knew how to make them feel ridiculous and so force them into crucial mistakes, knew how to set such a tone from the first round—later he was to know how to begin it a year before he would even meet the man. Clay knew that a fighter who had been put in psychological knots before he got near the ring had already lost half, three quarters, no, all of the fight could be lost before the first punch. That was the psychology of the body.

Now, add his curious ability as a puncher. He knew that the heaviest punches, systematically delivered, meant little. There are club fighters who look like armadillos and alligators—you can bounce punches off them forever and they never go down. You can break them down only if they are in a profound state of confusion, and the bombardment of another fighter's fists is never their confusion but their expectation. So Clay punched with a greater variety of mixed intensities than anyone around, he played with punches, was tender with them, laid them on as delicately as you put a postage stamp on an envelope, then cracked them in like a riding crop across your face, stuck a cruel jab like a baseball bat held head on into your mouth, next waltzed you in a clinch with a tender arm around your neck, winged away out of reach on flying legs, dub a hook with the full swing of a baseball hat hard into your ribs, hard pokes of a jab into the face, a mocking soft flurry of pillows and gloves, a mean forearm cutting you off from coming up on him, a cruel wrestling of your neck in a clinch, then elusive again, gloves snake-licking your face like a whip. By the time Clay had defeated Liston once and was training for the second fight, by the time Clay, now champion and renamed Muhammed Ali, and bigger, grown up quickly and not so mysteriously (after the potent ego-soups and marrows of his trip through Muslim Africa) into a Black Prince, Potentate of his people, new Poombah of Polemic, yes, by this time, Clay—we will find it more natural to call him Ali from here on out (for the Prince will behave much like a young god)—yes, Muhammad Ali, Heavyweight Champion of the World, having come back with an amazing commitment to be leader of his people, proceeded to go into training for the second Liston fight with a commitment and then a genius of comprehension for the true intricacies of the Science of Sock. He alternated the best of sparring partners and the most ordinary, worked rounds of dazzling speed with Jimmy Ellis—later, of course, to be champion himself before Frazier knocked him out—rounds which displayed the high esthetic of boxing at its best, then lay against the ropes with other sparring partners, hands at his

sides as if it were the 11th or 13th round of an excruciating
and exhausting fight with Liston where Ali was now so tired
he could not hold his hands up, could just manage to take
punches to the stomach, rolling with them, smothering them
with his stomach, absorbing them with backward moves, sliding along the ropes, steering his sparring partner with passive
but off-setting moves of his limp arms. For a minute, for two
minutes, the sparring partner—Shotgun Sheldon was his
name—would bomb away on Ali's stomach much as if Liston
were tearing him apart in later rounds, and Ali weaving
languidly, sliding his neck for the occasional overhead punch
to his face, bouncing from the rope into the punches, bouncing back away from punches, as if his torso had become one
huge boxing glove to absorb punishment, had penetrated
through into some further conception of pain, as if pain were
not pain if you accepted it with a relaxed heart, yes, Ali let
himself be bombarded on the ropes by the powerful bull-like
swings of Shotgun Sheldon, the expression on his face as remote, and as searching for the last routes into the nerves of
each punch going in as a man hanging on a subway strap will
search into the meaning of the market quotations he has just
read on the activities of a curious stock. So Ali relaxed on
the ropes and took punches to the belly with a faint disdain,
as if, curious punches, they did not go deep enough and after
a minute of this, or two minutes, having offered his body like
the hide of a drum for a mad drummer's solo, he would snap
out of his communion with himself and flash a tattoo of light
and slashing punches, mocking as the lights on water, he
would dazzle his sparring partner, who, arm-weary and
punched out, would look at him with eyes of love, complete
was his admiration. And if people were ever going to cry

watching a boxer in training, those were the moments, for Ali had the far-off concentration and disdain of an artist who simply cannot find anyone near enough or good enough to keep him and his art engaged, and all the while was perfecting the essence of his art which was to make the other fighter fall secretly, helpless, in love with him. Bundini, a special trainer, an alter ego with the same harsh, demoniac, witty, nonstop powers of oration as Ali himself—he even looked a little like Ali—used to weep openly as he watched the workouts.

Training session over, Ali would lecture the Press, instruct them—looking beyond his Liston defense to what he would do to Patterson, mocking Patterson, calling him a rabbit, a white man's rabbit, knowing he was putting a new beam on Patterson's shoulders, an outrageously helpless and heavy beam of rage, fear, hopeless anger and secret black admiration for the all-out force of Ali's effrontery. And in the next instant Ali would be charming as a movie star on the make speaking tenderly to a child. If he was Narcissus, so he was as well the play of mood in the water which served as mirror to Narcissus. It was as if he knew he had disposed of Patterson already, that the precise attack of calling him a rabbit would work on the weakest link—wherever it was—in Patterson's tense and tortured psyche and Patterson would crack, as indeed, unendurably for himself, he did, when their fight took place. Patterson's back gave way in the early rounds, and he fought twisted and in pain, half crippled like a man with a sacroiliac, for 11 brave and most miserable rounds before the referee would call it and Ali, breaking up with his first wife then, was unpleasant in the ring that night, his face ugly and contemptuous, himself well on the way to becoming Amer-

ica's most unpopular major American. That, too, was part of
the art—to get a public to the point of hating him so much
the burden on the other fighter approached the metaphysical
—which is where Ali wanted it. White fighters with faces like
rock embedded in cement would trade punch for punch, Ali
liked to get the boxing where it belonged—he would trade
metaphysic for metaphysic with anyone.

So he went on winning his fights and growing forever more
unpopular. How he inflamed the temper of boxing's white
establishment, for they were for most part a gaggle of avuncu-
lar drunks and hard-bitten hacks who were ready to fight
over every slime-slicked penny, and squared a few of their
slippery crimes by getting fighters to show up semblance-of-
sober at any available parish men's rally and charity church
breakfast—"Everything I am I owe to boxing," the fighter
would mumble through his dentures while elements of gin,
garlic, and goddess-of-a-girlie from the night before came off
in the bright morning fumes.

Ali had them psyched. He cut through moribund corus-
cated dirty business corridors, cut through cigar smoke and
bushwah, hypocrisy and well-aimed kicks to the back of the
neck, cut through crooked politicians and patriotic pus, cut
like a laser, point of the point, light and impersonal, cut to
the heart of the rottenest meat in boxing, and boxing was
always the buried South Vietnam of America, buried for 50
years in our hide before we went there, yes, Ali cut through
the flag-dragooned salutes of drunken dawns and said, "I got
no fight with those Vietcongs," and they cut him down,
thrust him into the three and a half years of his martyrdom.
Where he grew. Grew to have a little fat around his middle
and a little of the complacent muscle of the clam to his world-

ego. And grew sharper in the mind as well, and deepened and broadened physically. Looked no longer like a boy, but a sullen man, almost heavy, with the beginnings of a huge expanse across his shoulders. And developed the patience to survive, the wisdom to contemplate future nights in jail, grew to cultivate the suspension of belief and the avoidance of disbelief—what a rack for a young man! As the years of hope for reinstatement, or avoidance of prison, came up and waned in him, Ali walked the tightrope between bitterness and apathy, and had enough left to beat Quarry and beat Bonavena, beat Quarry in the flurry of a missed hundred punches, ho! how his timing was off! beat him with a calculated whip, snake-lick whip, to the corrugated sponge of dead flesh over Quarry's Irish eyes—they stopped it after the third on cuts—then knocked out Bonavena, the indestructible, never stopped before, by working the art of crazy mixing in the punches he threw at the rugged—some of the punches Ali threw that night would not have hurt a little boy—the punch he let go in the 15th came in like a wrecking ball from outer space. Bonavena went sprawling across the ring. He was a house coming down.

Yet it may have been the blow which would defeat him later. For Ali had been tired with Bonavena, lackluster, winded, sluggish, far ahead on points but in need of the most serious work if he were to beat Frazier. The punch in the last round was obliged, therefore, to inflame his belief that the forces of magic were his, there to be called upon when most in need, that the silent leagues of black support for his cause—since their cause was as his own—were like some cloak of midnight velvet, there to protect him by black blood, by

black sense of tragedy, by the black consciousness that the
guilt of the world had become the hinge of a door that they
would open. So they would open the way to Frazier's chin,
the blacks would open the aisle for his trip to the gods.

Therefore he did not train for Frazier as perhaps he had to.
He worked, he ran three miles a day when he could have run
five, he boxed some days and let a day and perhaps another
day go, he was relaxed, he was confident, he basked in the
undemanding winter sun of Miami, and skipped his rope in
a gym crowded with fighters, stuffed now with working fighters looking to be seen, Ali comfortable and relaxed like the
greatest of movie stars, he played a young fighter working
out in a corner on the heavy bag—for of course every eye was
on him—and afterward doing sit-ups in the back room and
having his stomach rubbed with liniment, he would talk to
reporters. He was filled with confidence there was no black
fighter he did not comprehend to the root of the valve in the
hard-pumping heart, and yes, Frazier, he assured everybody,
would be easier than they realized. Like a little boy who had
grown up to take on a mountain of responsibility he spoke
in the deep relaxation of the wise, and teased two of the reporters who were present and fat. "You want to drink a lot
of water," he said, "good cold water instead of all that liquor
rot-your-gut," and gave the smile of a man who had been
able to intoxicate himself on water (although he was, by re-
pute, a fiend for soft sweet drinks), "and fruit and good clean
vegetables you want to eat and chicken and steak. You lose
weight then," he advised out of kind secret smiling thoughts,
and went on to talk of the impact of the fight upon the world.
"Yes," he said, "you just think of a stadium with a million
people, 10 million people, you could get them all in to watch

they would all pay to see it live, but then you think of the hundreds of millions and the billions who are going to see this fight, and if you could sit them all down in one place, and fly a jet plane over them, why that plane would have to fly for an hour before it would reach the end of all the people who will see this fight. It's the greatest event in the history of the world, and you take a man like Frazier, a good fighter, but a simple hard-working fellow, he's not built for this kind of pressure, the eyes," Ali said softly, "of that many people upon him. There's an experience to pressure which I have had, fighting a man like Liston in Miami the first time, which he has not. He will cave in under the pressure. No, I do not see any way a man like Frazier can whup me, he can't reach me, my arms are too long, and if he does get in and knock me down I'll never make the mistake of Quarry and Foster or Ellis of rushing back at him, I'll stay away until my head clears, then I begin to pop him again, pop! pop!" a few jabs, "no there is no way this man can beat me, this fight will be easier than you think."

There was one way in which boxing was still like a street fight and that was in the need to be confident you would win. A man walking out of a bar to fight with another man is seeking to compose his head into the confidence that he will certainly triumph—it is the most mysterious faculty of the ego. For that confidence is a sedative against the pain of punches and yet is the sanction to punch your own best. The logic of the spirit would suggest that you win only if you deserve to win: the logic of the ego lays down the axiom that if you don't think you will win, you don't deserve to. And, in fact, usually don't; it is as if not believing you will win opens you

to the guilt that perhaps you have not the right, you are too
guilty.

So training camps are small factories for the production of
one rare psychological item—an ego able to bear huge pain
and administer drastic punishment. The flow of Ali's ego
poured over the rock of every distraction, it was an ego like
the flow of a river of constant energy fed by a hundred tribu-
taries of black love and the love of the white left. The con-
struction of the ego of Joe Frazier was of another variety.
His manager, Yancey "Yank" Durham, a canny foxy light-
skinned Negro with a dignified mien, a gray head of hair,
gray mustache and a small but conservative worthy's paunch,
plus the quick-witted look of eyes which could spot from a
half-mile away any man coming toward him with a criminal
thought, was indeed the face of a consummate jeweler who
had worked for years upon a diamond in the rough until he
was now and at last a diamond, hard as the transmutation of
black carbon from the black earth into the brilliant sky-blue
shadow of the rarest shining rock. What a fighter was Frazier,
what a diamond of an ego had he, and what a manager was
Durham. Let us look.

Sooner or later, fight metaphors, like fight managers, go
sentimental. They go military. But there is no choice here.
Frazier was the human equivalent of a war machine. He had
tremendous firepower. He had a great left hook, a left hook
frightening even to watch when it missed, for it seemed to
whistle; he had a powerful right. He could knock a man out
with either hand—not all fighters can, not even very good
fighters. Usually, however, he clubbed opponents to death,
took a punch, gave a punch, took three punches, gave two,

took a punch, gave a punch, high speed all the way, always working, pushing his body and arms, short for a heavyweight, up through the middle, bombing through on force, reminiscent of Jimmy Brown knocking down tacklers, Frazier kept on coming, hard and fast, a hang-in, hang-on, go-and-get-him, got-him, got-him, slip and punch, take a punch, wing a punch, whap a punch, never was Frazier happier than with his heart up on the line against some other man's heart, let the bullets fly—his heart was there to stand up at the last. Sooner or later, the others almost all fell down. Undefeated like Ali, winner of 23 out of 26 fights by knockout, he was a human force, certainly the greatest heavyweight force to come along since Rocky Marciano. (If those two men had ever met, it would have been like two Mack trucks hitting each other head-on, then backing up to hit each other again—they would have kept it up until the wheels were off the axles and the engines off the chassis.) But this would be a different kind of fight. Ali would run, Ali would keep hitting Frazier with long jabs, quick hooks and rights while backing up, backing up, staying out of reach unless Frazier could take the punishment and get in. That was where the military problem began. For getting in against the punishment he would take was a question of morale, and there was a unique situation in this fight—Frazier had become the white man's fighter, Mr. Charley was rooting for Frazier, and that meant blacks were boycotting him in their heart. That could be poison to Frazier's morale, for he was twice as black as Clay and half as handsome, he had the rugged decent life-worked face of a man who had labored in the pits all his life, he looked like the deserving modest son of one of those Negro cleaning women of a bygone age who worked from 6 in the morning to midnight every day, raised a family, endured and occasionally elicited the exasperated admiration of white ladies who would kindly remark, "That woman deserves something better in her life." Frazier had the mien of the son, one of many, of such a woman, and he was the hardest-working fighter in training many a man had ever seen, he was conceivably the hardest-working man alive in the world, and as he went through his regimen, first boxing four rounds with a sparring partner, Kenny Norton, a talented heavyweight from the coast with an almost unbeaten record, then working on the heavy bag, then the light bag, then skipping rope, 10 to 12 rounds of sparring and exercise on a light day, Frazier went on with the doggedness, the concentration, and the pumped-up fury of a man who has had so little in his life that he can endure torments to get everything, he pushed the total of his energy and force into an absolute abstract exercise of will so it did not matter if he fought a sparring partner or the heavy bag, he lunged at each equally as if the exhaustions of his own heart and the clangor of his lungs were his only enemies, and the head of a fighter or the leather of the bag as it rolled against his own head was nothing but some abstract thunk of material, not a thing, not a man, but thunk! thunk! something of an obstacle, thunk! thunk! thunk! to beat into thunk! oblivion. And his breath came in rips and sobs as he smashed into the bag as if it were real, just that heavy big torso-sized bag ranging from its chain but he attacked it as if it were a bear, as if it were a great fighter and they were in the mortal embrace of a killing set of exchanges of punches in the middle of the eighth round, and rounds of exercise later, skipping rope to an inhumanly fast beat for this late round in the training day, sweat pouring like jets of blood from an artery, he kept swinging his rope, muttering, "Two-million-dollars-and-change,   two-million-dollars-and-change," railroad train chugging into the terminals of exhaustion. And it was obvious that Durham, jeweler to his diamond, was working to make the fight as abstract as he could for Frazier, to keep Clay out of it—for they would not call him Ali in their camp—yes, Frazier was fortifying his ego by depersonalizing his opponent, Clay was, thunk! the heavy bag, thunk! and thunk!—Frazier was looking to get no messages from that cavern of velvet when black people sent their good wishes to Ali at midnight, no, Frazier would insulate himself with prodigies of work, hardest-working man in the hell-hole of the world, and on and on he drove himself into the depressions each day of killing daily exhaustion.

That was one half of the strategy to isolate Frazier from Ali, hard work and thinking of thunking on inanimate Clay; the other half was up to Durham who was running front relations with the blacks of North Philly who wandered into the gym, paid their dollar, and were ready to heckle on Frazier. In the four rounds he boxed with Norton, Frazier did not look too good for a while. It was 10 days before the fight and he was in a bad mood when he came in, for the word was through the gym that they had discovered one of his favorite sparring partners, just fired that morning, was a Black Muslim and had been calling Ali every night with reports, that was the rumor, and Frazier, sullen and cold at the start, was bopped and tapped, then walloped by Norton moving fast with the big training gloves in imitation of Ali, and Frazier looked very easy to hit until the middle of the third round when Norton, proud of his something like 20 wins and one loss, beginning to get some ideas himself about how to fight champions, came driving in to mix it with Frazier, have it out man to man and caught a right which dropped him, left him looking limp with that half-silly smile sparring partners get when they have been hit too hard to justify any experience or any money they are going to take away. Up till then the crowd had been with Norton. There at one end of the Cloverlay gym, a street-level store-front room which could have been used originally by an automobile dealer, there on that empty, immaculate Lysol-soaked floor, designed when Frazier was there for only Frazier and his partners to train (as opposed to Miami where Ali would rub elbows with the people) here the people were at one end, the end off the street, and they jeered whenever Norton hit Frazier, they laughed when Norton made him look silly, they called out, "Drop the mother," until Durham held up a gentlemanly but admonishing finger in request for silence. Afterward, however, training completed, Durham approached them to answer questions, rolled with their sallies, jived the people back, subtly enlisted their sympathy for Frazier by saying, "When I fight Clay, I'm going to get him somewhere in the middle rounds," until the blacks quipping back said angrily, "You ain't fighting him, Frazier is."

"Why you call him Clay?" another asked. "He Ali."

"His name is Cassius Clay to me," said Durham.

"What you say against his religion?"

"I don't say nothing about his religion and he doesn't say anything about mine. I'm a Baptist."

"You going to make money on this?"

"Of course," said Durham, "I got to make money. You don't think I work up this sweat for nothing."

They loved him. He was happy with them. A short fat man in a purple suit wearing his revival of the wide-brim bebop hat said to Durham, "Why don't you get Norton to manage? He was beating up on *your* fighter," and the fat man cackled for he had scored and could elaborate the tale for his ladies later how he had put down Yank who was working the daily rite on the edge of the black street for his fighter, while upstairs, dressed, and sucking an orange, sweat still pouring, gloom of excessive fatigue upon him, Frazier was sitting through his two-hundredth or two-thousandth interview for this fight, reluctant indeed to give it at all. "Some get it, some don't," he had said for refusal, but relented when a white friend who had done roadwork with him interceded, so he sat there now against a leather sofa, dark blue suit, dark T-shirt, mopping his brow with a pink-red towel, and spoke dispiritedly of being ready too early for the fight. He was waking up an hour too early for roadwork each morning now. "I'd go back to sleep but it doesn't feel good when I do run."

"I guess the air is better that hour of the morning."

He nodded sadly. "There's a limit to how good the air in Philly can get."

"Where'd you begin to sing?" was a question asked.

"I sang in church first," he replied, but it was not the day to talk about singing. The loneliness of hitting the bag still seemed upon him as if in his exhaustion now, and in the thoughts of that small insomnia which woke him an hour too early every day was something of the loneliness of all blacks who work very hard and are isolated from fun and must wonder in the just-awakened night how large and pervasive was the curse of a people. "The countdown's begun," said Frazier, "I get impatient about now."

For the fight, Ali was wearing red velvet trunks, Frazier had green. Before they began, even before they were called together by the referee for instructions, Ali went dancing around the ring and glided past Frazier with a sweet little-boy smile, as if to say, "You're my new playmate. We're going to have fun." Ali was laughing. Frazier was having nothing of this and turned his neck to embargo him away. Ali, having alerted the crowd by this big first move, came prancing in again. When Frazier looked ready to block him, Ali went around, evading a contact, gave another sweet smile, shook his head at the lack of high spirit. "Poor Frazier," he seemed to say.

At the weigh-in early that afternoon Ali looked physically resplendent; the night before in Harlem, crowds had cheered him; he was coming to claim his victory on the confluence of two mighty tides—he was the mightiest victim of injustice in America and he was also—the 20th Century was nothing if not a tangle of opposition—he was also the mightiest narcissist in the land. Every beard, dropout, homosexual, junkie, freak, swinger, and plain simple individualist adored him. Every pedantic liberal soul who had once loved Patterson now paid homage to Ali. The mightiest of the black psyches and the most filigreed of the white psyches were ready to roar him home, as well as every family-loving hard-working square American who genuinely hated the war in Vietnam. What a tangle of ribbons he carried on his lance, enough cross purposes to be the knight-resplendent of television, the fell hero of the medium, and he had a look of unique happiness

on television when presenting his program for the course of
the fight, and his inevitable victory. He would be as content
then as an infant splashing the waters of the bathinette. If
he was at once a saint and a monster to any mind which
looked for category, any mind unwilling to encounter the
thoroughly dread-filled fact that the 20th Century breed of
man now in birth might be no longer half good and half
evil—generous and greedy by turns—but a mutation with
Cassius Muhammad for the first son—then that mind was not
ready to think about 20th Century Man. (And indeed Muhammad Ali had twin poodles he called Angel and Demon.)
So now the ambiguity of his presence filled the Garden before
the fight was fairly begun, it was as if he had announced to
that plural billion-footed crowd assembled under the shadow
of the jet which would fly over them that the first enigma of
the fight would be the way he would win it, that he would
initiate his triumph by getting the crowd to laugh at Frazier,
yes, first premise tonight was that the poor black man in
Frazier's soul would go berserk if made a figure of roll-off-
your-seat amusement.

The referee gave his instructions. The bell rang. The first
15 seconds of a fight can be the fight. It is equivalent to the
first kiss in a love affair. The fighters each missed the other.
Ali blocked Frazier's first punches easily, but Ali then missed
Frazier's head. That head was bobbing as fast as a third fist.
Frazier would come rushing in, head moving like a fist, fists
bobbing too, his head working above and below his forearm,
he was trying to get through Ali's jab, get through fast and
sear Ali early with the terror of a long fight and punches
harder than he had ever taken to the stomach, and Ali in
turn, backing up, and throwing fast punches, aimed just a

trifle, and was therefore a trifle too slow, but it was obvious Ali was trying to shiver Fraizer's synapses from the start, set waves of depression stirring which would reach his heart in later rounds and make him slow, deaden nerve, deaden nerve went Ali's jab flicking a snake tongue, whoo-eet! whoo-eet! but Frazier's head was bobbing too fast, he was moving faster than he had ever moved before in that bobbing nonstop never-a-backward step of his, slogging and bouncing forward, that huge left hook flaunting the air with the confidence it was enough of a club to split a tree, and Ali, having missed his jabs, stepped nimbly inside the hook and wrestled Frazier in the clinch. Ali looked stronger here. So by the first 45 seconds of the fight, they had each surprised the other profoundly. Frazier was fast enough to slip through Ali's punches, and Ali was strong enough to handle him in the clinches. A pattern had begun. Because Ali was missing often, Frazier was in under his shots like a police dog's muzzle on your arm, Ali could not slide from side to side, he was boxed in, then obliged to go backward, and would end on the ropes again and again with Frazier belaboring him. Yet Frazier could not reach him. Like a prestidigitator Ali would tie the other's punches into odd knots, not even blocking them yet on his elbows or his arms, rather throwing his own punches as defensive moves, for even as they missed, he would brush Frazier to the side with his forearm, or hold him off, or clinch and wrestle a little of the will out of Frazier's neck. Once or twice in the round a long left hook by Frazier just touched the surface of Ali's chin, and Ali waved his head in placid contempt to the billions watching as if to say. "This man has not been able to hurt me at all."

The first round set a pattern for the fight. Ali won it and

would win the next. His jab was landing from time to time and rights and lefts of not great consequence. Frazier was hardly reaching him at all. Yet it looked like Frazier had established that he was fast enough to get in on Ali and so drive him to the ropes and to the corners, and that spoke of a fight which would be determined by the man in better condition, in better physical condition rather than in better psychic condition, the kind of fight Ali could hardly want for his strength was in his pauses, his nature passed along the curve of every dialectic, he liked, in short, to fight in flurries, and then move out, move away, assess, take his time, fight again. Frazier would not let him. Frazier moved in with the snarl of a wolf, his teeth seemed to show through his mouthpiece, he made Ali work. Ali won the first two rounds but it was obvious he could not continue to win if he had to work all the way. And in the third round Frazier began to get to him, caught Ali with a powerful blow to the face at the bell. That was the first moment where it was clear to all that Frazier had won a round. Then he won the next. Ali looked tired and a little depressed. He was moving less and less and calling upon a skill not seen since the fight with Chuvalo when he had showed his old ability, worked on all those years ago with Shotgun Sheldon, to lie on the ropes and take a beating to the stomach. He had exhausted Chuvalo by welcoming attacks on the stomach but Frazier was too incommensurable a force to allow such total attack. So Ali lay on the ropes and wrestled him off, and moved his arms and waist, blocking punches, slipping punches, countering with punches —it began to look as if the fight would be written on the ropes, but Ali was getting very tired. At the beginning of the fifth round, he got up slowly from his stool, very slowly.

Frazier was beginning to feel that the fight was his. He moved in on Ali jeering, his hands at his side in mimicry of Ali, a street fighter mocking his opponent, and Ali tapped him with long light jabs to which Frazier stuck out his mouthpiece, a jeer of derision as if to suggest that the mouthpiece was all Ali would reach all night.

There is an extortion of the will beyond any of our measure in the exhaustion which comes upon a fighter in early rounds when he is already too tired to lift his arms or take advantage of openings there before him, yet the fight is not a third over, there are all those rounds to go, contractions of torture, the lungs screaming into the dungeons of the soul, washing the throat with a hot bile that once belonged to the liver, the legs are going dead, the arms move but their motion is limp, one is straining into another will, breathing into the breath of another will as agonized as one's own. As the fight moved through the fifth, the sixth and the seventh, then into the eighth, it was obvious that Ali was into the longest night of his career, and yet with that skill, that research into the pits of every miserable contingency in boxing, he came up with odd somnambulistic variations, holding Frazier off, riding around Frazier with his arm about his neck, almost entreating Frazier with his arms extended, and Frazier leaning on him, each of them slowed to a pit-a-pat of light punches back and forth until one of them was goaded up from exhaustion to whip and stick, then hook and hammer and into the belly and out, and out of the clinch and both looking exhausted, and then Frazier, mouth bared again like a wolf, going in and Ali waltzing him, tying him, tapping him lightly as if he were a speed bag, just little flicks, until Frazier, like an exhausted horse finally feeling the crop, would push up into a trot and try to run up the hill. It was indeed as if they were both running up a hill. As if Frazier's offensive was so great and so great was Ali's defense that the fight could only be decided by who could take the steepest pitch of the hill. So Frazier, driving, driving, trying to drive the heart out of Ali, put the pitch of that hill up and up until they were ascending an unendurable slope. And moved like somnambulists slowly working and rubbing one another, almost embracing, next to locked in the slow moves of lovers after the act until, reaching into the stores of energy reaching them from cells never before so used, one man or the other would work up a contractive spasm of skills and throw punches at the other in the straining slow-motion hypnosis of a deepening act. And so the first eight rounds went by. The two judges scored six for Frazier, two for Ali. The referee had it even. Some of the Press had Ali ahead—it was not easy to score. For if it were an alley fight, Frazier would win. Clay was by now hardly more than the heavy bag to Frazier. Frazier was dealing with a man, not a demon. He was not respectful of that man. But still! It was Ali who was landing the majority of punches. They were light, they were usually weary, but some had snap, some were quick, he was landing two punches to Frazier's one. Yet Frazier's were hardest. And Ali often looked as tender as if he were making love. It was as if he could now feel the whole absence of that real second fight with Liston, that fight for which he had trained so long and so hard, the fight which might have rolled over his laurels from the greatest artist of pugilism to the greatest brawler of them all— maybe he had been prepared on that night to beat Liston at his own, be more of a slugger, more of a man crude to crude than Liston. Yes, Ali had never been a street fighter and never a whorehouse knock-it-down stud, no, it was more as if a man with the exquisite reflexes of Nureyev had learned to throw a knockout punch with either hand and so had become champion of the world without knowing if he was the man of all men or the most delicate of the delicate with special privilege endowed by God. Now with Frazier, he was in a sweat bath (a mudpile, a knee, elbow, and death-thumping chute of a pit) having in this late year the fight he had sorely needed for his true greatness as a fighter six and seven years ago, and so whether ahead, behind or even, terror sat in the rooting instinct of all those who were for Ali for it was obviously Frazier's fight to win, and what if Ali, weaknesses of character now flickering to the surface in a hundred little moves, should enter the vale of prizefighting's deepest humiliation, should fall out half conscious on the floor and not want to get up. What a death to his followers.

The ninth began. Frazier mounted his largest body attack of the night. It was preparations-for-Liston-with-Shotgun-Sheldon, it was the virtuosity of the gym all over again, and Ali, like a catcher handling a fast-ball pitcher, took Frazier's punches, one steamer, another steamer, wing! went a screamer, a steamer, warded them, blocked them, slithered them, winced from them, absorbed them, took them in and blew them out and came off the ropes and was Ali the Magnificent for the next minute and thirty seconds. The fight turned. The troops of Ali's second corps of energy had arrived, the energy for which he had been waiting long agonizing heart-sore vomit-mean rounds. Now he jabbed Frazier, he snake-licked his face with jabs faster than he had thrown before, he anticipated each attempt of Frazier at counter-attack and threw it back, he danced on his toes for the first time in rounds, he popped in rights, he hurt him with hooks, it was his biggest round of the night, it was the best round yet of the fight, and Frazier full of energy and hordes of sudden punishment was beginning to move into that odd petulant concentration on other rituals besides the punches, tappings of the gloves, stares of the eye, that species of mouthpiece-chewing which is the prelude to fun-strut in the knees, then Queer Street, then waggle on out, drop like a steer.

It looked like Ali had turned the fight, looked more like the same in the 10th, now reporters were writing another story in their mind where Ali was not the magical untried Prince who had come apart under the first real pressure of his life but was rather the greatest Heavyweight Champion of all time for he had weathered the purgatory of Joe Frazier.

But in the 11th, that story also broke. Frazier caught him, caught him again and again, and Ali was near to knocked out and swayed and slid on Queer Street himself, then spent the rest of the 11th and the longest round of the 12th working another bottom of Hell, holding off Frazier who came on and on, sobbing, wild, a wild honor of a beast, man of will reduced to the common denominator of the will of all of us back in that land of the animal where the idea of man as a tool-wielding beast was first conceived. Frazier looked to get Ali forever in the 11th and the 12th, and Ali, his legs slapped and slashed on the thighs between each round by Angelo Dundee, came out for the 13th and incredibly was dancing. Everybody's story switched again. For if Ali won this round, the 14th and the 15th, who could know if he could not win the fight? . . . He won the first half of the 13th, then spent the second half on the ropes with Frazier. They were now like crazy death-march-maddened mateys coming up the hill and on to home, and yet Ali won the 14th, Ali looked good, he came out dancing for the 15th, while Frazier, his own armies of energy finally caught up, his courage ready to spit into the eye of any devil black or white who would steal the work of his life, had equal madness to steal the bolt from Ali. So Frazier reached out to snatch the magic punch from the air, the punch with which Ali topped Bonavena, and found it and thunked Ali a hell and hit Ali a heaven of a shot which dumped Muhammad into 50,000 newspaper photographs—Ali on the floor! Great Ali on the floor was out there flat singing to the sirens in the mistiest fogs of Queer Street (same look of death and widowhood on his far-gone face as one had seen in the fifth blind round with Liston) yet Ali got up, Ali came sliding through the last two minutes and thirty-five seconds of this heathen holocaust in some last exercise of the will, some iron fundament of the ego not to be knocked out, and it was then as if the spirit of Harlem finally spoke and came to rescue and the ghosts of the dead in Vietnam, something held him up before arm-weary triumphant near-crazy Frazier who had just hit him the hardest punch ever thrown in his life and they went down to the last few seconds of a great fight, Ali still standing and Frazier had won.

The world was talking instantly of a rematch. For Ali had shown America what we all had hoped was secretly true. He was a man. He could bear moral and physical torture and he could stand. And if he could beat Frazier in the rematch we would have at last a national hero who was hero of the world as well, and who could bear to wait for the next fight? Joe Frazier, still the champion, and a great champion, said to the press, "Fellows, have a heart—I got to live a little. I've been working for 10 long years." And Ali, through the agency of alter-ego Bundini, said—for Ali was now in the hospital to check on the possible fracture of a jaw—Ali was reported to have said, "Get the gun ready—we're going to set traps." Oh, wow. Could America wait for something so great as the Second Ali–Frazier?

# THE
# UNSPOKEN

# THE
# UNSPOKEN

THOMAS FAHY

Simon & Schuster Books for Young Readers
New York  London  Toronto  Sydney

SIMON & SCHUSTER BOOKS FOR YOUNG READERS
An imprint of Simon & Schuster Children's Publishing Division
1230 Avenue of the Americas, New York, New York 10020

Book design by Daniel Roode and Karen Hudson
The text for this book is set in Fairfield.
Manufactured in the United States of America
2  4  6  8  10  9  7  5  3
Library of Congress Cataloging-in-Publication Data
The unspoken / Tom Fahy.—1st ed.
p. cm.
Summary: Six teens are drawn back to the small North Carolina town
where they once lived and, one by one, begin to die of their worst
fears, as prophesied by the cult leader they killed five years earlier,
and who they believe poisoned their parents.
ISBN-13: 978-1-4169-4007-4 (hardcover)
ISBN-10: 1-4169-4007-3 (hardcover)
[1. Cults—Fiction. 2. Murder—Fiction. 3. Dreams—Fiction. 4. Horror
stories.] I. Title.
PZ7.F14317Uns 2008
[Fic]—dc22
2007000850

For my nieces Tommi-Rose and Ellie Lynn,
whose futures are bright indeed.

# ACKNOWLEDGMENTS

I am deeply grateful and indebted to Elaine Markson and everyone at the Markson agency for their ongoing support. I also want to extend my sincere thanks to David Gale, his assistant Alexandra Cooper, and the dedicated staff at Simon & Schuster for making this book a reality.

I would have never crossed the finish line without the sagacious feedback of several dear friends—Daniel Kurtzman, Laura Garrett, and Susann Cokal. I can't thank you enough for your generosity and love.

I also extend my heartfelt gratitude to Tom and Eileen Fahy, Mike and Jen, and my enchanting nieces, Tommi-Rose and Ellie Lynn. I am so fortunate to call you family.

# CONTENTS

# PROLOGUE

Before Jacob Crawley arrived, the town of Meridian, North Carolina, was so small that most folks couldn't tell you where to find it. Even the state map skipped right over it, like it was too much trouble to write down the name, let alone make room for it on a map.

But Jacob changed all that. With an easy smile and a big voice he started to convince people that Meridian was destined for greatness. We just had to be ready for it, he said. We had to open our minds.

One summer afternoon Jacob invited the entire town to the abandoned church on Shady Grove Lane—one of the few streets in Meridian without a single tree on it. Allison once asked her daddy about that name being so out of place, but he was the kind of man who never answered a question directly.

"Some people don't have a good sense for naming things," he told her, and thinking back on Shady Grove Lane, Allison figures he was right.

As she and her daddy squeezed into the old church with the rest of the town, Allison remembers thinking that it was hot as the surface of the sun. Sure, she knew from science class that the sun was so hot that it didn't even have a surface. It was like molten lava all the time. But the heat was something awful that day, and everyone was sweating buckets. Ladies were fanning themselves. Men wiped their brows

with the backs of their hands, and little babies started to fuss.

When Jacob finally spoke from behind the podium, his voice seemed to soothe folks. Allison was ten and small for her age, so she could only see bits of him through the crowded pews in front of them. She doesn't remember much of what he said, but the sound of his words . . . now, that she remembers. They buzzed. People started swaying and nodding their heads. Some were even tapping their toes as they listened.

Soon everyone was caught up in the moment, moving their bodies and forgetting about the heat, about the street with no shade outside. That's when Jacob announced he was a prophet—a new prophet for a new age. Well, as you can imagine, those words stopped everything, kind of like the time Tommy Doyle belched in front of Baby Jesus during the Nativity scene at the school Christmas pageant—no one knew whether to laugh or to be real angry. So the church got quiet, and everyone waited for Jacob to say something else. To explain himself. Instead he left the pulpit, walked up the aisle to Allison's pew, and touched her daddy on the shoulder.

Jacob bowed his head slightly, and all she could see was his silver white hair. He was still for so long that Allison wondered if he'd fallen asleep. She had never known anyone who could sleep while standing up. Well, cows could, but not people. So she figured Jacob must have been concentrating real hard. Her daddy just got that strange half smile on his face—the same one he got after asking her for the "umpteenth time" to clean up her room. ("Umpteenth" was his word for a number that was too high for counting. Her daddy was a patient man, but that smile meant he was just about fed up.)

"Sometimes," Jacob began, lifting his head and looking at her daddy with those yellow eyes, "sometimes, we carry so much pain inside that we can hardly breathe. It's like our hearts just collapse. . . . That's what happened on the night

2

you lost your daughter, isn't it? On the night she was taken from you."

Allison's daddy didn't move. It was as if someone had slapped him in the face and he was too shocked to respond.

"I can help you breathe again," Jacob continued. "It's not too late."

Without waiting for a response, Jacob lifted his hand from her daddy's shoulder and moved farther down the aisle toward old Mrs. Haggerty. By then Allison wasn't paying attention anymore. She just looked at her daddy, who stood there with his mouth hanging open and his eyes blinking.

How could Jacob know about Melanie? Allison wondered. She was killed almost two years ago, and no one in town talked about it. Sure, everyone knew, but knowing and saying are two different things. It was possible Jacob had seen it in the news, Allison considered. The local paper had run a story about it, but Allison couldn't read it all the way through. To her, that night seemed too private . . . too painful for strangers.

After Jacob's first time at the pulpit Allison and her daddy started going to his weekly gatherings at the abandoned church. They weren't the only ones, either. Dozens of folks filled the church every week, listening to Jacob's ideas about our troubled times, about the fear infecting this country, about the end time and the new world that would come. Allison assumed it was powerful stuff because all of the grown-ups started to think Jacob was right. But she couldn't stop thinking about Shady Grove Lane and how it sounded like the name for a cemetery.

A few months later Jacob invited all of them to live in several cabins outside of town, not far from the old church. That was the day Jacob decided on a name for his ministry—the Divine Path. And that's what they started calling themselves.

The Divine Path.

That was two years ago, and in the last two years Allison has thought about that story too many times for counting. Once a week Jacob insisted that everyone share a "moment of enlightenment" with the other believers. Allison wasn't exactly sure what that meant, but she always told this story because that day in the church was the first time since Melanie's murder that her father seemed to have hope. It was the first time he seemed like her daddy again.

Now—with the fire raging behind her and Ike Dempsey gripping her hand so tight that she can't feel her fingertips— it's the only story she can think about. The heat from the blaze starts to make her back sweaty, and she leans forward. Standing in a circle with the only friends she has ever known, she looks around at the six of them, heads bowed as if they are too ashamed to look at one another.

*We did it,* she thinks. *All of us.*

Except it was her idea. She was the first one to say it out loud: "We have to kill Jacob. We have to destroy this place."

They were too late to save their parents, though. Jacob must have poisoned everyone else hours before the blaze started. Moments later angry winds carried the flames to the main hall, and it caught fire like dried autumn leaves. There is nothing they can do to stop it from burning, but they can't watch, either. It's just too painful to see your whole life—your family, your home . . . everything you thought you cared about—disappear in an instant. So they stand in a circle, facing one another instead, and listen to the sounds of the crackling flames.

What scares Allison most is the idea that Jacob somehow knew what was going to happen. That he knew the six of them would do this. Hadn't he told everyone that the Divine Path

would be devoured in a wall of flame? That someone would betray him just as Judas betrayed Christ?

He made other predictions too. He foresaw terrible things happening to them—visions of their worst fears coming true.

"In five years' time," Jacob told each of them privately, "your greatest fear will consume you. It will rob you of your last breath."

Listening to the fire sizzle and gasp behind her, Allison wonders if he wasn't just trying to scare them.

"What if it comes true?" she asks to break the silence, her voice hoarse and unsteady.

But no one looks up or says a word. They just hold hands as the air around them fills with smoke and the white ash of burning flesh. . . .

Five years later . . .

# 1
# DREAMCATCHER

The bright red blood on Allison's pillow reminds her of "Snow White"—not the watered-down Disney version with magic kisses, dwarfs named Dopey, and singing animals. The older story with a hateful queen who wants to eat a young girl's lung and liver. The one that ends when the queen is tortured to death in red-hot iron slippers.

*Now, that's a good story,* Allison thinks with a sly smile. Better than the image that woke her—a boy being swallowed by black green waters. Mouth open. Bubbles where a scream would be.

As she sits up, the sickly-sweet taste of blood fills her mouth, and she can feel the bumpy surface of her tongue. She must have bitten it in her sleep, she realizes. Her eyes are stinging bad, and her forehead pounds like the drum set that her pimply foster brother plays in the garage every afternoon.

She looks back at the red stain on the pillow, trying to remember if she took her medication yesterday. She has some kind of seizure every few weeks now. They're so common that they don't faze her much anymore. Sometimes she's surprised how much a person can get used to. How much pain and fear and heartbreak.

But that dream was different. She hasn't had one like that for years.

Since right before the fire.

Of course, she probably wouldn't be sick anymore if Jacob

hadn't taken away her pills back then. He thought the medication would interfere with her dreams, so he kept it from her.

"Dying might interfere with them too," she always wanted to say, but Allison was too afraid of Jacob for that. Jacob had ways of punishing that stayed with you.

Mostly, Jacob thought the seizures made her dreams more vivid, more prophetic—a word he used lots to explain away the things that folks didn't like about the Divine Path. Allison could never remember anything after a seizure anyway, but sometimes when she came to, an image would flash before her eyes, like the way a lightbulb flares up before it burns out forever. That's what happened when she was first diagnosed with epilepsy—seven days before her sister's murder. She was sitting at the kitchen table, flicking milky Cheerios at Mel's face, when her body went cold and hard.

Later, Daddy told her how she suddenly fell to the floor and let out a cry. "Like someone was squeezing the air right out of you," he said. "Then you started shaking something fierce."

Allison doesn't remember any of those things. But she does remember Doc Hillerman coming over to see her. That made her nervous. Doctors never come to your house—even in a small town where the nearest hospital is thirty miles away. Besides, she didn't want anyone around, let alone Doc Hillerman, who always smelled like olives, but it wasn't up for discussion, Ma said.

Doc Hillerman got there quick, and he didn't waste any time chitchatting, either. He walked right over to Daddy's leather chair in the living room, where Allison was sitting, and he asked her how she was doing. That made her nervous too because Doc Hillerman usually liked to play around first—pretending that he couldn't remember her name or giving her candy for medicine. But instead of trying to make her laugh,

he took out his stethoscope and leaned in close to listen to her heart. She could smell the olives on his body, and it made her stomach turn. Then he flashed a little white light in her eyes.

That's when it happened. In an instant she saw a picture of her sister lying in bed, black blood covering her throat like a scarf.

Allison screamed so loud that Doc Hillerman dropped his penlight.

She didn't care, though. She was convinced that something terrible had happened to Melanie. Struggling to get off the soft cushions that seemed to be swallowing her, Allison blurted out her sister's name—"Mel!"

"Where's . . . ," she started to say, still trying to push herself away from the chair, but before she could finish, her sister came running into the room with Ma.

She was just fine . . . for seven more days.

"Allison," her foster mother calls up the stairs. "You're going to be late for school. Hurry up."

The voice startles her, as if someone has just shaken her awake, and Allison looks at the clock on her bedside table: 7:14.

"Crap," she mutters. Math class is first period, and her precalculus teacher, Mrs. Jenkins, has the patience of a rabid pit bull. Allison won't just get detention for being tardy. That would be too easy. She is going to get another lecture on personal responsibility and God knows what else. "There are two types of people in the world, Miss Burke"—Mrs. Jenkins always begins the same way, her narrow glasses perched at the tip of her nose and a silver pendant of the Virgin Mother dangling between her freckled breasts—"those who show up and those who don't. . . ."

*Blah, blah, blah,* Allison thinks as she gets out of bed and

stumbles toward the bathroom. Her tongue throbs, and her head is still spinning from the seizure and from the memories of her sister. She needs her medication. She needs to *not* be thinking about Mel right now. Sometimes it feels like too much, Allison admits to herself. Melanie and Daddy. Ma. Jacob and the terrible things that happened back then. All of these memories feel like a weight that's too heavy for one person to carry.

In the bathroom the cold tile floor stings Allison's feet as she stands in front of the medicine cabinet and grabs the pills from the top shelf. Standing here, she also looks at her reflection in the mirror—the brown, shoulder-length hair, the green eyes, and, of course, a new spot of acne above her upper lip.

"Double crap," she says, before popping the pill into her mouth and chasing it with a handful of water from the faucet.

Stepping back into the bedroom, she glances down at her slender body and long white legs. Some of the guys at school stare at her on the days she wears skirts and tight jeans, but they mostly seem to notice the strange mark across her neck. She hasn't gone out without necklaces or scarves in five years. But they don't always cover everything. Sure, she can tell when people at school are whispering about it. But she doesn't care what they think.

Just Bo.

Bo is the boy she has been seeing for about a month now. Six days ago he gave her a silk scarf. He called it a "just-because gift." That's the first time she really let him see her scar. He even ran his fingertips across it that night, while they were making out in the front seat of his father's Mercedes. His touch sent goose bumps down Allison's body.

She wonders what her neck felt like to him. Yeah, she has touched it a thousand times, but your own body never feels the same to someone else. That's what makes being touched so

nice. Your flaws disappear, for a while at least, and your body tingles—not just from the feeling, but from knowing that someone else wants to touch you.

"Allison?" her foster mother calls out again.

"Okay," she hollers back. "I'm coming."

Allison doesn't want to say anything about her seizure. She doesn't want to involve her foster parents at all. This illness is part of *her* and her past—the part she wants to control and forget. She can handle it on her own.

In truth, she doesn't really mind her foster parents much. They're nice enough—though they won't win an award for Parents of the Year anytime soon. Like the day Mrs. Packer set fire to the kitchen while trying to kill a cockroach with hair spray. She was screaming and spraying the roach as it scurried across the gas stove, where she was boiling water. Allison isn't sure if Mrs. Packer killed the roach that day, but half the stove and the wall behind it are still black with scorch marks from the flaming hair spray. Or the time Mr. Packer ran the lawn mower over his own foot. He only lost his small left toe, but before going to the emergency room, he insisted on finishing the lawn. "Heck, there was only one more row to cut," he enjoys saying when he retells the story. "And nobody wants to see an unkempt lawn."

"Especially with human toes in it," Allison always wants to add, but she knows better.

Mr. Packer takes lawn maintenance very seriously.

Yeah, they're nice enough, but crazy things happen in the Packer house about once a week. This doesn't bother Allison much. It's kind of entertaining, actually, and most of the time Mr. and Mrs. Packer are too busy managing their own chaotic lives to give much notice to Allison. Which is fine with her. Now, if she could just get eleven-year-old Brutus Packer Jr. to stop practicing the drums . . .

Allison plops down in front of her desk and turns on the computer. Her day doesn't begin until she's checked e-mail. Like coffee or a cold shower, it's the thing that kick-starts every morning.

The connection is molasses slow as usual, but Allison doesn't mind so much today. She feels better sitting down—the dizziness stops, and her head doesn't pound so hard. She looks at the rest of her desk, which is an absolute disaster. Random stacks of CDs. Her cell phone. School textbooks and folders that look like they were just poured out of a bucket. And a can of Diet Coke that's at least five days old.

A dreamcatcher hangs above it all from the desk lamp, and she touches it with her fingers. The circle of yellow and orange cloth reminds Allison of a bright summer day and the orange-haired boy who gave it to her just over five years ago—Ike Dempsey. He had a crush on her, and though Allison liked him, she didn't like him *like that*. She wanted quiet David Holloway, the boy who always lowered his eyes when he smiled, to notice her. She almost kissed David one night in the old tree house—but as Brutus Packer Jr. is fond of saying, "almost" only counts with hand grenades and nuclear war.

The Internet connection finally goes through. Only one message is waiting in her in-box, but she doesn't recognize the e-mail address. The subject line reads: "A Voice From The Past." Allison opens the message and finds a forwarded newspaper article with today's date.

### *Meridian Herald*
Mystery Surrounds the Drowning of a Teenage Boy
by Marcum Shale
The bizarre circumstances surrounding the death of Harold Crawley, a seventeen-year-old boy found in a tobacco field off Route 78, has local authorities baffled.

According to Sheriff Cooper of the Meridian Police Department, an anonymous phone call alerted him to the body two days ago. The cause of death was not immediately apparent, but the county coroner's preliminary findings suggest that Harold Crawley drowned—even though he was found more than thirty miles from the nearest body of water, Lake Haverton.

"Five liters of fluid were found in his lungs," Sheriff Cooper told reporters this morning. "But that doesn't prove anything. This may or may not be a homicide. Right now we have no crime scene and no concrete evidence of foul play."

Sheriff Cooper refused to comment on Harold Crawley's link to the infamous cult the Divine Path, which was founded in Meridian, North Carolina, about seven years ago. Harold was the only son of the cult's leader, Jacob Crawley, and in the summer of 2002 he was one of six children who survived the fire that claimed the lives of Jacob and the other adult members of the Divine Path.

Harold's legal guardian, Ms. Janet Wilton, reported him missing several days ago from their home in Atlanta, Georgia. According to the director of Cicely's Funeral Home, Ms. Wilton has decided to bury Harold in Meridian, where Mr. Crawley purchased a plot for his son a few months before the fire.

A brief memorial service will be held tomorrow at five in the afternoon.


Allison pushes away from her desk with a jolt. Goose bumps run down her spine, and she can feel her stomach dropping away.

"Oh, my God," she mutters.

Allison scans the message again, then studies the user name of the sender: lazarus6. "Lazarus," she says to herself. Like the guy in the Bible that Jesus raised from the dead?

Allison tries to figure out who would send this article. Someone from school? Not likely. She has worked hard to keep

her past a secret. When she first moved in with the Packers, her teachers were told that Allison's real parents had died in a car accident, and that story has been around long enough to pass for truth. But if no one from school sent it, who did? Someone from Meridian? Someone who knew about the Divine Path back then? The possibilities make her uneasy. She can tell that the message has been forwarded to several undisclosed recipients. And she wonders if the rest of her old friends have gotten it too. If Ike and David might be reading it right now. If Jade Rowan and Emma Caulder have seen it. If all of them are remembering Jacob's promise.

Allison pictures Harold's face on the night of the fire—his cheeks flushed bright red from the heat. Then she remembers something she hasn't thought of in years. Trees. Harold loved to climb trees. He could scramble up the tallest trunk in the blink of an eye and without ever getting a scratch on his body. Some of the other kids called him Monkey Boy, but that didn't seem to bother him. Allison always thought that he liked being able to get away from time to time. To go where Jacob couldn't find him.

But something is missing from this article. Something that a reporter and the police would never know: Harold couldn't swim. In fact, he was terrified of the water.

A wave of dizziness makes the room shift out of focus, and Allison has to close her eyes to feel steady again. When she opens them, everything is back in focus. She can see the glowing computer screen. The chaotic mess on her desk. The Diet Coke. And the dreamcatcher, which sways slightly from her lamp. She takes it in her hand.

That's what Jacob tried to do—to catch their dreams. Not to keep them safe or to protect them from nightmares. He wanted them to see ugly, horrible things and, more than that, to be afraid. It was fear that fueled his prophecies about the

end of the world, about his promise that they would all die from their worst fears.

She wonders if the drowning is just a coincidence, if the thing that Harold was most afraid of killed him. Then Allison recalls the sound of Jacob's voice when he told her that she would die in five years.

"Your greatest fear will consume you. It will rob you of your last breath," he said with a kind of cold pleasure, each word harsh, like metal scraping against cement. The memory makes her shiver.

"Let's get a move on up there," Mrs. Packer says loudly, and Allison looks at the clock again: 7:26.

She is going to be way late for school now, but she doesn't care. She has more important things on her mind. She gets up from the chair slowly, and her entire body feels unsteady and off balance.

*What if it's true?* Allison asks herself. She glances around her room, unsure of what to do next. She tries to stay calm, to clear her head, but Jacob's promise keeps pressing in around her. She wants to go back to Meridian but is afraid—afraid that Jacob could be right and that all of them are about to die.

But she has to go, she thinks. She needs to see her old friends again. They are the only ones who understand what's about to happen.

# 2
# SCARS

Allison wakes up the next morning with a craving for key lime pie. Sure, she has always had a sweet tooth the size of the Mississippi Delta—which, as any map will tell you, is pretty big—but she usually wants chocolate. Ding Dongs. Double chocolate chip cookies. Hot chocolate. Chocolate chocolate chip ice cream. Chocolate fudge brownies. In a pinch she'll even eat a Hershey's Bar—which, as any chocolate lover will tell you, is second-rate stuff. But recently Allison has been thinking more about key lime pies than chocolate, and she isn't sure why.

Key lime pie was her ma's favorite treat, and she always let Allison and Melanie help with making desserts. "There are two things you need to know about a good key lime pie," her ma would never forget to remind them. "You gotta have *real* key limes from Florida. And you need just the right amount of juice." That last part might sound obvious, but balance is everything. You need enough tartness to make your mouth pucker up and enough sweetness to make you want another mouthful.

And another.

And another.

Balance. Ma, Daddy, Mel, and Allison. Together the four of them were like ingredients. Each one made up an essential part of their family, but when Melanie was gone, nothing tasted right anymore. Ma got real quiet. Daddy stopped laughing. And Allison became invisible, at least to her folks.

Most days when Allison got home from school, her ma would be sitting in front of the television, staring. That may not sound strange at first, but the television was completely broken. You couldn't see anything but your own reflection on the black screen. A few weeks earlier Daddy had plugged one too many things into the same electrical socket, and something inside the TV made a loud popping sound. He liked to joke that Ma's favorite shows were so bad that the TV finally exploded in protest.

But after Mel died, nothing seemed funny anymore. In fact, nothing seemed to work in the Burke house after that—broken towel racks, burned out lightbulbs, leaky faucets. It was as if the entire house was falling apart too.

Three months later her ma wasn't sitting in front of the television, or anywhere else in the house, for that matter. She disappeared on a Saturday afternoon, along with her clothes and jewelry and her favorite cookbook for desserts.

It was the weekend of the state fair, and ma didn't want to go. No amount of persuading would change her mind, either, so Allison and Daddy went without her. It was good to be away, Allison remembers thinking—outside and in the warm sunlight. At the fairgrounds they ate funnel cake and fed the largest pig in the world. They even got tickets for one of those spinning rides whose only purpose is making people dizzy. By the time they got home, Allison's stomach ached from all the spinning and eating—especially the chocolate-dipped Rice Krispies Treats and the rainbow lollipops.

She and Daddy called out when they walked through the door, but no one answered. All the rooms were half empty, and Ma wasn't anywhere to be found. Allison wanted to call the police.

"No," her daddy said, staring at his shoes and speaking in a whisper. "Sometimes people need to disappear for a while . . . she'll come back for you."

Allison figured those words must have hurt a ton—thinking that Ma would return for her daughter but not for her husband. No matter. It turns out he was wrong anyway.

Ma never came back for either one of them.

Before that day Allison had always assumed that disappearing would be hard—that only magicians, CIA agents, and serial killers could do it. But in the Burke house eight years ago Allison learned that disappearing was about as hard as making key lime pie.

And that's not hard at all.

Allison gets out of bed, relieved that there isn't any blood on her pillow. She feels mostly back to normal this morning, though her tongue is sore and swollen, and her head throbs as if Brutus Packer Jr. has been using it for a drum solo. Her duffel bag is ready and sitting by the bedroom door. The gas tank in her car—the ancient car that Mr. Packer gave her when she turned seventeen—is full. And she has left out plenty of crunchy food for John Donne, the Packers' enormously puffy cat.

Now she just needs to get dressed and check e-mail before hitting the road. She hopes Bo has sent his usual good-morning-I'm-thinking-of-you e-mail. For the last month he has written her something every night so she has it first thing. But today her in-box is empty. She's not that surprised, though. Yesterday when Bo asked her why she needed to leave town all of a sudden, Allison couldn't answer.

"It's just something I gotta do," she said.

He got real quiet after that.

How could she tell him—or anyone—about the terrible things that happened back then? About her fear that she might die soon? And if she couldn't explain it to Bo, there was no way Mrs. Packer would understand. So Allison did the only thing she could think of.

"I really need to stay at Heather's place this weekend," she said yesterday after school.

A lie.

"Heather Montgomery?" Mrs. Packer asked, as if Allison knew so many Heathers that it was hard to keep track.

"Yes, Heather Montgomery." *The only Heather I've known my whole life,* she wanted to say. *My only real friend at school.* Instead Allison added, "We have a big history test on Monday."

Another lie.

Allison hates lying. It reminds her of Jacob Crawley and the lies that brought Daddy and her to the Divine Path. The lies that led up to the night of the fire. But Allison doesn't have any other choice right now. She needs to go to Harold's funeral, and there's no way that her foster parents would allow it. As Mrs. Packer would say, "N-period-O-period." So Allison has told two lies. She figures it's better than disappearing like her ma did. She'll never do that to anybody. Ever.

It hurts way too much.

Besides, Heather will cover for her. That's what best friends do. Heather has long blond hair, sky blue eyes, and cheerleader good looks, but she doesn't act like it. She reads books and plays the cello. She's also the only other girl in school who thinks Bill Stringfield, the quarterback of the football team, is the biggest loser in the world. Which he is—and not just because he thinks he's God's gift to women and one time in English class he spelled "potato" with an *e* on the end.

Heather is the only one whom Allison has told about the Divine Path. Well, little bits here and there. But Heather has heard enough to know that Allison has to go back to Meridian. Pronto.

Like Allison, Heather also has a scar, but hers resembles jagged glass and runs from the palm of her hand to the bend in her elbow. She got it in a car accident several years ago

when her stepfather-no-more, Tony, drank too many beers at a neighborhood barbecue and insisted on driving Mrs. Montgomery and Heather home. He crashed into an oak tree less than two blocks from their house, giving his wife three broken ribs and cutting up Heather's arm real bad.

And Tony . . . well, he didn't have a scratch on him.

Heather says she doesn't mind the scar so much anymore, but then again, she mostly wears long-sleeved shirts. Allison doesn't mention this. She understands that Heather hates having a permanent reminder of Tony on her body—especially since he left her mother and her about a year after the accident.

Allison knows all about wanting to forget the past.

She knows all about scars, too. . . .

The Confessional was about six and a half minutes from the campsite—far enough away to be out of earshot but close enough to remind you that it was always there. It was the place where Jacob gave penance to those who sinned. At least, that's what Jacob liked to call it—"giving penance."

Allison walked that six and a half minutes enough times to do it blindfolded and backward. She can still picture every step—where the fallen tree blocked most of the stream, where the strange black rocks formed an X on the side of the hill, where you could first see the Confessional under a canopy of thick branches and leaves.

From the outside the Confessional looked like a dilapidated shed with wood as dark as the night sky and walls tilted unnaturally far to one side. It seemed as if a gust of wind could knock the whole thing over. If only. But the inside appeared both bigger and smaller at the same time. Mirrors of different shapes and sizes covered each wall, and even the ceiling was made up of reflective glass. It was like everything was looking back on itself.

A deep, circular pit took up most of the space where the floor should have been. For a long time no one—not Allison or Harold or any of the other kids—got close enough to see inside. They had all sorts of theories about what was there, though. Sharks. Bats. Killer bees. Monsters. Even terrorists.

Once Allison thought she heard a gasping sound like someone choking. Harold heard things too. But he was convinced that something was gurgling, like it was trying to come up for air. No matter. They all had different theories until the day Allison got caught stealing. Until the day she sneaked into Jacob's room to find the box with David's asthma medication.

Jacob's bedroom was more boring than she had expected. A bloodred candle glowed in the far corner, its light flickering across the desktop, and the shelves overflowing with books and yellowing papers. A rectangular rug with faded patterns covered most of the floor, and thick purple drapes hung from the windows. Jacob's bed was against the opposite wall.

Allison hurried across the room to look underneath the bed. The golden box was there—just like Harold had said. She dragged it onto the rug, and its surface held a distorted reflection of everything in the room, like a dirty fun-house mirror. There was no lock or latch on the box. No lid or visible opening. But it wasn't solid wood, either.

Allison tapped on the surface, and she could hear its hollowness. Nothing but four smooth sides. She ran her hands over the entire box again but couldn't figure out how to open it.

*It has to be in here,* Allison remembers thinking.

Jacob had mentioned the box many times. It was the place where he kept their past—tokens from their lives before the Divine Path, tokens he held on to as if they had some magic power over them. She started to pound the box against the floor, but nothing happened. Not even a dent. She stood up

with it in her arms, planning to run outside for a rock or something heavy to smash it open.

That's when Jacob walked through the door.

Her heart stopped beating.

"Good evening, Allison." Jacob smiled, and a slow, easy expression crossed his face. She knew what that meant—another trip to the Confessional.

Less than fifteen minutes later the Doctor brought Allison to the shed. In fact, the Doctor always took "penitent" children to the Confessional. No one had seen him before Jacob moved his followers to the campsite. The Doctor came after that. He just appeared one morning at services, when Jacob brought him up to the podium and introduced him as "the Doctor." Since no one knew what else to call him, the name stuck. He mostly handled basic medical stuff at the camp—bandaging cuts and sprains and that kind of thing. Jacob didn't allow the use of any medicine. He said that God took care of the sick, and that was that.

No one was sure how the Doctor felt about this. He didn't say too much. Besides, his drooping face, unshining black eyes, and grayish skin didn't make you want to strike up a conversation with him. Still, the Doctor always looked worried when someone started coughing or running a fever. He wore that same worried expression every time he escorted Allison to the Confessional. He'd tell her that everything would be fine, that Jacob was doing this for her own good. But she could see that he didn't believe a word of it.

Adults can be the worst liars.

This visit to the Confessional was different from the start. The Doctor walked Allison to the edge of the pit and told her to look inside. She thought it was some kind of trick. Jacob had never said you *couldn't* look inside, but he'd never said it was okay, either. It was as if he just wanted you to wonder, to

worry about what was down there. But the Doctor waited . . . waited until she leaned over the uneven edge of the pit and peered down.

Nothing. Empty. *A big black zero,* Allison thought with relief. After all that time she'd spent imagining the terrible things down there, it was only in her head. Either that or the hole was too deep to see anything. She turned back to the Doctor, but he was gone. Instead Jacob stood in the corner of the room, his body reflected in the dozens of mirrors around him.

"What do you want with the box, Allison?"

She didn't answer. In truth, she was sick to death of talking to Jacob.

"I said, what do you want with the box?" Jacob stepped forward, and so did the dozens of Jacobs in the mirrors. His white linen suit and silver hair made his entire body shine.

"I . . ." She hesitated. "Nothing."

Jacob nodded. In an instant he grabbed her shoulders and held her at the ledge.

"Look into the pit again, Allison," Jacob said. "This time I want you to open your eyes. I want you to see what's really down there."

Allison had no choice because Jacob was holding her over the opening now. It wasn't the idea of falling that scared her. It was the realization, maybe for the first time since Daddy and she had become part of the Divine Path, that Jacob would really hurt her. And even worse, that he *wanted* to hurt her. Bad.

"Think about the thing that you're most afraid of, Allison. Concentrate."

Jacob's grip squeezed tighter, and that's when she saw something moving in the darkness below. Allison stared into the pit, trying to see more clearly. The shadows shifted again. Then she could hear a scraping sound, like someone sharpening

metal. It got louder and louder, moving closer to the surface. Allison struggled to pull away from the opening, but Jacob held her firmly in place.

"Why do you want to bite the hand that feeds you, Allison?"

Beneath her, something started to glow in the darkness. Red and hot and burning. Then she heard more scratching. Her eyes started to sting and tear. Smoke was suddenly coming up from the pit. It was filling the entire room and scorching the inside of her throat.

"Please," Allison begged. "I can't breathe."

That's when Jacob released her, and Allison fell into the darkness.

"What are you doing?" Brutus Packer Jr. practically shouts across her room, and Allison almost drops the scarf in her hand.

"How many times do I have to tell you to knock, Brutus Packer Jr.?"

He hates the fact that Allison always uses his full name, and his face turns pinkish red. He then glances at the duffel bag by the door and taps it with his foot.

"You're leaving?" his voice cracks somewhat.

Allison suddenly realizes that her neck is not covered, and she wraps the scarf around it, hiding her scar—the scar Jacob put there that day at the Confessional.

"I'm spending the weekend with a friend," she says, and for the first time since she has lived here, Brutus Packer Jr. seems disappointed, almost sad. "I'll be back soon," she adds, and his face brightens briefly.

"Whatever, stinky-pants," Brutus Packer Jr. blurts out before hurrying out of her room.

Allison smiles as she grabs her bag and walks downstairs.

It is still early in the morning, and she can sneak out before Mr. and Mrs. Packer get up. Allison considers waiting around to say good-bye, but she's too anxious for that. It's going to be a long drive, she reminds herself. It's going to be a long trip back to a place she doesn't want to go, to a place that could be dangerous.

She thinks again about Harold and Daddy and Mel and the other kids she used to know. She thinks about key lime pie and how the little things in life make you ache the most for home. And as she starts the engine of her car, she even thinks about Brutus Packer Jr.—her new family, her new life . . . a life she hopes she'll live long enough to come back to.

# 3

# REUNION

Only one road goes into Meridian, and it leads to the town square, which is actually a circle with a thirsty-looking park in the center. If you decide not to stop, the dusty road will loop around and send you right back the way you came. That's how most people think of Meridian—as a town that's more like a revolving door than a place to sit down for a spell.

Not that there is much to stop for. Sure, if you're lucky, you might stumble across the Glory of God Breakfast Barn or the No-Name Tavern, with its maroon pool table and a juke-box that doesn't play music written after 1985. There's even an ice cream parlor at the back of Sutter's Pharmacy. Every summer, on days that were too hot for moving around or thinking, Allison would take Mel there for a root beer float. The red vinyl barstools always felt cool and sticky against your back-side, and the icy sodas were almost too big to finish. Almost.

But the truth is that a town with emptiness at its center is like a body without a heart, and Meridian never had much of a pulse—before Jacob, that is.

Allison drives around the town circle, but not too slowly. Small towns have long memories, and someone might recognize her. Most folks would take notice of a car like hers any-way—an off-white 1967 Plymouth Barracuda with a black vinyl top. She looks at the sagging park benches with splinter-ing wood and the mossy green statue of a Confederate soldier. The plaque at his feet is too faded to read, but all of the high

school kids used to call him Porn Star because of the way his sword looks when you're standing on either side of him.

Allison turns up Cottonwood Drive and passes by a row of houses that hasn't changed a bit since she left five years ago. On the nearest corner is Mrs. Pinkerton's place, which everyone called Mrs. P.'s Beauty Porch because of the salon at the back of the house. Wiley, her husband, had been the only dentist in Meridian when Allison was a kid, and after he died from a bee sting in the spring of 1998, Mrs. Pinkerton had the two dentist chairs from his office moved to their sunporch. That's when she first started "stylin'," as she liked to call it.

"Those are the nicest things we ever owned, me and Wiley," she always said, pointing to those chairs. "Damn expensive, too."

Mrs. Pinkerton never had a gift for hair, but none of the local women had the heart to say anything . . . or to go anywhere else, for that matter. Needless to say, an appointment at Mrs. P.'s Beauty Porch was risky business. Once you sat in one of those dentist chairs, you never knew how things were going to turn out upstairs, especially if Mrs. Pinkerton started talking about the bee sting. For a long while she swore that Wiley didn't have the brains that God gave a tree frog—*snip, snip, snip*. Otherwise, he wouldn't have been out there in the yard with no shoes on—*snip, snip, snip*.

"Wiley just stepped on the little guy, and the next thing you know, both Wiley and the bee are dead." *Snip, snip, snip.* "Damn waste of a bee."

The shears always snipped more angrily when Mrs. Pinkerton mentioned that bee. Sometimes Allison gripped the arms of that chair so tight that she thought someone would have to pry her off when it was all over. And you could always tell which days Mrs. Pinkerton had gotten to telling that story by the haircuts in town. It wasn't a pretty sight.

A few years later, when Mrs. Pinkerton was less angry about Wiley being gone and she had had time to start missing him something bad, she told folks that he'd been in the garden that day gathering flowers for her.

"Wiley Pinkerton was such a romantic at heart, girls," she'd say with a tear in one eye.

In truth, no one could remember Wiley ever saying or doing anything romantic in his entire life. Other than cleaning teeth and holding the No-Name Tavern's unofficial record for longest belch, Wiley Pinkerton was a regular guy who didn't care much for flowers, love poems, or Hallmark cards.

Allison used to wonder why folks didn't say anything about the new story being so different from the old one, but now—after Mel and Ma and Daddy and the things that happened with Jacob—she understands. It doesn't really matter how Mrs. Pinkerton remembers her husband. Everyone changes the way they see the past at some time or another. It's just something you got to do to make moving on a little bit easier.

As Cottonwood Drive pulls away from town, sycamore trees crowd both sides of the road—thick and green and huddled close together. Allison looks up at the late-afternoon sky. Gray white clouds stretch across the treetops like pulled cotton, and the moisture in the air turns some of the leaves black.

Soon the road seems to give up on the idea of going any-where at all, and it becomes narrow and rough from neglect. If Allison hadn't been here a thousand times before, she'd think she was lost for sure. But right when most people would turn around, the road spills into a clearing that serves as the only cemetery in Meridian.

Marble slabs and stone markers cover the uneven field. Some even date back to the early 1800s, a fact that Allison knows from all her visits to Mel. She and Daddy used to walk past dozens of tombstones before finding her sister's place.

She wasn't far from Lt. James Riley, 1896–1917, and Baby Hawks, who died at three weeks old in 1809.

Sometimes days and even weeks go by before Allison gets that strange feeling in her stomach from missing Mel—like an elevator dropping so fast you almost believe you can fall up. But not a single day passes without some memory of her sister. On the swing that hung from the oak tree in their backyard. At the piano during lessons with Ma. In her room playing with Blue Lizzy, her favorite doll. Or just the mental image of her name carved into that cold black stone:

# MELANIE CARMEN BURKE
## BELOVED DAUGHTER AND SISTER
### 1991–1998

Allison has that feeling now as she digs her fingernails into the steering wheel for support. But she knows better. Real pain always sneaks up on you, and there's no bracing for that.

Her stomach starts to settle back down as she pulls into the parking lot of Cicely's Funeral Home—an unremarkable building of worn, almost colorless brick. A handful of cars are parked near the side entrance, including a police car, but otherwise the place is empty.

Allison has been thinking about her friends for most of the drive. She remembers how the six of them were inseparable. How they helped one another get through those years with Jacob, when the world seemed to turn upside down.

It has been strange remembering so much so fast. For five years Allison has been trying to forget, trying to put them out of her mind because she had to. Some memories just hurt too much.

She knows that killing Jacob was the right thing to do, but

there are days when the guilt presses down so hard on her chest that she can't breathe. She took a life. What if that makes her as bad as Jacob somehow? What if that's the reason he killed their parents that day? He could have overheard their plans to burn down the camp. Or maybe he figured it out from studying their dreams. He had said someone would betray him.

Despite the rush of painful memories, Allison is curious about who else may be coming back for the funeral. She has been imagining how each of them received the news of Harold's death. David—the first boy she ever had a crush on—reading the e-mail on a computer at school. Sitting perfectly still and thinking about Jacob's promise. Maybe thinking about her, too. Ike checking it on his phone and feeling the receiver almost slip out of his hand. Emma finding a quiet place—an empty park bench or a library cubicle—and waiting until no one else was around before reading the printout several times. Digesting each word. And Jade skimming it at home—angry enough to tear her computer to shreds.

Allison's legs feel stiff as she gets out of the car. The air is crisp to the point of stinging, and mist dampens her face. She adjusts the maroon scarf around her neck without thinking.

Right now the loose gravel on the ground makes each step feel like Allison is moving through mud. Thick and heavy. She is almost at the side door of the chapel when she hears several low, somber tones behind her.

She turns around.

At the far end of the lot a man wearing a wide-brimmed hat and a black overcoat leans against a car. Only his purplish lips are visible as he presses them against the mouthpiece of a flute. The silver instrument is dull, and it seems too small for his thick, knotted fingers.

Sure, it's possible that Allison didn't notice the rust-colored

car at first—old, junky cars don't stand out much to her. Daddy used to work on them in the backyard every weekend. But she is certain no one was standing there before now. One hundred percent certain.

She is still wondering where the man came from when the tune ends and starts all over. This time she sees his upper body moving in small circles with each note. The hollow, breathy sounds are steady like a ticking clock, and they sound somewhat familiar.

Suddenly the melody stops. An uneasy silence follows, and the man lowers the flute.

Though his eyes are still hidden under the rim of the hat, Allison can tell that he is watching her, close. He places the flute on the hood, stands up, and slips his hands into his coat pockets.

"Hello?" Allison asks, and she is surprised by the thin, fragile sound of her voice.

The man doesn't say anything or move an inch. She is about to speak again—this time with her What's-your-problem? voice—when he starts toward her with slow, deliberate steps.

There is something ominous about his body now. He moves as if he knows he can catch her no matter what. The courage drains right out of her, and Allison realizes that this isn't a game.

Maybe he had something to do with Harold and now he's after her, too, she thinks in a panic.

*Crunch, crunch, crunch . . .*

Her heart is racing now. She tries to move her legs but can't at first. It's as if the gravel has become quicksand. She can feel the sweat on the backs of her legs, and her breathing gets short and hard. The scarf seems to tighten around her neck. The man is only a few feet away now, getting closer with each step.

*Crunch, crunch, crunch . . .*

An image of the man who killed her sister—still standing over her lifeless body—breaks Allison from the trance. She gets to the door and yanks it open.

"What the hell," she mutters, keeping her eye on the door as she steps backward into the chapel.

She expects the man to burst through at any second, to grab her, to squeeze the air from her with his knotted hands. Her body tenses. She can feel her throat tighten and her heart crash like thunder. She stops moving, waiting and looking around at the people sitting quietly inside. They don't seem to notice her.

Ten seconds pass. . . .

Twenty . . . forty-five . . .

Sixty . . .

Nothing. The door doesn't rattle or shake or swing open. The man doesn't appear. Everything is quiet.

Allison exhales for the first time in what feels like forever, and once again she looks around Cicely's Funeral Home.

The cool darkness feels safe somehow. *Safer.* It has been a long time since she has been here. At best, the place makes a halfhearted attempt at being a chapel—the two stained-glass windows at the front don't let in much light on cloudy days, and the white benches remind her more of cheap lawn furniture than of church pews. It is quiet except for her thudding heart, and the whole place smells of old things, mothballs, and layers of dust.

The chapel is mostly empty. An older woman sits near the front. Her shoulders are straight and hard, not curled forward in grief, and Allison wonders if that is Harold's foster mother, Ms. Wilton. Three other people are in the front row, two dark-haired girls and a tall boy with narrow shoulders. Allison immediately thinks of Jade, Emma, and David. *They've come*

*back too,* she tells herself, but she isn't sure. She hasn't seen them in so long that she's afraid to go up there. Sheriff Cooper stands at the back. He hasn't changed one bit since her days in Meridian. He's almost as round as he is tall, and his stomach still pushes out against his brown uniform as if it's ready to make a break for it. Sheriff Cooper nods to Allison, and she smiles back—not as a greeting or because she's happy to see him. She's definitely *not* happy to see the man who shoved her and her friends into police cars five years ago and shipped them to different parts of the country. No, her feelings about Sheriff Cooper fall somewhere between hating his guts and hating his guts, but she smiles out of relief—relief, perhaps for the first time in her life, that a cop is nearby.

Allison doesn't have any more time to wonder about the people in the front row before the side door swings open with a swoosh. There is a flash of white light. Allison squints, and her stomach seems to drop to her knees.

It takes a few seconds to realize who's there. It's not the man from outside, the man who moves like a hunter of people. It's Ike Dempsey, breezing toward her with a swagger. His bright orange hair sticks up like he just rolled out of bed, and his blue eyes remind her of the Carolina skies in springtime. Ike's face is still narrow and kind and sprinkled with freckles, and he walks right up to her as if no time has passed since they last saw each other.

"You just gonna stand around all day or what?" he asks with a smirk before plopping into the nearest bench.

Allison sits next to him, still a bit shaky and dazed from the scare. She also can't believe her eyes. Ike Dempsey. After all the time she spent trying to forget, she started wondering if her old life didn't exist at all, and now it's only six inches away. She wants to poke him in the shoulder—just to be sure he's really real—but instead she blurts out, "Did you see that guy outside?"

"What guy?"

"In the parking lot . . . by the crappy car? I saw him after I pulled in."

Ike shakes his head, and Allison can tell from the look on his face that he thinks she's one step away from the loony bin. But instead of asking her what kind of medication she's on, he whispers, "This totally sucks."

"What?"

"Having practically no one show up," he says, looking around the room and fidgeting in his seat. "How do you think Tom Sawyer would've felt if only seven people showed up to his funeral?"

Allison can tell that Ike is just talking foolish to hide his nerves, but she understands. She hasn't felt right ever since being back in Meridian—the town circle, the cemetery, the man in the parking lot, and even this cheap funeral parlor. It all feels a bit unreal.

And dangerous.

"At least we're here," she offers, but Ike only shrugs.

Allison glances around the chapel and realizes that he's right. More people should be here—crying or blowing their noses or falling over with grief. Sad music should be playing in the background. Instead the building is quiet as a library.

Allison wonders about her own funeral. With Mel and Daddy and Ma gone, who would show up? Heather would find a way to get there. Allison spends most of her meaningful time with Heather—after school at the mall or just hanging around Insomnia, the wannabe Starbucks on Kingston Street. Bo works there. He may not be the sharpest knife in the drawer, but he can kiss in a way that warms your whole body. During breaks they hang out in the back, kiss, share cigarettes, and sip from their free café mochas.

Yeah, Bo would probably make it to her funeral, but

Allison doesn't think he'd miss her for long. Sure, his touch makes her happy, and she likes the way he kisses deep, because you have to be completely in the moment for that kind of kissing. But Bo isn't her forever someone. From their very first kiss she has known something is missing. Some feeling that should be there.

Maybe Sheriff Cooper would show up to her funeral, she considers next, but no one else from Meridian, that's for sure. She can picture Mr. and Mrs. Packer wearing black and sitting by her coffin, but she can't imagine them crying. Not that they wouldn't be sad. Allison is pretty sure that Mrs. Packer and Brutus Packer Jr. would miss her. But being sad and weeping from real pain are different things.

No, Allison can't think of one person who would cry hard, painful tears for her like she has for Mel, and that makes her realize something: She's no Tom Sawyer. She would never risk going to her own funeral.

It'd be way too depressing.

A tall man in a flowing black gown appears from a small door at the front of the chapel and approaches the podium. The yellowish wood of the coffin seems cheap and flimsy to Allison. Next to it, on a small table, there is a black-and-white photograph of Harold.

She recognizes the smile on Harold's face. He would get that expression after scurrying up trees faster than anyone else. That's when he was happiest. Away from Jacob and his words . . .

"The outside world knows only corruption and intolerance, violence and hatred," he preached. "We have chosen a different path. A divine path. Most other folks don't understand, as we do, that the time is near, that every hour, every minute, every second, it gets closer. And we need to prepare. We need to distinguish ourselves from the lot, to

show our readiness to be leaders in the next life."

Allison tries to push Jacob's voice out of her head. The rise and fall of it, the changing rhythms . . . it has a way of sticking with you. Sometimes she hears him in her dreams, as if he's lying right next to her, whispering.

"We are gathered here today to mourn the loss of Harold Crawley," the preacher begins flatly, as if he's reading from note cards for the first time. "It always seems particularly sad when a young person dies. But . . ." The preacher pauses to look out at the group.

"But let's face it," Ike whispers, mimicking the preacher and leaning close to Allison. "You're all going soon. So get used to it."

Ike laughs nervously, but Allison can't bring herself to join in. Some things cut too close to the bone for laughing. She looks at the preacher again, pretending to listen, but instead of his voice she only hears Jacob's final promise:

"In five years' time, your greatest fear will consume you. It will rob you of your last breath."

For the first time all day Allison remembers her vision of Harold in black green waters. Screaming where no one could hear. Drowning.

What if Jacob is responsible somehow?

No, Allison tells herself. It's not possible. Jacob's dead. Someone else drowned Harold and dragged him into the tobacco field. Someone brought him to Meridian so that Allison and the other survivors would come back. That must be it.

But why?

The service ends as quickly as it began. The preacher makes the sign of the cross to no one in particular and retreats to the door at the front of the chapel. Everything gets quiet, until one of the girls in the front row steps into the aisle. It's Jade Rowan. Her raven hair has streaks of blue, matching her

eyeliner and nail polish, and the silver rings on her hands make them look thick. Her black skirt stops several inches above her knees, and she wears high black leather boots. She walks right up to Allison and Ike.

"Hey." Her voice is softer than her look, and this reminds Allison of the Jade she knew from five years ago. Quiet, scary smart, and never far from a piano. She liked Beethoven and Liszt the best. Big pieces with big sounds. Even back then Allison could tell that Jade enjoyed shocking folks. No one could believe such a tiny body could make so much sound, and almost every jaw in Jacob's congregation dropped clear to the floor the first time she played.

Allison doesn't know what to say, so she gives Jade a hug. Wrong move. She can feel Jade's body get stiff, and Allison lets go. She's not sorry, though. It feels more right than talking.

David Holloway and Emma Caulder are right behind Jade. Emma stands back from the rest of them. Her thick glasses seem too wide for her face, and she mostly stares at the floor. Her bangs cover her forehead like one of those soapy curtains at a car wash, and her baggy black sweater gives her body a shapeless quality. Under it she wears a loose black dress that hangs to the floor.

"Hi," David says hoarsely, and his voice sends a chill down Allison's back.

David is taller than the rest of them by at least six inches, and Allison has to tilt her head to see his hazel eyes with golden flecks. He has wavy brown hair and a narrow nose that makes his face look serious but not too serious. He loosens his tie and then lets his long arms fall to his sides. He's uncomfortable, not just because no one knows what to say to one another, but because his suit is way too small. The jacket sleeves stop a couple inches above his wrists, and the collar of his shirt appears to be strangling him. But this only

makes him more cute, Allison thinks. More handsome.

"I gotta get out of this damn thing," David says to every-one. "I haven't worn it in two years."

"Let's go. I have some booze back at the hotel," Jade pipes up. "I say we drink."

"Hell yes," Ike chimes in, and Allison can feel him stand-ing close to her, his body almost touching hers.

"Dave and I will lead the way," Jade continues. "We're stay-ing at the Winds. Room twelve."

*Together?* Allison practically blurts out, but she manages to keep her mouth shut. Thankfully. Allison didn't think much about where she'd stay once she got to Meridian. She didn't know what to expect—if anyone else would show up to the service or if she could find out more about Harold's death here. She dreaded the idea of coming back and didn't want to think about staying. That changed once she saw David—though she sure doesn't like the sound of Jade's "Dave and I," as if they've been planning a vacation to the Bahamas.

Before anyone else can speak, Sheriff Cooper's big belly pushes its way into their circle.

"It was nice of y'all to come," he says in a strained whisper, as if to remind them that they're in a chapel. "I'm sure Harold would've been very appreciative." Sheriff Cooper squints with each word, and Allison wonders if he needs glasses. He hesitates before adding, "Are y'all planning to stay around long?"

"Why the hell would we do that?" Jade snaps before turn-ing to David. "Let's go."

Jade doesn't wait for a response before storming toward the side door. She slaps it open with both hands and disap-pears into the parking lot. The sheriff's face gets slightly red, but whether it's from embarrassment or just being plain annoyed, Allison can't tell.

"Well . . . ," he begins again, "I've gotta tend to Ms. Wilton."

With that, Sheriff Cooper steps over to Harold's foster mother. She hasn't moved since Allison's arrival, but when he puts his hand on her shoulder, she bows her head and starts to weep quietly.

"Do you guys need a ride? We all came from the hotel together," David says to Allison and Ike, but she wonders if he's really just asking her. He still has that sweetness that made her want to kiss him a long time ago—one summer afternoon in the old tree house.

But before she can respond, Ike says, "No, that's cool. I'll go with Allison. And Emma, you can come back with us if you want."

"Didn't you drive here yourself?" Allison snaps.

"No," Ike replies, unfazed. "I took a cab from the train station. Besides, I think it's better to travel in packs."

Outside the mist has gotten thicker and colder. Allison looks around for the man with the flute but doesn't see him or the rust-colored car anywhere. This doesn't make her feel any better, though.

She has never been comfortable with disappearing acts.

Jade's red Jeep is idling by the exit, and she honks twice, leaning partway out of the window. David turns to Allison one more time.

"See you there, right?" he asks.

"Yeah, do you want my cell—"

"There's no reception."

"What?" Ike blurts out, taking the phone from his back pocket and checking for himself.

"Jade and I haven't been able to get a signal anywhere in town," David adds.

Allison glances at her own cell phone. Nothing.

"This totally sucks," Ike says. He steps away from them,

holding up his phone, still looking for reception.

Jade honks again.

"I better go. See you there," David says to Allison before jogging to the passenger side of the Jeep, pulling himself inside, and speeding away in a cloud of gray dust.

The sound of the Jeep fades away almost as quickly.

Ike snaps his phone closed and pauses.

"So . . . ," he says, looking at the Barracuda in the center of the lot. "That must be yours."

"Yep," Allison says absently. She isn't in the mood for old-car jokes right now, so she doesn't encourage him. Even though her head is spinning with thoughts of David and the strangeness of seeing all her old friends, there is something she has to do first. Something that can't wait.

Allison walks past her car toward the cemetery. The sign at the entrance reads: REMEMBER. But she doesn't think that needs much reminding, though. It's forgetting that's the hard part.

"Where are you going?" Ike calls out.

Allison turns partway around and sees him standing there with his palms up, as if he's about to catch something. Emma waits behind him, looking at her feet.

"To see my sister," Allison says.

# 4
# BLOOD ATONEMENT

Mel's grave is just like Allison remembers it. She was worried that it might be overgrown with weeds or wildflowers, but the gardeners here keep the grounds up nice. They're a lot cleaner than Allison's room at the Packers' house, that's for sure. Mel's name, etched in white against the black stone, is clear as crystal, not scratched up or faded like on some of the older graves, and there are even a few fresh flowers by the headstone.

It doesn't feel right having Ike and Emma standing behind her. Ike fidgets like he has to pee, so Allison cuts the visit short. *I'll come back,* she says to herself and to Mel. *I promise.*

With that, she leaves the cemetery.

Allison is still annoyed with Ike. He's acting like there's something between them, like he did when he gave her that dreamcatcher years ago. He's acting like a boy with a crush.

*Maybe I'm no better,* Allison admits to herself. It took her less than one tenth of a second to get a butterfly stomach in front of David and to think about the day that they almost kissed. Allison isn't sure if those feelings and daydreams are love. Maybe loving someone is natural as the way a person laughs. It comes from somewhere inside, and you just can't change it.

Allison unlocks the car. Emma climbs into the passenger seat, and Ike slides into the back. In the rearview mirror Allison can see him fidgeting again—his head nodding as if music were pumping through the speakers. Allison wonders if

he is ever still, but from the looks of it, she doesn't think so.

They all stay quiet as Allison starts up the car. Gravel grinds beneath the tires as they pull away from Cicely's Funeral Home and start down the rough, uneven path toward the highway. Emma folds her pale hands in her lap. Her shoulders curl slightly forward, and she seems to be studying something on the floor.

"So, Emma . . . ," Allison begins after a few minutes, though she still isn't sure what to say. "How are things going?"

Ike laughs, and pretty soon Allison and Emma join in. Maybe it's the ridiculous question or the weirdness of being back in Meridian or not knowing whether to be sad or scared because of Harold's death. Allison isn't sure, but it doesn't matter. The laughter feels good.

It *sounds* good too.

"Things are fine," Ike says through a cough. "I've spent five years in Cults Anonymous and haven't missed a meeting. Of course, my sponsor tells me that I get a little negative when I talk about the end of the world. But other than that, I'm fine. . . . How are you?"

Emma covers the smile on her face with both hands, and she leans back in the seat. Tears gather in Allison's eyes, and she can't remember the last time she cried from something other than sadness.

The laughter fades in a few moments, and though they're silent again for a while, it isn't awkward like before.

"Seriously," Allison tries again, her voice still light from laughing. "What are you up to now?"

Emma begins tentatively, like a turtle poking its head out of a shell. She goes to Immaculate Conception High School and spends the rest of her time volunteering for a local library. School is boring. But school and learning are different things, and most of her classes aren't hard at all.

"I mean, we were doing tougher math problems and studying more history and stuff with Jacob than most seniors do at my high school," Emma says with a touch of pride.

Allison remembers all the hours of schooling at the compound. They worked from eight thirty in the morning to three in the afternoon, just like normal school, except with breaks for lunchtime prayers and afternoon meditation. Since there were only six kids, you had to carry your own weight in every class and with every assignment. The Doctor handled all the science and math classes. He was patient and soft voiced and a lot nicer than Jacob when you slacked off. Jacob taught everything else—religion and English and history and philosophy. They read Socrates and Sartre, Dickens and Shakespeare. Basically, they read until their brains hurt, like when you eat ice cream too fast and the chill goes to your head.

*Emma's sure right about one thing,* Allison thinks. *All that work has made high school a breeze.*

"Of course, my foster parents think something's up because I spend so much time away from home," Emma continues. "They figure I'm one step away from being a drug dealer or a prostitute or even a Catholic. I don't know . . . maybe it'd be easier for them if I started dealing drugs. Proof positive that I'm the screwup they always thought I'd turn out to be. Instead, they go to church three times a week to pray for me, and Mrs. Weaver, my foster mom, gets so upset about all the books in my room that she calls them 'the devil's dictation.'"

"The devil's dictation?" Allison echoes incredulously, about ready to burst out laughing again.

"Yeah, it's hard to believe how stupid stupidity really is," Emma says flatly, without a hint of humor. "Basically, she's never read a book in her life, so she figures that anything in them has to be bad."

Emma's world couldn't be more different from Allison's.

Classes and libraries are the last things Allison would talk about. Not that she doesn't do well in school. She got an A on Mr. Bernstein's chemistry midterm, and she hardly gets any red marks on her English papers. But school isn't where her heart is.

It's clear that Emma's big love affair is with the Lynchburg Public Library. Checking out books. Working in the stacks. Ordering from the catalog. Helping the patrons find what they're looking for even when they don't have the first clue. And when it comes to libraries, Emma isn't shy about talking at all.

"'Do you have something on the solar system?' It always starts that way," Emma says eagerly, "but you gotta ask the right questions to find the right books. That's what I do. I help people ask the right questions, instead of telling them what to do."

"You must really like to read," Ike says, and Allison can hear the utter boredom in his voice, as if he'd rather be sentenced to life in prison than spend one hour in a library, let alone work in one.

"I love books," Emma says, then pauses to think. "They're just what they seem to be."

Emma gets quiet, and for the first time Allison understands. Books do have a certain honesty to them. What you see is what you get. And in that way they're everything that Jacob wasn't. . . .

When Jacob caught Allison trying to take the golden box from his room, she expected to go to the Confessional. She had broken one of the rules—well, several rules, actually. She'd lied, pretending to be sick so she could leave evening prayer service early and sneak into Jacob's room. Then she got caught stealing the box where Jacob kept things from each child's past. For Allison, it was her epilepsy medication and a silver

locket with Mel's picture inside. She used to wear it around her neck.

So Allison had committed a double whammy of sin in less than five minutes. She knew she'd have to pay a price, but when she was thrown into the pit, she didn't expect to see the end of the world that day.

Allison hit the dirt floor of the pit. Hard. Suddenly her body burned all over. Hot coals were biting into the palms of her hands, her breasts, her stomach, her knees. Everywhere.

She tried to scramble away from the glowing cinders, half crawling and half rolling until she hit something. A wall. She got to her feet fast. Clouds of hot, strangling smoke were everywhere. She covered her mouth with one hand, but she had already swallowed mouthfuls. She could feel it.

Allison moved along the uneven stone wall, guiding herself with one hand. The pit was getting warmer, and her head started to spin. She stumbled from the dizziness and confusion. Tears streamed down her cheeks.

Then she fell again—this time through an opening in the wall. The air felt cooler here, as if she had fallen into a room or passageway of some kind. She stayed on her knees for a moment, trying to breathe through the smoke and her own coughing.

That's when she heard the growling. It seemed to be all around her—hungry and fierce.

She struggled to see through the grayness, but shadows moved everywhere in the smoke. She had to get away, to run . . . even if it was right into the mouth of a lion.

The growling surged. Allison got to her feet, wobbling unsteadily. But before she could take her first step, something grabbed her hair and pulled. Her head tilted back with a sudden jerk, and an icy coolness slid across her neck, quick and even.

Whatever had grabbed her disappeared in a flash. She fell

to the ground, her body folding in on itself like a discarded puppet. Her heart was sputtering. A palpable fear pulsed through her.

She was okay, though. She could make it out of there, she told herself. She was sure of it.

But something *was* wrong. Allison couldn't get up. She touched her throat where the cold had been and felt a thick warmness spilling down the front of her body. It covered her hands and dripped onto her wrists and forearms.

Blood. Everywhere.

Her throat had been cut, and she was bleeding bad. It was pouring out of her. The room was getting darker, and then she realized something. . . .

She was going to die.

That's the last thing she remembers thinking before passing out. . . .

She woke up in the infirmary, a small room with only two beds and a narrow window that looked out onto the compost heap. It smelled rotten and dirty all the time. Thick bandages were wrapped around Allison's neck, tight enough to make it hard to move, and her throat felt desert dry.

The Doctor was the only one allowed to visit her. He brought glasses of water with colorful straws and books that were more fun than what they read for Jacob—Agatha Christie mysteries and *Dr. Jekyll and Mr. Hyde*.

"Jacob said that you were running away from your penance, that you fell into the ravine," the Doctor said one day, after she had been in the infirmary for more than a week. "Jacob had to climb down there to get you, to carry you back. You hurt yourself pretty bad."

The Doctor cut one side of her bandages with a pair of long, shiny scissors and lifted the bandages off in long strands.

Each one was stained brown and yellow and red. "You shouldn't have done that, Al."

Allison was shocked. *How can someone be so kind and so stupid at the same time?* she thought angrily. The Doctor had taken her to the Confessional in the first place. He knew what had happened. This was his fault too.

The Doctor unwound a new strand of gauze, but before he put it on her neck, Allison pointed to the wound.

"You think I got this from falling?" she said hoarsely, but the Doctor didn't look. He just closed his black eyes for a moment and exhaled.

"Sometimes we have to atone for our sins with blood," he said as he laid the clean dressing on her neck. It felt cool and soft against her skin.

Allison had heard all of this before from Jacob. "Blood atonement," Jacob called it. But the Doctor didn't have Jacob's sinister poetry in his voice. He just sounded a bit sad and lost. Still, Allison couldn't figure out why Jacob had let her live, why he had come so close to killing her, then stopped.

"You're going to be just fine," the Doctor said all of a sudden, but Allison wondered if he was trying to convince her or himself. "Jacob forgives you."

The Doctor finished dressing the wound and left the infirmary without another word. Allison had another twelve days to think about what had happened to her and what the Doctor had said. About what truth she discovered that day.

Before it was all over, Jacob would terrorize all of them. They would all be made to atone with blood and fire. And even though Allison didn't realize it then, she had seen a glimpse of the end of the world that day. The end of the Divine Path. The end that Jacob had been planning for them all along.

# 5

# THE WAKE OF
# HAROLD CRAWLEY

Along Route 54 the sign for the Whispering Winds Hotel can be seen for almost a mile in either direction. It peers above the line of trees like someone looking for a seat in a crowded movie theater. In fact, the sign is the highest point in Meridian, and it is made higher by the fact that the hotel is perched on the town's only hill. *"Hill" might not be the right word*, Allison thinks as she drives up the gentle slope. *"Hotel" might not be the right word either.* Fifteen rooms, no continental breakfast, and no HBO. That doesn't sound like much of a hotel to her, but it's the only place to stay for miles.

The Whispering Winds got its name from the high-pitched whistling sounds that whip through the doors and poorly insulated windows late at night. It doesn't take more than a breeze to get the whole place singing, and the folks in Meridian used to joke that it was near impossible to sleep through the night there.

"It's the perfect place to send your in-laws," Sutter Jones would tell his customers at the pharmacy, and the grown-ups always laughed at that, no matter how many times they'd heard it.

Allison pulls into the parking lot, and even in the twilight the Whispering Winds looks like a dump—cracked, faded paint and a paper-thin rooftop. She wouldn't be surprised if the whole place just fell over one day—exhausted from so many years of neglect.

"Camelot," Ike mutters as they get out of the car. He

stands with his hands on his hips, looking at the flickering neon sign overhead.

They start looking for room 12, but the numbers don't follow any logical order—7, 3, 9, 6. . . . Allison wonders if it is some kind of prank, if some guest—angry and sleepless from the whistling winds—decided to rearrange them one night.

"I thought I sucked at math," Ike mutters without slowing his pace, and Emma falls in step behind him, close enough to be his shadow.

Allison wonders if Ike gives her the butterfly stomach.

Probably.

As they turn the corner, Allison sees the rust-colored car from the funeral, and it stops her cold. That man again. There are no other cars in the lot. Just *his*, parked near a pile of cardboard boxes and a Dumpster. She looks for the man, her heart racing once again.

Nothing.

A light breeze pushes through the trees, and for a second Allison thinks she hears a faint melody. Her throat starts to tighten. Ike and Emma are several doors ahead of her now, and Allison considers yelling out to them. But to say what, exactly?

"Watch out for freelance flute players?"

"Speed kills?"

No, there's nothing to say because there's nothing here, she admits. No melody lingers in the wind. No one leans against the hood. There is only an empty car and some trash.

Ike reaches the other end of the lot and calls out to Allison, "What's up?"

She shakes her head and then hurries past several rooms to catch up: 1, 5, 15, 4. . . .

At the back of the hotel Jade's red Jeep is parked in front of room 12. Like every other side of the building, the room

faces out onto miles of dense trees, and Allison wonders how anyone decided to build something here. So isolated. So closed off from the rest of the world.

Ike knocks on the door twice.

"Enter," Jade says, swinging open the door, and she hands him a beer.

The room is one bad motel cliché after another—a cheap particleboard desk with a matching dresser, gray carpets, floral wallpaper, and a lumpy bed with a multicolored comforter that, as far as Allison can figure, is trying to achieve a whole new level of ugliness. David sits by the nightstand, searching for a radio station on the alarm clock there. The sight of him on the bed bothers Allison. She wonders if maybe he is staying with Jade after all, if they hooked up as soon as they found their way back to Meridian. Or worse—if they reconnected long before now and are together.

Seriously together.

Jade plops down on the bed next to David, leaning against the wooden headboard and stretching her legs out in front of her. She picks up the open beer on the nightstand and takes a long gulp.

As soon as she comes up for air, she says, "There's more in the fridge."

Ike takes a seat in the chair by the desk, and Allison can tell that he's staring at Jade's legs. Emma slinks past them, but instead of getting a drink, she drops into the puffy chair on the other side of the room.

The hissing from the clock radio stops, and a faint song without words crackles through the speaker. It sounds like the jazz that Daddy used to listen to after supper. Every night he'd tune the stereo to the same jazz station, pick up a newspaper, and sit in his favorite chair. Its worn leather was the softest thing Allison had ever touched, even softer than Ma's hair

after it was clean and she'd brushed it straight. Sometimes Allison would sit in his lap, and he'd read something to her before bedtime. But that was before they gave up the house and everything in it to become followers of Jacob.

"This is the only station I can find," David complains softly, and he turns to everyone with an apologetic smile, as if he's to blame for the bad reception. He has changed into a pair of jeans and a black T-shirt that hugs his chest. Allison can see that he's more muscular than she first thought, more muscular than Bo.

"No thanks on the elevator music," Jade says, and Ike laughs in that polite way boys laugh when they're hot for you.

"It's not elevator music. It's Miles Davis," Emma corrects. Her eyes flutter at Ike, but he doesn't notice.

"Who?" Jade asks after another sip.

"Never mind," Emma replies, downcast. With Ike staring at Jade's legs, and the rest of them not having the first clue about Miles Davis, Emma slumps farther into her chair in defeat.

David turns off the radio and stays seated on the bed, close to Allison and Emma. The squareness of his face reminds Allison of those marble statues in museums. Heroes and gods and warriors carved in stone. Handsome. Strong.

"Do you think . . ." Allison's voice cracks, and she begins again. "Do you think it's safe here?"

"In the hotel?" Ike asks sarcastically, his eyes still on Jade.

"No, in Meridian."

"It's safe enough," Jade says sharply.

"How do you know?" Allison asks.

"Look," Jade begins, leaning her head back and glancing at the stained ceiling, "what happened to Harold sucks. But that doesn't mean we have to relive everything. What's done is done."

Allison hesitates. "But what if it's not done?"

Jade shakes her head, then takes a long sip of beer.

Allison looks around the room, but everyone seems far away now. Eyes lowered. Fingers peeling the paper labels off beer bottles. Bodies shifting uncomfortably. No one speaks. Until seeing all of them together again, Allison didn't realize how dangerous coming back to the funeral might be. Maybe she came back to Meridian to convince herself that that danger was just in her head, that everything would be okay and that Harold's death was a strange accident, not a portent. Maybe that's why they all came back. To lie to themselves a little longer. But now she is convinced that something is wrong.

"So . . . ," Jade says, turning her attention to Ike. Her forced, bright tone announces the change of subject. "What's your story?"

"My story?" Ike echoes, as if he'd rather not be distracted from looking up her skirt.

"Yeah, your story," she continues with a smirk, watching him watch her and basking in it. "What you've been up to for, I don't know, the last *five* years? And don't give us some one-minute, G-rated version. We want the real deal."

Ike mutters through some general things at first—about recently dropping out of high school and not getting along with his foster parents. But once Jade rolls her eyes, he shifts gears and starts talking about airplanes.

"I know lots of people who are afraid of flying—afraid because they can't think about anything other than the fall. But all sorts of things can happen at thirty thousand feet," he explains. "Turbulence. Electrical storms. Air pockets. Crying babies. That's the whole point. Flying is about taking chances. It's about letting your feet off the ground."

Ike leans forward in his chair, closer to Jade. "To see people and cars from the tops of buildings is one thing.

But to be so far up that you can look down on clouds—
*clouds*—now, that's just badass."

Almost every part of Ike's life seems to involve defying
gravity. He tells them that he just started working on the tallest
buildings and handling the toughest inclines for Mountain High
Cleaners. That he never loses his footing on a slick surface. Not
even close. He practically started the company, anyway. Well,
his buddy Jake came up with the money and manages the business side of things. But it was Ike's idea to specialize in office
buildings and skyscrapers.

Technically, Ike doesn't turn eighteen for another few
months, but Jake fudged the books so he could get started
early. They first met on the rock-climbing wall at Arnold's
Gym, so Jake knows that Ike can handle standing on a wooden
plank forty stories above the asphalt. That Ike can keep his balance when the winds start whipping at his body. No problem.

He pauses to sip his beer. "The bottom line is—I love every
minute of it."

This should come as no surprise, though, Allison thinks.
After all, his full name—Icarus—is all about flying.

She has never forgotten the story of his parents. He told it
many times when they all lived at the compound. The
Dempseys were traveling in Greece when they first found out
the news: Elena, his mom-to-be, was pregnant. They had been
trying to have a baby for a long time, so this was good news.
His parents were so excited that they wanted to name their son
something important, something special. But they couldn't
make up their minds until the day he was born.

Only when his dad was holding him for the first time,
looking down at that bright orange hair and aerodynamic
body (his father was an engineer before they started living
with the Divine Path), did he name his son: Icarus. The
nurses looked at him funny, but as he told Ike much later,

"It was just the first word that popped out of my mouth."

So that's how Ike was named after some guy in Greek mythology who liked to fly. Apparently, Icarus flew so high that he almost touched the sun—before the wax on his wings melted and he fell into the sea and drowned.

Allison doesn't like flying herself. She'll do it, but she'd rather be behind the wheel of a car, where you can change course with just a turn and where the tires never leave the ground. Driving is all about taking control—leaving when you want, going where you want, and stopping when you want along the way.

Right now Allison wants David. To talk. She wants to ask him about *his* life and all the missing time between them. But not here, not in front of everyone else. She tries to imagine what his voice sounds like up close in the dark—when you're talking to someone in sweet whispers and you can smell the mix of soap and sweat on his body. The good kind of sweat.

She also wants to know where he's sleeping tonight.

But before Allison has a chance to ask David anything, Jade decides to talk about her busy social calendar—though Allison can't remember anyone asking.

"My boyfriend back in the city doesn't like heights. He's kind of a wuss that way. But Silo isn't much better. . . ."

By "the city," Jade means Washington, D.C. By "boyfriend," Jade means one of three guys who seem entirely interchangeable in that department—Gene (a high school senior whose biggest claim to fame is a television commercial he did for Tide detergent at the age of seven), Silo (a violinist who played a concert with Jade last year and sneezed during the finale), and Danny (who lives in "the city" and supports himself by working as a supermarket cashier).

Jade doesn't talk much about school or her family up in Washington. She doesn't mention best friends, favorite

movies, or annoying foster brothers. From the sound of it, you'd think she does only one thing—juggle guys. And as Allison watches how the names of Jade's boyfriends deflate Ike like needles in a balloon, she can tell that Jade has a serious talent for juggling.

Ike slumps back in his chair and grabs another beer. He takes longer swigs now as he listens to stories about Danny's narcolepsy and the time Gene got caught smoking a joint during lunch break at their high school. Allison listens too, but all she hears is a girl who knows how to perform—hiding behind funny stories and a tough attitude, talking without really saying anything.

Allison wonders if guys, like Ike, find her mysteriousness as sexy as her clothes. But Allison would rather get a glimpse of the real Jade. She has had enough of fast-talkers to last a lifetime.

"Yeah," Jade continues, "Gene doesn't seem to be able to do *anything* without some pot. Being mellow is, like, his whole thing—"

"Do you love any of them?" Emma blurts out, and everyone turns to her, surprised.

The words don't sound mean, but they stop Jade in her tracks. There is something about the sincerity of Emma's voice that sucks the air out of the room. She could have asked if Jade was just having sex with them, if it was nothing more than hormones and feeling good. Anyone could understand that. And Jade would probably have answered in her cool, hip, self-assured way. No sweat. But Emma asked about Love with a capital *L*. She said "love" like someone who has read every fairy tale ever written and is waiting her turn for castles and princes and white horses.

"I . . ." Jade hesitates, and the performer in her falters.

Allison completely understands. Love, with or without a

capital *L*, isn't the stuff of casual conversation. One day you have it, and you're driving everybody else crazy from showing it off too much—like Heather did when she was all over her first boyfriend before he dumped her for some theater chick at school—the next day it's gone. Someone steals it or you lose it. That's something Allison has learned. You can lose love just as easily as car keys or a cell phone. Some boyfriends cheat. Some mothers run away. But getting back lost love . . . well, that'll probably break your heart, Allison thinks—whether it's in little bits over time or all at once.

Jade finishes the rest of her beer in one fast chug and slaps the empty bottle on the night table. Her blue fingernails shimmer in the light. "What the fuck, Emma? We're just hanging out."

With that, Jade springs off the bed and grabs another beer from the fridge. Everyone is silent, and this is the first time since getting to the hotel that Allison can hear the whistling winds. They don't sing at all, she realizes. They start as a faint howling through the door—long, sustained, unnerving—and they get louder and louder, until you think you can't stand hearing them anymore.

And then they stop. All of a sudden.

This time the quiet in the room is nothing more than a pause before the next howl gets going. A chill runs up and down Allison's arms.

"So much for sleeping tonight," Ike mutters, but he says the words while staring at Jade, and Allison doubts that he's thinking about the whistling winds at all.

"Maybe . . . ," David begins tentatively, and stops to clear his throat. "Maybe we should have a toast or something for Harold. I mean, that's why we're here."

He holds up his beer, and everyone else does the same; even Emma grabs one of the empty bottles next to her.

"To Harold," David says, his voice kind and sincere, and each of them echoes the same before drinking.

Allison wonders what Harold would have been like after all these years—probably as different and awkward as everyone else tonight. Trying to move on changes a person, and that's what they've been doing. They've been living new lives with new families and new friends. They've been trying to forget the Jacob part of their past, but here they are. In Meridian all over again. It's like stepping into a time machine that only takes you back to the worst moments in your life, Allison thinks.

"So, are you staying a little while?" Ike asks Jade with a slight smirk on his face. "I hear the Meridian Cult Museum is worth a visit."

Jade holds the beer bottle close to her lips and blows into the rim until it wheezes like a foghorn. "Hell no. I'm outta here first thing tomorrow."

"You're leaving?" Allison asks, surprised.

"Ye-ah." Jade drags out the word as if she just heard the stupidest question in the world.

"What about Harold?"

"What about him?"

"Don't you think . . ." Allison hesitates, screwing up the courage to ask the question on her mind. "Don't you think it's strange that he drowned? That he died this year—the year Jacob said he would?"

"Not again," Jade mutters.

"You don't think it's strange?"

"He couldn't swim," Jade snaps, before blowing into the bottle again, and Allison can't decide which is more annoying—her smart-ass comment or the foghorn.

"Yeah, but they found him in a tobacco field," Allison presses.

"Whatever."

"*Whatever?*"

Jade leans forward aggressively. "What are you planning to do—make a vacation out of it? Or do you just want to hang out long enough to hook up with Dave?"

Allison can feel her cheeks burn with embarrassment, but she's not going to take the bait, she tells herself. She knows girls like Jade, always trying to impress guys with a big attitude and a short skirt.

"I think we should ask around a bit," Allison says, looking at everyone but Jade. "Find out what Harold was doing back here. If anyone had seen him around—"

"What for?" Jade snaps.

"Well . . ." Allison hesitates. "To be sure that Harold's death was an accident."

"O-kaaaay," Jade says, glancing at Ike and David. "You do realize that this isn't an episode of *CSI*, right?"

Allison shoots her a hard look before tuning to Ike, who is still slumped in the rickety desk chair by the fridge. "How did you find out about Harold?"

"What?" Ike asks, shifting uncomfortably in his seat.

"How did you hear about his death?"

"Look, I still can't believe my cell phone doesn't work—"

"Ike!"

"I don't know," he says. "I got an e-mail. A newspaper article."

"Forwarded from a stranger, right?" Allison turns to Jade. "What about you?"

Jade doesn't answer, but David does. "That's how I heard."

"Ditto," Emma says.

Allison faces Jade. "Do you think that's just another coincidence?"

Jade shrugs, her confidence fading.

"Whoever sent them wanted us to come back—"

"Wait a minute," David interrupts, moving toward the edge of the bed, closer to Allison and the puffy green chair that seems to be swallowing Emma. "You think someone wanted us *here*?"

Allison nods, looking at David's eyes. She sees a tiredness there that makes her wonder if the same kind of guilt keeps him up at night too. The winds start howling again, louder than before, and the sound is almost piercing. Ike marches over to the door and slams on it with the palm of his hand.

"Shut up!" he yells, before turning around to face Allison. "So, what are you saying?"

"They're coming true, aren't they?" Emma blurts out, using the thick arms of the chair to pull herself forward. "All the things Jacob said. They're going to happen to us."

"Bullshit!" Jade snaps.

"Why is it bullshit?" Emma asks. "Because you'd rather drink?"

"Now, that is the first good idea you've had all night." Jade reaches for the drawer of the nightstand and pulls out a bottle of tequila.

"What are we going to do?" Emma asks, her voice tense and high.

Allison wants to say something to Emma, to everyone, but she doesn't know what. Sometimes there just aren't words for things.

"What are we going to do?" Jade echoes as she takes out several plastic cups from the same drawer. She then opens the bottle and starts pouring. Allison can smell the sourness of the tequila almost immediately. It reminds her of Mexican restaurants and greasy fried beans.

"I'll tell you what I'm going to do," Jade continues as she passes around the cups. Even Emma takes one. "First I'm going to get drunk. Then I'm going to get the hell out of here

tomorrow. I've spent too much of my fucking life thinking about God and Jacob and the end of the world. Not anymore."

Jade holds up a cup and takes the shot fast. Ike follows. Allison looks at David for a moment, and his eyes narrow. Allison drinks. The tequila burns her throat, and she sticks out her tongue from the sourness.

"Ugh." Allison shudders.

"Damn, I forgot something," Jade says as she gets off the bed and steps over to her suitcase. "Gene got me all this stuff as a going-away present," she explains, taking out a bag with several limes and a saltshaker.

She smiles and starts pouring the second round.

Eventually Allison loses count of the shots and the hours. It's nice to be so close to old friends, she thinks. To listen to everyone laughing and telling stories. To be surrounded by the people who understand what it was like with Jacob, who live with the memories of what happened. Even Emma is drinking—reluctant at first and then eager, like she's racing someone.

Soon the room gets dark. The low-watt lightbulbs seem to get weaker as the night goes on, and without wanting to, Allison can feel herself being pulled into sleep. The voices around her fade. . . .

She wakes up, startled. The light still glows, but no one is moving. Jade and Ike have passed out on the comforter of the bed. Their bodies face opposite directions, and Ike's hand touches her ankle. David is stretched out on the floor beside the bed. Allison slumps in the puffy chair. She glances around for Emma but doesn't see her. Everything gets dark again. . . .

Later the howling winds half wake her. They seem distant and close all at once. As she listens, they remind her of fire

engines. The Packers live near a firehouse, and Allison has gotten used to the way sirens start far off and get louder before dropping away.

Soon the howl changes into a melody. A hollow, breathy tune.

Allison is almost certain that it's the sound of a flute. . . .

# 6

# THE WATERLESS WELL

*The horse looks as dusty as the road. Its rider slumps forward in the saddle, and the reins dangle loosely from her pale white hands. The gray sky overhead rumbles with storm clouds. It is a mean, hungry sound.*

*Then a flash. Fire from the sky, scorching the rider's face. Her skin burns red, and her eyes go coal black. She screams as her body falls hard to the ground. Smoke rises from the empty spaces where her eyes used to be.*

*She screams again, but the sound is swallowed by thunder.*

*There is no rain, just dryness and crying without tears. The ground shakes—*

Allison wakes with a jolt. David is right in front of her, holding her hand. Stubble dots his chin and the sides of his face. Ike stands next to him, and his orange hair is even more disheveled than the day before. Jade hovers behind them, holding her forehead with one hand.

"Are you okay?" David asks. "You were shaking."

"I . . ." Allison tries to get up, but her head is still spinning from the seizure. She can taste blood in her mouth. "I'm fine. I just need my pills."

"Pills?" Jade's voice is as heavy as her eyelids.

"They're in my bag. In the car."

"I'll get them," David says, and he hurries out the door before she can say thanks.

Allison leans back in the puffy chair and closes her eyes to

ease the dizziness. Her head throbs—some from the seizure, some from the tequila.

"I need an Advil," Jade mutters as she lumbers toward the bathroom. The faucet turns on with a snap, and Allison can picture her drinking from the spout.

"So . . . ," Ike mumbles, his voice hoarse and sleepy, "what happened?"

Allison opens her eyes and sees him sitting on the very edge of the bed, his feet tapping quietly against the floor and his fingers twitching.

"Sometimes I get the shakes when I dream. That's all."

"Like you used to for Jacob?"

Allison tilts her head back and exhales. "I guess. . . ."

All of the children met with Jacob in the early morning. He would come into the cabin and wake them with a start. Before sunrise. Before any of the adults were up.

"Rise," his voice boomed. "It's time to reveal what you've been seeing in your dreams. Every detail. Every image."

Then Jacob brought them to the waterless well—one at a time. The stone well had been there long before Jacob came to Meridian, but no one could get any water from it. Not a drop. It was just a dry hole in the middle of camp—a dry hole that made most folks thirsty. The way seeing something you don't have makes you want it even more.

"Close your eyes, Allison," Jacob began with a soft, sleepy voice. It was cold and damp in the early mornings, Allison remembers, but Jacob never seemed to notice. He was always warm enough for ten people. Sweating in his white linen suit as he spoke in front of the congregation. Turning red in the coolest weather. And fanning himself as he taught school. "I want to hear about your dreams."

Jacob asked Allison to talk more than anyone else, especially

after her seizures. Her dreams were the most vivid then. Sounds and smells and faces. They were so real that sometimes Allison worried about getting lost in them forever. About never waking up.

That's why Jacob took away her medication. He wanted those dreams to continue. He was most interested when they were violent—filled with blood and fire, shadows and pain. Jacob's yellow eyes glistened when he heard these visions—that's what he usually called them, "visions." Every once in a while he'd touch her forearm or her knee. His hands clammy and moist with sweat. Allison wanted to pull away, but she was too afraid of what might happen.

"Praise be," he'd mutter before removing his hand and walking quickly to his cabin. "Praise be."

Even the memory of those words make Allison's chest feel tight.

The door of the room opens, and David rushes in with Allison's duffel bag. He wears the same jeans and black T-shirt from last night. His wavy hair is mussed in a way that makes her want to run her fingers through it. Just the sight of him makes her feel better. Calmer. Safer somehow.

"I brought the whole bag," he says, handing it to her.

Allison shuffles through it quickly, trying to hide most of what's inside. She doesn't want David to see her private things—underwear, bras, her retainer, which she is supposed to wear at night. *As if wearing braces for nineteen months wasn't bad enough,* she thinks. Allison finds the bottle of Tegretol at the bottom of the bag, takes it out, and cups it in her hand so no one can see the label.

"I should probably get something to eat," Allison says as she stands up slowly.

"Good. I'm fucking starved," Jade blurts out from the bathroom. "There has got to be a Denny's around here."

"Yeah, right," Ike says. "Or maybe a Hooters."

"Do they even serve breakfast?" David asks, playing along.

"Who cares?" Ike replies.

Allison turns to David. Her vision blurs somewhat, but at least she doesn't feel fall-over dizzy. "Where's Emma?"

"She went to her room last night—around two or so." David's body is so close that she could reach out and wrap her arms around him.

"She has her own room?"

"Yeah. So do I . . . I just didn't make it out of here last night."

Allison smiles. She is so relieved that David and Jade aren't together that she could do one of those dorky *Riverdance* numbers that Mrs. Packer likes to watch over and over again on DVD.

Suddenly the vision from this morning flashes before her. The pale woman on a horse. Her black hair falling to her shoulders. Eyes burning from a fire in the sky. That familiar face . . .

Allison shakes her head. "What room?"

"What?" David reaches out to touch her arm.

"What room is Emma in?" Allison's words are crisp, and David pulls back.

"Eleven, I think."

Allison can see the weirded-out expression on his face, but she doesn't have time to explain. She pushes past him and rushes out the door.

There are no whistling winds this morning, no winds at all. The sun is bright when it pushes through the scattered clouds, but it's not high enough to be warm yet. Allison hurries along the side of the building, unsteady and still somewhat off balance. She follows the random sequence of numbers—8, 10, 14, 2—until she finds 11.

She pounds on the door with one hand and uses the other

to lean against it for support. David and Ike rush up behind her.

"What are you doing?" David asks.

"I . . ." Allison thwacks the door again with her fist. "Emma's not answering."

"It's seven thirty," Ike mutters in a voice that sounds like he's rolling his eyes at the same time. "In the morning."

Allison turns to David. "We've gotta get in there."

"Okay . . . but—"

"Please," she says.

"I'll . . . I'll get the manager," David replies before jogging toward the front of the hotel.

Allison knocks on the door again. "Emma?"

Ike exhales audibly, as if he's too annoyed for words, and Allison turns.

"What?"

"Good question," Ike says impatiently. "What are you doing?"

"I'm worried about Emma—"

"Why?" Ike's steady, tired expression doesn't change.

"Why *what*?"

"Why are you worried about her? She probably passed out."

Allison leans back against Emma's door for balance. *Maybe Ike's right,* she thinks. Once Jade brought out the tequila last night, Emma started drinking with the rest of them. But not to fit in or to laugh louder or to make flirting with Ike easier. Allison could tell that Emma was drinking because of fear. Maybe they all were. Something about Jacob's prediction seemed to terrify Emma all over again—as if it was the first time she ever considered that it might come true, that she might be next.

"I . . . I saw her," Allison says. "In my dream."

"This morning?"

"Yeah. She was riding a horse and . . . lightning struck her."

"Lightning?"

Allison can hear the sarcasm creeping back into Ike's voice. She knocks on the door again. "It was Emma's face."

"I don't understand the big deal," Ike says.

"I saw Harold, too," Allison explains desperately. "Before I got the e-mail. I saw him drowning."

Allison's eyes sting with tears, and she turns away from Ike. She doesn't want dreams and seizures and the taste of blood in her mouth. She doesn't want her past to define her entire life—running away only to end up where she started. She has given enough to Jacob in blood and fear, that's for sure. She just needs Emma to be okay. She needs Jacob to be wrong about everything so she can go home.

Ike steps in close to her and tries the doorknob. The door opens slightly, but the chain stops it.

"Emma," Allison calls out, pressing her face close to the opening and trying to see inside.

"Move," Ike commands.

As Allison steps away, he throws his body, shoulder first, into the door. It swings open with a pop, and the broken chain falls heavily to the floor.

The early-morning sun lights only the entryway, leaving the rest of the room dark and shadowy. The curtains hang heavy and thick over the windows. The room smells of a smoldering campfire.

"Emma," Allison calls out as she steps inside.

It takes a few seconds before her eyes adjust and she can see Emma's body on top of the bed, white against the darkness. Emma wears only black panties and a matching bra. Her arms extend out from her sides, and her head is turned away from the door. Her long black hair hides most of her face.

*Ike shouldn't see her like this,* Allison thinks suddenly. He should wait outside. But before she can say anything, he snaps on the light. The weak bulb glows overhead, making everything a sickly yellow color.

"Emma?" Allison asks again, approaching the far side of the bed. "Are you all . . ."

Allison's words get lost in her sudden gasp for air. She can feel herself falling backward, knocking over the frail nightstand and the stack of books on top. She moves back against the wall, and something cracks loudly under her feet. She looks down: Emma's glasses. Ike is next to Allison now. He blinks repeatedly, and she can see the strength leaving his body.

Emma's face has deep, black caverns where her eyes should be. The skin around them is scorched black and red.

Allison's stomach turns as she realizes that the burning smell is from Emma's skin.

"Her eyes," Ike mutters. "They're gone."

# 7

# STRANGERS

From the outside the Meridian Police Station doesn't look much like a police station. You'd walk right past it and never guess. The white pillars and big front porch remind most folks of the South you read about in history books. White masters in rocking chairs, drinking sweetened iced tea and fanning themselves. Slaves working in tobacco fields.

History always seems to be about two types of people, Allison thinks. Those who have power and those who don't.

Apparently the mayors of Meridian used to live in this house until 1981. In that year Kimball King, the mayor at the time, decided it was no longer appropriate for government officials to live in an old plantation house. So he gave it to the police and built a mansion with a swimming pool on the other side of town.

Allison wouldn't have known any of this if it weren't for the newspaper articles on the walls of the lobby, which is actually a den with a fireplace, cloth-covered chairs, and a not-so-comfortable couch. She is waiting for the sheriff to wrap things up with David and Ike and Jade. She wants to keep her mind busy, to stop herself from thinking about what she saw this morning.

Sheriff Cooper's questions weren't all that bad, Allison admits. He didn't act like those cops on television who lose their temper and throw someone against a wall. Sheriff Cooper never even raised his voice. He mostly asked the

basics: "How was Emma acting at the party last night?" "Did she drink?" "What time did she leave y'all?" "What was she wearing?" "Was she upset about anything?"

But with each question Allison kept seeing Emma's unclothed body on the bed, eyes black and empty. Her body laid out like a crucifix.

*Emma.*

At the end of the interview he asked: "Is there anything else you can tell me about her?"

Allison hesitated. In truth, she couldn't think of a single thing. Not a phone number to call or the name of a best friend. Not a story about her new family or a cute guy at school. Nothing. After all these years Emma was just a stranger. They were all strangers to one another.

"She loved to read," Allison said at last. It was the best she could do.

He nodded. "Okay, then. Why don't you wait in the lobby and—"

"Sheriff?"

"Yes?"

"What happened?"

He stepped away from the table and opened the door for her. "We're trying to figure that out."

"Best guess," Allison pressed.

"Pardon?"

"Best guess about what happened?"

"I wish I knew." His voice was flat, almost sad, but his eyes narrowed as if making an accusation.

"You don't think I . . . that one of us—"

"You can wait in the lobby for your friends," he said.

The interview was over.

*Friends?*

Allison should have spit the word back at his pudgy face.

Sheriff Cooper had stolen her friends. He had cut them off from one another and sent them away, as if moving far distances could erase the past. Allison remembers crying herself to sleep for a long time after that. Sure, those tears came for lots of reasons—Daddy, Mel, Ma, and all the things that happened with Jacob. But losing her friends—her best friends— meant that she had no one left in the world.

She was totally alone.

Allison sits on the stiff couch in the lobby, her body still tired from the seizure and from being hungry. She feels a headache building.

"Hey," Ike says as he walks into the room. His voice has lost its breezy quality from yesterday.

"You okay?" Allison asks.

Ike shrugs as he plops onto the couch next to her. She can feel his leg shaking, but neither of them looks at each other. Allison figures it's better this way. It's not easy to look at someone when you're hurting. It makes it harder to hold back the tears somehow.

"Sheriff Cooper thinks one of us killed Emma," Allison says, and the gravity of this accusation hits her for the first time. She could go to jail. She could be sent away from everything she knows—again. No. She wraps her arms across her chest and squeezes tight, trying to stave off the panic.

Ike turns to her, his blue eyes shimmering and intense. "The windows were painted shut," he whispers. "They didn't open in Emma's room. I heard the manager telling the sheriff before we left."

"So?"

"So? The door was chained from the inside, and the windows didn't open. How could we have done it?" Ike's face reddens with frustration. He glances around the room before reaching into his pocket and pulling out a crumpled piece of

paper. "I found this on the floor by her bed."

He hands the paper to Allison, and it feels moist and dirty from being in his pocket. She unfolds it carefully:

And now, behold, the hand of the Lord is
upon thee, and thou shalt be blind, not seeing
the sun for a season. And immediately there
fell on him a mist and a darkness; and he went
about seeking some to lead him by the hand.

Allison knows the story by heart. It was one of Jacob's favorites. Saul, a disbeliever, was traveling on the road to Damascus when God struck him with lightning and blinded him. Three days later his sight was restored, and he converted, changing his name to Paul.

Jacob saw himself as the bolt of light that lifted blindness from his followers. "We have all been blind to the truth at one time or another," he preached. "The truth is painful. It's not something all of us are ready to see. But there comes a day when we must take the road to Damascus.

"We must all be struck down to rise up again. . . ."

Ike sits forward now, watching Allison read. "Do you think it happened like that?"

"Like what?"

"With lightning. The way you saw it in your dream?"

"God doesn't leave notes," Allison mutters drily, trying to mimic Ike's sarcasm, but he doesn't seem to notice.

"Her books," Ike says softly, as if he's talking to himself. "I mean . . . that must be what she was most afraid of, right? Going blind." He pauses, and for the first time his body becomes still.

"I guess."

He doesn't speak.

"What is it?" Allison asks, uneasy about the faraway look in his eyes.

"Ever since this morning I've been thinking about Jacob's promise that we'd all die. Do you remember the day I went to the Confessional?"

For a long time Ike talked about it only in bits and pieces. Then one night he showed Allison the scars. She can still picture the shapes of the burn marks on his arms. They reminded her of constellations.

"Yeah." Allison's voice is soft. There are some things you can't forget.

No matter how hard you try.

Ike ran away from camp—but not for real, not for good. He just slipped out early one morning because he missed things. They all did. So Ike put on his jeans with the secret money pouch, which his mother had sewn there for summer camp years earlier, and he sneaked off to town for all of them. He was going to spend on them the only money he had kept hidden.

For Ike it was baseball cards and rock candy. Allison missed chocolate candy bars and root beer floats—but there was no way Ike could bring back a root beer float. Jade wanted some CDs, even though she had no way to play them. Piano music, mostly, and some Britney Spears. Emma asked for the newest Harry Potter book. And David . . . he didn't want anything. He didn't want Ike to get in trouble.

Jacob caught Ike on his way back from town, his mouth full of rock candy and a bag with goodies swinging from each arm.

Later that day Jacob would reveal that not all of them would be with him at the end. That the six children—all born in the same year—would die in the same year. That their

deaths would signal God's plan for the end.

"On the day that the last of the six shall die, God will destroy the earth and all its wickedness with fire. He will begin again with a new garden and a new paradise. And the Chosen will be reborn as rulers and lawmakers.

"Praise be."

Still chewing candy, Ike stumbled back to camp, Jacob pulling him by the arm until they reached the Doctor's cabin.

"Take him to the Confessional for penance," Jacob ordered, before storming away with Ike's bags.

As always, the Doctor led Ike to the old shed, but this time he didn't speak. Not a word. The only sounds came from the woods and the dried leaves crunching under their feet.

At the Confessional the Doctor turned around and started back toward camp.

"Where are you going?" Ike called out, but the Doctor didn't answer. He just kept walking away.

Ike didn't know what to do, so he reached for the shed door to let himself in. That's when someone grabbed him from behind. A damp rag was pressed against his mouth.

Ike tried to pull it away, but the grip was heavy and solid like stone. A sweet smell filled Ike's nose. He kicked his legs and flung his arms about, trying to break free, but he couldn't breathe. His head started to spin. His arms dropped to his sides. Everything faded away. . . .

Ike woke up inside the smoky pit, cold and dizzy. His naked body strapped to a thick wooden chair—rope tied tight around his wrists and ankles. A hazy light came from the circular hole above him.

"You wish to leave?"

The voice echoed throughout the pit. Then there were footsteps behind him. Getting louder.

And louder.

Jacob passed by the chair so close that he almost bumped into it. He turned to Ike, his face expressionless and distorted in the smoke. A cigarette rested between his lips. The end glowed orange.

Ike had never seen Jacob smoke before. As far as Ike knew, no one was allowed to smoke or drink at the campsite. "One must not pollute the body," Jacob told the congregation often.

"What are you doing?" Ike asked, his voice wobbling with fear.

"I've seen a new vision, Icarus. One that involves a sacrifice—"

"I want my clothes!" Ike yelled, pulling and twisting at the ropes.

"The Divine Path will be consumed in a wall of flame, and I will be betrayed as Christ was by Judas," Jacob continued with steady, calm words. "But you . . . you and your friends will survive. For five years. The rest of us need time—time to prepare for the new world."

With this, Jacob stepped back and disappeared in the smoke. Ike strained to see the orange glow of his cigarette, but that, too, was gone.

"Let me go!"

Ike yanked his right arm. The rope slipped somewhat, but it only seemed to cut into his skin. Then he pushed his feet hard against the floor, trying to knock the chair over. But it wouldn't move. His throat was burning from the smoke, and Ike could feel tears streaming down his cheeks.

"Smoking is bad for you!" Ike screamed. He wanted to say something hurtful, but that was the only thing he could think of through the fear and the anger and the humiliation of being naked.

Jacob chuckled directly behind Ike.

"You're right," Jacob said, his lips inches from Ike's ears,

his breath hot and moist. "I should put this out."

Suddenly Jacob pressed the glowing end of the cigarette into Ike's left forearm. Ike writhed and screamed.

"No!" Ike cried. *"Please . . . stop!"*

Jacob used his other hand to hold Ike's arm in place. The smell of burning flesh filled Ike's nose.

"You tried to fly away, Icarus. On wings of wax . . . ," Jacob intoned as he blew on the tip of the cigarette. Ike watched it glow bright orange again. "This is what happens when you don't listen."

The cigarette burned a new place on his arm, and Ike screamed until his voice went hoarse. . . .

Yes, Allison remembers the story. She remembers Ike's night-mares after that day too. He'd yell in his sleep or start moan-ing real loud, and when he woke up, all he could remember was being burned alive. Sometimes he was trapped in a house fire or a burning building. Other times he was being held over the flames of a campfire.

It frightened Allison to see how much Ike changed after that trip to the Confessional. A week earlier he had given her the orange yellow dreamcatcher. "I made this for you," he said, his smile bright as the sunlight. How he'd found time to make it and where he'd gotten the string, she never knew. But she knew it made her feel special. Sure, she didn't *like* him like him, but it was nice to feel the heat of someone's crush. To think that she could make someone's heart beat faster.

That was special.

But Ike's face and eyes never looked the same after Jacob burned him. They were distant, shaky.

And now Ike looks back at Allison with those same tor-tured eyes.

"Emma's room smelled that way this morning, you know.

Like burned skin," Ike says, swallowing hard. "When I was standing there looking at her, all I could think of was myself. I was more afraid for *me* than I was sad for Emma. Can you believe that?" Ike lowers his head.

"We're all scared," Allison says, and then she realizes this might be her problem too. It's not that Emma was practically a stranger that bothers Allison so much. It's that she wants to *feel* something more for her. All her sadness is mixed with terrible memories and uncertainty. It's mixed with fear, and fear just makes you selfish.

Emma deserves more, Allison admits. A lot more.

"Hey," David calls out as he and Jade step into the lobby.

David is wearing the same jeans and black T-shirt from yesterday. In fact, everyone is wearing the same clothes except Jade. She must have changed before following them to Emma's room. Her short red skirt sparkles with shiny beads, and her black lacy top is almost see-through.

Sheriff Cooper watches for a moment from the doorway before speaking. "Y'all need to stay around for the next few days. You're material witnesses to this crime, and we'll have more questions that need answering. Understand?"

Sheriff Cooper doesn't wait for them to answer. He just hooks his thumbs into his belt and turns slightly when another officer enters the room. This man is tall like David, except with blond hair and blue eyes. He doesn't look much older than seventeen himself.

"This is Deputy Archibald," the sheriff announces. "He's going to take you"—he points to Jade—"and Ike back to the hotel. I'll drive you two," he says, looking at David and Allison.

"Just give me a minute," Sheriff Cooper adds before leaving the room. His footsteps sound heavy and labored as he walks down the hall.

Deputy Archibald opens the front door quickly. "Come on.

Let's go," he says, his voice high and thin like a tightrope.

Jade mutters, "Later," over her shoulder, and Ike quickly follows her through the doorway.

David stands close to Allison now. This is the first time that they've been alone since she got back to Meridian. It is what she has wanted. To be alone with him. To be close to him. But now she doesn't know what to say.

"I need to know something, Allison." David's words break the silence. "The truth, okay?"

Allison nods.

"Who's next?"

"What?"

"In your dreams, which one of us dies next?"

Allison can't believe the question.

It feels as if someone has just kicked her in the stomach and knocked the air right out of her. She looks at David, wishing that her heart didn't change rhythm every time she noticed the sadness in his eyes.

"I . . . I have no idea." The words stumble from her mouth as she steps away.

"What's wrong?" David asks.

*"What's wrong?"* Allison snaps. "What kind of person do you think I am?"

"I—"

"Don't you think that I would have done something if I knew Emma was going to die? Don't you think I would have warned her? Or Harold?"

David lowers his eyes, sorry.

"I didn't mean it that way," he says sheepishly. "I thought you might be trying to protect us, you know? Trying not to freak us out or something."

"No," she mutters. But really, she wants to shake him. She wants to be able to say: "Don't you know *me* well enough?"

But of course, he doesn't. How could he? And this makes her feel hurt all over again.

Before Allison can say anything at all, Sheriff Cooper enters from the hall door. "Y'all ready?"

"Definitely," Allison says fast, without even glancing at David.

Like Jade, she barrels out of the station, not looking over her shoulder to see Sheriff Cooper or David. Right then she misses her car. The freedom to hit the road. To go anywhere. To get as far away as possible.

# 8

# TALKING WITHOUT WORDS

Jade's suitcase is on her bed and mostly packed when David and Allison get there. The hotel's cheap furniture and hideously ugly bedspread aren't amusing now. They're just cheap and hideously ugly. Emma's room was identical to Jade's, and Allison has to work hard not to picture Emma's body on the bed. Her white skin and missing eyes. The horrible smell—

Allison stops. She wants to sit but can't bring herself to use the puffy chair that Emma was on yesterday. It wouldn't feel right, she thinks. It just wouldn't. Instead she stands by the end table. Across from her, Ike leans against the wall, watching Jade pack.

"You sure you have to leave so soon?" he asks.

Jade steps out of the bathroom and shoves a small toiletries bag into the suitcase. "No, I thought I'd hang around until someone burns my eyes out."

"The sheriff told us we have to stay for a while," David says earnestly. He lingers by the open door.

"Well, he can drive his fat ass up to D.C. and arrest me." Jade closes the suitcase and sits on the bed. Like everyone else, she avoids the puffy chair as if Emma were still sitting in it.

"Maybe Jade's right. Why don't we just get out of here?" Ike asks.

*"Thank you,"* Jade replies.

"Do whatever you want, Ike," Allison says more harshly than she expected. She wonders if Ike and Jade think the same

thing that David does, the same thing that Jacob did all those years ago. That Allison can see the future in her dreams. "We can't just go home and pretend none of this ever happened. We all know what this could mean. . . ."

"What?" Ike pushes.

Allison expects Jade to chime in with her trademark rudeness, but instead she is quiet. Her body is still, except for her fingers. They start dancing quietly on her thighs. Some hovering in the air, others pressing into the skin. Jade must be playing some piece of music, Allison thinks. But that's not all. There is something oddly beautiful and sad about those fingers with the blue nail polish. The way they move and stay slightly curved. Any boy could fall in love with her hands, Allison admits.

"Well?" Ike insists. "What could it mean?"

Allison looks up at him. "That Jacob's prophecy is coming true."

*Finally,* Allison says to herself. *Someone said it.* Ike's fear. Jade's attitude. David's hurtful question. Even her own dreams. They're all about the same thing. They're afraid Jacob might be right.

"But what if someone is doing this to make it *seem* that way? I mean . . . what if someone else survived the fire that night? One of the adults," David says thoughtfully, and Allison can tell that he isn't looking for a fight. He has been listening to her. Really listening, she realizes. In a way that no one else ever has. He treats her words and ideas with respect.

She considers his question while wishing that he weren't standing so far away, his loose body leaning against the doorframe. "You mean, to convince the people that Jacob's prophecies are coming true?" she asks. "To revive the cult?"

"I'm still not hearing a good reason to stick around," Ike says.

"Emma." The word slips out of Allison's mouth, and Ike tucks his hands in his pockets.

"Look," Allison continues. "We can't let Jacob's cult start up again, Ike. You remember the things he did. We can't let that happen to anyone else."

With those words Jade's fingers stop moving.

"You can't be fucking serious," she snaps as she stands up and holds out her hands for everyone to see, her fingers spread apart. Most of them are crooked and twisted, and they remind Allison of the old map in her history teacher's class. The parchment cracked and yellow with age. Its texture sturdy and fragile.

"Nothing supernatural did this," Jade continues, her eyes fierce. "Jacob did. Jacob cut Allison's neck. He burned Ike's arm. He almost drowned Harold several times. That's torture, not the hand of God. And the world isn't going to end just because some crazy man said so five years ago!"

Jade reaches for her suitcase again. As she puts her hands against it, she stops for a second. Staring at them.

"I still play, you know. I might even go to a conservatory one day," she says quietly. "They can't move as fast, and they hurt when it gets cold out. But I'll never stop playing. I won't let Jacob take that away from me. . . ."


The upright piano in the main hall was the perfect instrument for the end of the world. Dusty and old and falling apart. Many of the plastic keys were cracked or melted with cigarette burns. A few at the top didn't make any sound at all when Jade pushed on them, but she didn't really mind.

*You hardly play up there anyway,* she told herself.

As far as being in tune . . . well, it wasn't even close. It could still be played, though. You just had to get used to it. Jade always figured the instrument had its own language that way, and that she'd learned it so well that most folks thought she was a native speaker.

The piano made her special at the compound, Jade

explained to them. Everyone got real quiet when she played. Grown-ups talked about her after supper. And old Mrs. Haggerty often took her aside to lament the day she stopped taking lessons.

"My mother always told me I'd regret it," old Mrs. Haggerty said with her wobbly voice.

Blah, blah, blah . . .

There might not have been any music teachers at camp, but Jade wasn't going to stop playing anytime soon. That was for damn sure. This was one thing she could do better than anybody else there. Even Jacob.

And Jade liked it that way.

Her parents did too. They were never much in the talking department. Her father, Bruce Rowan, preferred grunting as his primary means of communication before the days of the Divine Path. While Mrs. R. smiled so often you had no idea what she was thinking. But both of them listened to Jade with a *look, that's my daughter* expression on their faces—especially when the congregation gathered around.

Although being prideful was probably a sin (though Jacob never really talked about that), Jade could tell they were proud. Her father would cross his arms in front of his chest and lean back in a way that made him look like someone who'd just finished eating an enormous meal. Her mother . . . well, she smiled, of course.

And on the days that something deep in Jade's chest hurts from missing her parents, she's glad to know she made them happy at least a few times in her life.

Jacob allowed her to practice every afternoon in preparation for Sunday service. Soon this became Jade's favorite part of the day. For thirty minutes it was just she and the music.

Almost everything else at the camp involved other people— sleeping in one-room cabins, sharing meals, going to classes,

praying. Even the crappers, the outdoor toilets that the grown-ups called privies, were crowded with folks. No, you never had a minute for yourself, Jade remembers. No time to think. To be on your own. To dream about the days before the Divine Path.

Except at the piano.

Jade was practicing Brahms the day Jacob visited. The thick, C major chords of the intermezzo filled the empty hall. They were bright and energetic, but with a touch of sadness, like seeing gray clouds on a sunny day.

She wasn't used to anyone coming around during practice, so Jacob's voice startled her. It made her heart accelerate and her jaw tense. Still, without thinking, Jade kept her hands on the keyboard right where she left off, the way some people use bookmarks when they read.

"I want to speak with you," Jacob said, his voice clashing with the beauty of the notes still hanging in the air.

"Yes, Jacob."

He leaned against the piano, looking down at her. His eyes were yellow, though her mother called them hazel, and his chin came out to a point, making his entire face look like a crescent moon.

"It is about your faith." Jacob paused, and Jade could smell the sweat of his body. It reminded her of hard-boiled eggs. "Recently your voice has been silent during prayer. You don't call out with the others in praise. You don't seem moved by his Word."

Jacob reached down and pressed one of the keys that made no sound.

"Your mind is elsewhere, Jade . . . but not when you play." Jacob lifted his eyebrows and waited in the way that grown-ups wait when they want you to spill the beans about something.

Jade remained silent. Unreadable. She'd learned that from her father.

"Faith is not a gift," Jacob continued. "It is something you

must work at. Like playing Schubert's music."

"Brahms," Jade corrected.

"Excuse me?"

"It's Brahms, not Schubert," Jade said, keeping her voice flat and even.

The half smile on Jacob's face faded, and he stepped away from the piano. "It would be tragic to lose your faith *and* your ability to play, don't you think?"

Jade nodded, and without another word he left.

After that Jacob prevented her from getting anywhere near the piano. New chores filled the late afternoon—sweeping floors, setting possum traps, gathering firewood for the kitchen, and helping David and Ike take garbage to the compost heap.

Jade wasn't asked to play for Sunday services, either. Mr. Jenkins, who could hardly see a thing with or without his glasses, pounded out some hymns, and the congregation sang along. No one seemed to care that he knew only three songs. Worse than that, no one seemed to miss Jade's playing.

At least, no one said anything to her.

Even her mother didn't appear troubled by the change— until Jade complained that it wasn't fair, that she still had faith but didn't want to be a damn phony about it.

*Slap.*

It was the first time her mother hit her.

The shock hurt more than her open palm. Her mother had always been gentle as silk.

"We are doing something far more important here," she told her daughter, without a smile or a hint of compassion. "Don't ruin it with your selfishness and complaints."

She shuffled off to evening prayers, and her footsteps kicked up hardly any dust. That was the first time Jade understood the power that Jacob had to change people.

The next day Jade went by the main hall around the time

she used to practice. She thought Mr. Jenkins might be there, refining the art of wrong notes and crappy playing, but not a single sound came from inside. A lock was on the door.

*What the hell?*

Jade had obeyed Jacob. She did her lousy chores and put off doing the one thing that made her happy. But she hadn't seen this before. None of the other doors on the compound were locked. Everything was open, even Jacob's cabin.

Something about the lock lit a fire deep inside her. She dropped the garbage pail in her hand and hurried around the side of the building. The window on the back left was always stuck halfway between open and closed, and she knew she could squeeze through.

The interior of the hall felt cool, and Jade wiped the sweat from her forehead.

There it was. The piano. Dusty and old and falling apart as always. But it looked different to her now. It was the thing that Jacob had tried to take away from her because . . . because music was more important to Jade than Jacob, the Divine Path, or anything else.

It had become her religion.

She touched the keys, and her fingers came to life. She played the loudest, fastest pieces she could. Beethoven. Brahms. Chopin. Big chords that made the entire piano shake with beautiful fury.

*Anything but Schubert,* she thought with a smile, and closed her eyes to listen. . . .

The lock and chain rattled before the door of the main hall swung open. Jade looked over her shoulder and saw the Doctor standing there. He didn't move. He just motioned to her in the way he always did when it was time to go to the Confessional.

Jade didn't care, though. She closed the lid with the same

care Jacob gave to the Good Book after a sermon. Then she marched right out of the hall and toward the Confessional. She wasn't going to let the Doctor take her there. She wasn't going to let him or Jacob think that she was afraid.

Hell no.

Inside, the Confessional was thick with smoke. The mirrors made the room feel enormous and claustrophobic at the same time. With each step your own reflections seemed to push in around you. Crowding and watchful.

"Hello?" Jade called out as she walked toward the pit.

Her voice echoed below and faded quickly. There were no other sounds. No birds or cicadas singing outside. No hint of the gurgling stream in the nearby ravine. Only the late-afternoon darkness seeped through the walls.

Then Jade heard something sizzle beneath her, like water being poured on hot coals. The smoke billowed up more heavily now. She leaned over the edge for a better look.

Slowly.

Her eyes were stinging from the smokiness when—

A hand latched on to her ankle. It yanked her forward in one violent motion. She tumbled headfirst into the pit. . . .

Jade's head throbbed when she finally opened her eyes. She must have hit the ground hard. The rotten taste of dirt filled her mouth.

She tried to touch her face but couldn't move. Her arms were trapped—buried inside the dirt wall in front of her. She tried pulling them out, but they wouldn't budge. Not an inch. The holes were deep and not much wider than her arms. The muddy soil pressed against her skin.

She couldn't get any leverage to pull away, either. She was on her knees, her chest and the right side of her face against the wall.

Jade wanted to scream and to cry at the same time, but she

was too afraid at first—afraid of drawing attention to herself. She tried pulling away again and realized that her hands were free and uncovered on the other side of the wall. Something cold and metallic was fastened around each wrist, though. Handcuffs or chains of some kind, she figured.

That's when she first heard the sound behind her. Steady, nasal breathing. Someone was watching her, but she couldn't turn her head far enough to see.

"Jacob?" she mumbled.

The sounds stopped for a moment, then continued. This time she could hear feet sliding in the dirt as well. He was moving away from her now. Into another room, it seemed. With one ear pressed against the wall, though, Jade couldn't make out the faraway sounds. She tried to yank her arms free in one big motion.

Nothing.

The struggle only made her feel more trapped.

An icy coldness suddenly touched her hands.

She screamed.

The cold pressed against her fingers and wrists, prodding at first. Someone was trying to grab them . . . trying to hold her still. Jade could feel the tears streaming down her cheeks and chin as she shook her hands. Her mouth still tasted of dirt and smoke.

The strong, icy grip on the other side finally tightened around her right hand. Two hands wrapped around one. Enveloping. Suffocating.

A few seconds passed and nothing happened. Enough time for her to get still, to breathe more easily, to wonder what was happening. Until—

*Snap.*

Her index finger shattered.

Jade screamed so loud she thought her throat was on fire. She pulled and squirmed and yelled: *"No!"*

But the grip on her right hand didn't loosen. He moved to her next finger.

*Snap.*

Each finger. One at a time.

The bones breaking.

*Snap.*

*Snap.*

Not the thumb. Just the fingers.

It stopped. A few seconds passed, and she could feel warm urine spilling down her legs. Her screams had become sobs. Everything became still.

Then the man on the other side of the wall started on her left hand. . . .

Before that day Jade had preferred to talk without words. Maybe she got it from her father. Except she used a piano instead of grunts and disapproving stares. But after that Jade spoke with her voice more, not less. She didn't give Jacob any reason to question her belief. She called out the loudest "Amen's" and "Hallelujah's" at services.

Not from faith. But from anger. From the hope that the force of her unbelieving words would pummel him.

Long after her fingers healed—healed as well as they could—she continued to use words like fists. To lash out first. To keep her distance. That way, she figured, no one could know what you really cared about.

That way, no one could take it away.

"Some*one* is trying to kill us," Jade says coolly as she lifts her suitcase off the bed. "Maybe you're right, Allison. Maybe it's about reviving Jacob's cult and convincing people that the world is about to end. I don't know."

Jade steps past Ike and David and pauses at the door. "But I don't really give a fuck. I'm going home."

"What about Harold and Emma? Don't we owe them . . .

something?" Allison asks, struggling to find the right words, the right reasons.

"Like what? A higher body count?" Jade looks at Ike, but he doesn't respond. "Don't you get it?" she asks all of them. "This is it. This is our chance to get out of here for good. To leave all of this shit behind. The town. The memories—"

"Five years," David says, with his eyes lowered and his shoulders curled forward. "It's been five years, and I haven't forgotten a thing. I mean . . . we killed a man. I know we had to, but . . ." He pauses, looking up. His eyes are watery and distant. "How are we supposed to get over that?"

"Well, hanging around here isn't going to help," Jade says.

"Okay, forget about Harold and Emma." Allison turns to Jade, though she is still thinking about David's words. How true they are. How many times she's wished she could wipe away her past like words on a chalkboard. To erase the guilt and the fear. "Forget about the cult and what it did to us. What about you?"

"What about me?"

"You think you're safe? You think that whatever is doing this won't come after you? That it won't find you?"

Jade adjusts her grip on the suitcase. "I prefer to be a moving target."

"None of us are safe," Allison continues. "Not until we stop what's happening."

Jade exhales but doesn't move.

"Look," Allison presses, and her voice cracks slightly. "Let's find out the truth about what happened. Let's end this."

"How?" Ike blurts out. He has been watching the conversation like someone at a tennis match, and now he shifts uneasily from one foot to the other.

Allison walks across the room to her bag. "I want to talk to this guy," she says, pulling out the newspaper article about

Harold's death and handing it to Ike. The name Marcum Shale is circled at the top.

"I Googled him," Allison explains. "He works at the Meridian Public Library. He might know something about Harold—about why he came back here."

"And if he doesn't?" Ike asks, concentrating on the paper.

Before Allison can answer, a whistling wind starts to push its way through the door, and it howls like a lonesome dog looking at the moon. She waits for it to quiet down.

"I'm not sure." Allison shrugs. "At least it's a start."

"Well, that all sounds like a blast," Jade says as she opens the door. "But no thanks. I'm outta here."

Jade hesitates, and as she looks around at everyone, Allison sees something sad cross her face, something genuine.

"It's been real," Jade says quickly. "Later."

With that, the expression is gone.

And so is Jade.

# 9

# NUMBERS

The Meridian Public Library is connected to the town hall, which is nothing more than a one-room building with wood floors and a portrait of George W. Bush on the south wall. The library building gets used for everything from school bake sales to hoedowns for retired folks. The library itself is L shaped, wrapping around two sides of the town hall. The longer side is almost entirely filled with books about the Civil War. Mr. Beederman, the librarian for more than thirty years, considers the War of Northern Aggression the only real war worth reading about in U.S. history. He also thinks "Yankee" is just about the worst thing you can call a person—that and "liberal."

Since Meridian Elementary doesn't have a library of its own, every kid in every grade has to go to Beederman's Book Barn at some point. That's what most folks call it—the Barn, for short, since the library was originally a stable and it still smells like hay.

The Barn hasn't changed much in five years, Allison observes. The circulation desk is still no bigger than her desk at the Packer house, though it's a lot cleaner, and a faded poster hangs on the wall by the door. Yellow letters at the top spell out the word READ. The rest shows an open book with a pair of glasses on top.

The glasses remind her of Emma.

Emma would have felt right at home here, Allison thinks. Sitting behind the desk and helping folks find books on the

neatly ordered shelves. She turns to David and Ike to say something, to see if they might be thinking the same, but they aren't looking at her. They seem lost in their own memories.

"Can I help you?" a young woman with shoulder-length brown hair asks. She sits behind the desk with a book in her lap, and the badge on her lapel reads: LINDA, VOLUNTEER.

"Yes," Allison says. "We're looking for Marcum Shale."

"Mr. Marcum?" Linda asks, closing her book. "He doesn't come in on the weekends. But he'll be here bright and early Monday morning."

Allison hesitates, unsure of what to say. "We might not be around then. You see, we're just visiting. . . . We grew up here."

"Oh," she says, glancing at Ike and David with a smile. "I knew I didn't recognize y'all. I'm kinda new here myself. About three months now, since my grandma got sick. I'm from Tallahassee. Well, I still am. I'm just here helping Gran for a while." She pauses. "So, you knew Mr. Marcum a while back, then?"

Allison nods. "Yeah."

"We didn't want to leave without saying hi," Ike says as he steps up to the desk, and Allison is relieved for the help.

"I could try calling him," Linda says, opening the top drawer of the desk and shuffling through some papers. "I don't see a number here. Maybe it's in the back office." She looks up and chuckles. "Well, it's more like a storeroom."

"A storeroom?" Ike echoes, running his hand through his hair, and Allison suddenly wonders if he's flirting with Linda the Volunteer.

"Yeah, I can show you, if you'd like. It's where Mr. Marcum keeps all the town records—birth certificates, newspaper articles, census reports, things like that." Linda stands up from the desk. "Yeah," she continues. "He's got file cabinets filled with stuff. He's quite the collector, you know."

She leads them around the corner, past the stacks of Civil War books. The corridor seems to get narrower with each step, as if the building is coming to a point, and they have to follow her in a single-file line. Ike stays closest to Linda, then Allison and David. There are no windows here, just metal shelves and fluorescent lights overhead. The library is empty except for them.

Linda steps into the last aisle and pauses in front of a door. It is in the farthest-away, darkest place in the building.

"Let's see," she mutters, opening the door with a brass key and snapping on the light switch by the entry.

A single bulb buzzes overhead, giving off more noise than light. The low ceiling curves slightly downward, and as they step inside, David has to duck his head. The room is narrow and much longer than Allison expected. Newspapers and books are stacked precariously against every inch of the walls.

It smells strongly of horses.

Linda walks across the room and starts leafing through some papers on the desk. "It should be here," she says.

Dozens of yellow pads are piled on top of one another, and they seem to be filled with handwritten notes. At one corner a space has been cleared for a framed black-and-white picture. But it's too faded to make out.

Two steel-gray file cabinets lean against the back wall. On top of one there is an old, metallic fan that doesn't look like it has worked since 1865. More newspapers are piled on top of one another.

"I keep telling Mr. Marcum that he should straighten things up a bit. How he can find anything in this mess is beyond me," Linda says, still looking through the papers. "I'm sorry. I'm just not seeing anything. . . ."

"Maybe it's out front somewhere?" Ike suggests, his voice rough like bark yet sincere. It reminds Allison of the way men talk to women in movies, not real life.

"Well . . . it could be on the new schedule," Linda says as she puts her hands on her hips. "We can run back over there and check—"

"I can come with you," Ike offers, and he moves toward the door before she can answer. "Allison hasn't been feeling well all day. It'd be better if she could stay here and rest a bit."

"Well . . . ," Linda starts.

"I'd really appreciate it," Allison says in her trying-to-sound-sick voice.

"We'll be along in a few minutes," David adds.

After hesitating for a moment, Linda nods, then she leaves with Ike right behind her.

Even though Allison figures that Ike is trying to give them some time to snoop around the office, she can tell that he *is* flirting with Linda too. Part of her wants to remind him that Jade left only ten minutes ago. Of course, it didn't take Allison long to put Bo on the back burner when she first saw David. For Ike, it might be his overcharged hormones that have him following Linda back into the hall like a puppy dog.

Or maybe he has a rubber-band heart. Flexible enough for anyone at any time. Flexible enough to snap right back into place after being stretched out and let go. But not Allison. Her heart has always felt like a fruit that bruises too easily. Sure, she doesn't love Bo, but she has never pretended to. She also doesn't know what she's feeling for David. Whether or not it's love, she wonders how much more bruising she can take.

As soon as Linda and Ike are out of sight, David steps over to the file cabinet and opens the top drawer.

"What are you looking for?" Allison asks.

"The library lady said that Marcum keeps town records," David says over his shoulder. "There's gotta be something here about Jacob, right?"

As David flips through the first few files, Allison starts

looking through the other cabinet. Being this close to him makes her think of Bo again. Those nights behind the coffee shop. Kissing instead of talking. His fingertips running along the scar. That would make things a lot easier right now, Allison thinks. If she could just kiss David and they didn't have to talk at all.

She glances over at him. His long, strong fingers shuffle through several folders, and she wishes he would hold her hand again. Just for a second. Then, all of a sudden, he turns to her with a quick smile.

Her heart flutters.

David returns to the manila folders beneath his fingers, and she does the same. They don't have much time before Linda and Ike get back.

All of the cabinet drawers seem to be organized by date: 2000–2001, 2002–3, 2004–5. . . . Allison focuses on 2002–3.

"Allison?" David asks. This time he doesn't look at her.

"Yeah?"

"I'm sorry about earlier."

Her heart flutters again.

"Me too."

At the back of the drawer she finds a file marked JULY 2002. The file feels heavy in her hands, and the outside is more soiled than the others. Dozens of newspaper articles crowd the front. Papers from all over the country—*New York Times*, *San Francisco Chronicle*, *Raleigh News and Observer*, *Denver Post*. . . . All of them feature stories about the fire that killed Jacob Crawley and the adult members of the Divine Path. Several include a grainy picture of him—his silver white hair and a smile that could hide the greatest sins.

Allison has never seen any news coverage on the cult. She never wanted to. But she can't believe all of this. Somehow it doesn't seem real that the whole country was reading about

*them.* To her, the world seemed a lot smaller then. Meridian. Daddy. Mel. Jacob. Her friends. That was pretty much it. But these newspapers make what Jacob was doing bigger somehow, she thinks.

Bigger and more frightening.

"Look at this," Allison says to David, handing him a few of the clippings.

He stands closer to her now, and she can breathe him in. His smell reminds her of Mr. Packer's garden. Fresh soil and leafy plants. As he reads, she continues looking through the folder. There is a faint wheezing sound every time he exhales.

The next sheet of paper in the file is burned slightly at one end, and she wonders if it was salvaged from the fire. The handwritten text is discolored and somewhat smudged:

And round about the throne were four and twenty seats: and upon the seats I saw four and twenty elders sitting, clothed in white raiment; and they had on their heads crowns of gold.

It was Jacob's prophecy about the end time and the new world to come, she remembers. He often read to the congregation from the book of Revelation, but this was one of the few passages that he asked his followers to know from the heart. It was the passage they recited before Jacob preached for the last time.

His final words, his final two promises, have stayed with Allison like handprints dried in cement. Permanent. Hard. She can picture Jacob that day. He wore the same white linen suit he always wore, even though the air was so thick and humid that you practically had to swim through it. Sweat drenched his body, and his yellow eyes flickered like candlelight.

It was three days before the fire.

"I have seen the end, brothers and sisters. I have seen it in my dreams and in the visions of our children—visions that are still pure and uncorrupted by too many years on this earth." He gestured to Allison and David and Ike and Jade and Emma and Harold. They sat in the front row, as always.

"In five years' time God will destroy the earth and all its wickedness with fire. But there will be no ark. No Noah. No animals carried to safety.

"Not this time.

"This time it must all be destroyed. It must burn for the Lord to begin again with a new garden and a new paradise. It must burn so the Chosen can be reborn as rulers and law-makers.

"The revelation of the Lord tells us that twenty-four elders will reign over the kingdoms of the earth. And I tell you once again that we are the twenty-four. We are the Chosen who will rise up from the ashes to govern the new world with justice and wisdom, with vengeance and mercy.

"Praise be, I say.

"Praise be."

Even back then Allison understood that Jacob never promised salvation. He only promised power. He promised the grown-ups that they would rule the earth. That they would have the kind of power that they had never felt in their own lives. The power not to be fired from a job or to be left by a wife or husband. The power to see the good rewarded and the wicked punished. The power to start over.

*And who doesn't want that every once in a while?* Allison thinks.

Her Daddy even promised her that men like the one who killed Mel would be punished in the next world. An idea that didn't sound bad at all, Allison remembers.

What sounded bad was saying good-bye. That's the second thing Jacob promised:

"The Divine Path will be consumed in a wall of flame, for we, too, must be cleansed. As we prepare for the new world, our children, the Visionaries, will stay behind. They will wait until the Lord is ready to reunite us, until he takes their lives on this earth as a sign that the end is here.

"Do not be afraid.

"Do not shed any tears.

"It is his will."

"Whose will?" Allison wanted to scream. Jacob was asking her to say good-bye to Daddy, and that was the last straw. She had said good-bye too many times in her life. Not again.

Something had to be done. She had to stop him.

"They got it wrong," David says, and Allison looks up from the folder in her hands. "All of them."

"What?"

"Look here." He points to a line and reads: "'A fire in Meridian, North Carolina claimed the lives of twenty-three people yesterday, all of whom were members of a cult known as the Divine Path.'"

"Twenty-three?"

"Yeah, they all say twenty-three."

"But that would mean . . ." Allison stops, still staring at the papers in David's hands. Twenty-four adults. Six children. Those were prophetic numbers for Jacob. Something he talked about often. Something that only cult members would know about.

"Someone else *did* survive the fire," David says with a whisper.

Allison's mind starts to race. Someone—not some *thing*, not the power of some prophecy—must be chasing them. But how? She still can't explain what happened to Emma and Harold.

Before she can say anything else to David, Linda calls out across the room. The shrill sound of her voice makes Allison jump.

"What's going on here?" Linda says more as an accusation than a question. "I don't think you should be touching Mr. Marcum's things."

She hurries toward them and takes the folder from Allison's hands. "He's very particular." Linda shakes her head the way parents do when they want to make you feel bad and guilty at the same time. She then grabs the clippings from David, shoves them inside the file, and presses it against her chest. "Very particular."

"Sorry," David mutters, his eyes lowered.

"Yeah," Allison adds. "We didn't mean to upset you."

"Not me," Linda corrects. "Mr. Marcum."

"He seems really interested in the Divine Path," David says in a pleasant, almost casual tone.

Linda nods.

"So many clippings," David adds.

"Well, he's not the only one," Linda begins tentatively. "Lots of folks have been talking about Jacob again. Mr. Marcum. Sheriff Cooper. Smiley Peters. Jennifer—"

"Talking how?" Allison blurts out.

Linda's body stiffens a bit. "Not the way you might think."

"I'm surprised anyone is talking at all," David says coaxingly. "It seems like ancient history to me."

Linda leans forward, and Allison can tell that this woman enjoys telling secrets. A thin smile brightens her face.

"Oh, they're talking, all right," Linda continues. "But not like you might think. Not about him being crazy. It's just the opposite. They talk like Jacob was this great man or something. They say he saw the future—"

"Wait a minute," Allison interrupts again. "Where's Ike?"

"What?"

"Ike." Allison's voice tightens. "Where is he?"

"He said he'd wait for you outside. I guess he was feeling a bit claustrophobic. Some folks don't take well to bein' in quiet places."

"He left?"

"Why, yes." Linda's eyebrows furrow, and she gestures toward the door. "I think it's time you leave too . . ."

But before she can finish, Allison rushes out of the office and into the long corridor of books. It doesn't make sense, she thinks. Ike "I Think It's Better to Travel in Packs" Dempsey wouldn't leave. Not even to try his cell phone again or to step out for some air or to knock back a shot of tequila.

No way.

She can hear David closing in behind her, their footsteps slapping loudly against the floor. As she turns the corner, Allison almost knocks over a small table with library flyers. She was hoping to see Ike in the lobby, with a smirk on his face and his orange hair sticking up as if his whole body were charged with static. But he's not here. The lobby is empty. Only the poster of eyeglasses without eyes looks back at her.

*Something is wrong,* Allison says to herself. She can feel it in her somersaulting stomach as she pushes open the front door.

The white light outside is blinding. She squints, but it doesn't seem to help. The brightness only seems to get worse.

Suddenly her legs buckle. Allison can feel herself falling down. Falling into a hard, burning light . . .

*White light reflects off a silver blade. It is long, with jagged edges. Silver teeth. Hungry and savage.*

*They bite down hard, and red blood spills out of the white skin. The jagged blade stops, stuck against the bone. It starts again.*

*Back and forth . . .*

*Back and forth . . .*

*The girl's hands are bound to a steering wheel, tight. She tries to pull free. Her mouth open, screaming without sound. Only soft piano music can be heard in the distance.*

*Rain starts to fall, but it is not cool. The thick, heavy drops coat the windshield red until the girl disappears from view. . . .*

# 10

# TAKING PICTURES

"Allison?"

David's voice seems far away, but when her eyes come into focus and the whiteness fades, she can see him kneeling by her side. Her legs feel stiff and rubbery, her throat dry. Everything around her—David's face, the library door, her car parked on the street—is blurry, as if she were watching an out-of-focus film.

As David helps her to her feet, she notices the medication bottle in his hand.

"I found this in your pocket," he says.

She twists off the cap and puts a pill in her mouth. It tastes bitter on her tongue. "Thanks."

"Maybe you should see a doctor," David says as he takes the cell phone from his back pocket and presses some buttons. "Damn . . . I still can't get a signal. . . ."

"It's okay. I'm fine," Allison mutters, trying to ignore her throbbing headache and the fear of what's happening to her. The seizures. The visions. It's all getting worse, she thinks. "Really."

"No, you're not fine," David snaps. "You're not even close to fine. You're, like, the opposite of fine." He pauses. "We need to get you to a hospital."

"We don't have time for that," Allison says, her head spinning like water down a drain. "I saw something . . . Jade, I think. Tied up in her car. I think she's still in town. I—where's Ike?"

"I don't know. He wasn't out here when you fell."

"Crap." Allison tries to hurry to her car but stops at the rear bumper. Her legs shake unsteadily. She is out of breath. "I can't drive."

"No kidding," David mutters.

"Look, we need to find them."

"*How*, Allison?" David asks angrily. There is a hard quality to his face. "Jade's gone. Ike's gone. And if you keep passing out on the street . . . well, I don't even know what. We need a doctor."

"There's nothing a doctor can tell me that I don't already know. I have epilepsy. Period."

David recoils slightly. "That . . . that doesn't mean we can't do something—"

"There's no cure, David. There's no changing it. So all I can do is take my pills and hope for the best. Most of the time they keep me from having seizures—"

"Most of the time?"

"*Yes*, most of the time." She leans against the trunk for support. "Maybe something about this place is making them worse. I don't know. But right now you have to trust me, okay? I can handle it."

Without waiting for him to respond, Allison reaches into her pocket and pulls out her car keys. "Maybe Ike went back to the hotel to wait for us."

David takes the keys reluctantly. His face seems heavy—heavy with exhaustion and fear and doubt. Allison can tell that he doesn't believe for one second that Ike is safe. She doesn't either.

Inside the car Allison leans back in the seat. Her body aches, and her head still pounds. The hum and vibrations of the engine are soothing. It's strange being in the passenger seat of her car, though. It feels familiar and different at the

same time, like trying on your best friend's clothes.

"I've never let anyone drive my car before," Allison says. "It's weird."

"I'll try not to crash, then."

"Funny." She glances at him, and there is a smirk on his face.

As they leave town, the trees get thicker. Allison closes her eyes, and the pounding of her head seems to lessen. The tires thump along the uneven road. The wind whistles through the poorly insulated windows.

"Talk," she says.

"Talk?"

"Yeah."

"About what?"

"Anything," she tells him. "I just want to hear the sound of your voice."

After a moment, David starts talking.

"Cameras. I have lots of them: a couple of Nikon digital SLRs, some old Nikon film cameras with everything from a fish-eye lens to a four-hundred-millimeter telephoto like the ones that sports photographers use. I even have a medium format Hasselblad. But my favorite is the Leica M3 with a simple fifty-millimeter lens."

"Sounds complicated to me," Allison replies.

"It was my dad's," David continues. "He loved taking pictures—before we moved to Meridian, that is. Photography was his favorite thing next to falling asleep on the couch and watching Jimmy Stewart films.

"'Who's that?' I'd ask, as if Dad hadn't forced me to watch *It's a Wonderful Life* a thousand times.

"'The last great actor,' he'd say with the same tone he'd begin his most-repeated sentence of all time: 'Back in my day . . .' Then

fill in the blank with whatever you just did wrong. 'Back in my day we had manners.' 'Back in my day we respected our elders.' 'Back in my day we cared about getting good grades.'. . .

"But I figure Grandpa dished out a whole bunch of 'Back-in-my-day's' too, and Dad was simply carrying on the family tradition.

"Mom preferred Sean Connery to Jimmy Stewart. Especially the old James Bond films. But mostly she kept her unrequited love for Sean Connery a secret. She didn't want to encourage Dad to spend any more time with films and photographs.

"Especially photographs.

"'Jack, this hobby of yours is gonna put us in the poorhouse,' she'd scold. 'If you like that camera so much, why don't you follow around some movie stars with it? Like those pop-rot-zees?' Mom had a habit of mispronouncing words because she didn't care enough to learn them right.

"'What exactly is a "pop-rot-zee," Helen?'

"'Someone with a lot more money than us,' she'd snap.

"But Dad mostly ignored her. He thought that photographs should capture something special about the world. Something you can't put into words.

"'You know it when you see it,' he always told me. 'Like love. It's just there or it isn't.'" David pauses.

He doesn't look over at Allison. His eyes stay fixed on the road ahead. Even with everything that has happened, he has a calmness, an easygoing looseness that rubs off on Allison. It reminds her of the David she knew five years ago. Whenever she got scared or uneasy, she'd find David. He always knew what to do—like taking a walk to the creek to catch fogs or hiding out in the old tree house that Harold found. Those times were filled with talk about the past. About their lives before Jacob. About what they dreamed of doing when they

grew up. David wanted to be a surgeon. Allison, a dancer.

"Your dad . . . ," Allison begins. "Your dad must have taken some great pictures."

"Well, he said he only took four pictures in his whole life that were worth a damn. And when he got to talking about those, he'd count them off: 'One, the way the sky looked on the day your grandma died; two, you asleep in your crib at seven months and twelve days; three, an empty milk bottle on the kitchen table in the late afternoon; and four, a homeless man asking for food in Atlanta.'

"'Why the last one?' I asked once.

"'There are no right words for the look on a man's face when the whole world has given up on him,' Dad said. 'No right words at all.'

"But the Leica M3 isn't my favorite just because of him," David says. "It's my favorite because it takes the most alive pictures you've ever seen. So alive that you wonder if you saw the real thing to begin with.

"At school there's an old-fashioned darkroom I can use for free. Well, it's more like a broom closet with aluminum foil over the window, but it's got all the equipment you need for developing black-and-white photos. The reddish light over-head. The chemicals that smell like opening a new textbook and sticking your nose right against the pages. Miss Garrett, the art teacher, lets me in after last period. She says that hardly any-one else uses it, and what a shame this and what a waste that. But I like having a quiet place to go to. Time practically stops in there. No sounds. No outside light. No one else around. It's just you and your pictures."

"That sounds nice," Allison says.

"Yeah." He nods. "I've taken thousands of pictures, but only one is worth a damn so far. Last spring I was in D.C. with my U.S. history class, and I saw this woman sitting on the

steps of the Lincoln Memorial. She was by herself, dressed in a suit and smoking one of those clove cigarettes. There was something about her face that made me take a picture. About the way her left eyelid was heavier than her right.

"It's an honest moment. You can just see it." David pauses. "Dad would have liked that picture.

"I figure that's what he was looking for. Truth. You know, the capital *T* kind. The kind you only get glimpses of here and there because it doesn't come along very often. Just like taking a picture, I guess. It happens in a split second, and the rest of the time people are just pretending—pretending to be smarter or hotter or funnier or more important than they really are.

"Dad always said that it's damn important to be honest. That the world needs honest people right now more than ever. I believed him for a while. And when I saw how much he believed in Jacob, I did too."

Allison remembers feeling the same way about her own Dad. But faith is a tricky thing. It asks for more and more all the time. And everybody has to figure out just how much they can give.

Jacob taught her that. He taught all of them that.

As the road curves slightly ahead, Allison spots Jade's red Jeep parked at the side. The driver's door is open, and the brake lights glow red. There is nothing else around except trees.

"Look!" she yells.

But David already sees. He pulls up behind Jade's Jeep, and the car slows to a stop. When the engine shuts off, Allison can hear the forest buzzing with sound. A chorus of cicadas. Loud and fast. Coming and going. It's a frantic, urgent sound, she thinks.

Allison gets out of the car, and a thick humidity presses in around her. It's the kind that's so sticky you can hardly move.

The kind that makes you want the rain something bad.

She moves toward the Jeep and calls out, "Jade?"

Her voice echoes in the trees.

She takes another step and stops suddenly. David is right behind her.

"What?" he asks, looking at her face, then over to the Jeep.

Allison doesn't answer. A pool of blood stains the road. Red and thick. It drips from the car like a slow, leaky faucet.

David inches forward, as if someone might jump out and grab hold of him at any second. One step. Then another. He's about to reach the door when Jade's brake lights flicker.

Allison tenses.

The cicadas burst into a new scream, louder than before. She wants to cover her ears and scream herself. She wants to disappear, to be someone without any of this happening. Someone without a past that won't let go.

David leans into the open door now, slowly. He grabs the roof for balance, and Allison notices the blood pooling at his feet. He looks inside.

The color leaves his face.

Allison rushes forward to see for herself. Blood has sprayed all over the dashboard and front seat. Some has splattered on the windshield as well. It drips from the rearview mirror and the steering wheel. It covers the stick shift and the stereo.

But no one is in the car. Jade isn't here. Only her suitcase is in the backseat.

Allison is about to turn away when she sees something on the floor by the brake. It's hard to make out at first. Curled and jagged and bulky. She reaches down to pick it up. . . .

The silver rings.

The crooked fingers.

The blue nail polish . . .

It's Jade's hand. Cut off at the wrist.

Allison staggers, falling backward into a sitting position on the ground. Her hands and jeans are now sticky with Jade's blood.

She screams.

David helps her up, wrapping his arm around her shoulder and leading her to the car. Allison stumbles forward, heavy and awkward, and she can tell that David is practically carrying her. She collapses into the passenger seat, closing her eyes.

David hurries to the other side. She hears him fumbling with the keys, slamming the door behind him, and starting the ignition.

The engine roars.

The tires screech as they lurch onto the road.

Allison starts wiping her hands on her jeans, faster and faster. She wants to get the blood off, but it doesn't seem to help. It's as if her fingers are stained red. Permanently. There's blood on the leather seat beneath her too. She tries to wipe it away, but it seems to be everywhere.

David is speaking now. She can tell from the tone of his voice that he's trying to soothe her, but she can't make out the words.

Instead she imagines the photograph that he might have taken here. The red color of the Jeep bleeding onto the ground. And the strange beauty of Jade's tortured, twisted fingers.

# 11

# DREAM JOURNALS

As soon as they get to David's room at the Whispering Winds, Allison rushes into the bathroom. She scrubs her hands in a kind of fever, rubbing the bar of soap hard against her palms. Rubbing until her hands practically disappear in the lather. Jade's reddish brown blood starts to run into the sink. Swirling around and around. Clinging to the rim. It's all over her clothes, too. Her shirt. Her jeans. Her shoes.

Allison yanks them off and throws them on the floor.

She is crying now.

The tears have been building since the news of Harold, since finding Emma's body. And now with Jade's Jeep. Hard, round drops slide down Allison's face. She can taste the saltiness of some on her tongue; others fall into the basin and mix with the blood and the soap.

She watches the water for a few moments and waits—until her eyes dry a bit. Until the blood disappears into the drain. Soon there's just a steady stream of water pouring from the faucet. Clear and cool.

As if nothing happened.

Allison splashes her face

In the mirror she sees herself standing there in her underwear, her hands dripping with water. They still feel dirty to her, and she rubs them hard with a towel. She looks tired and *much* older than seventeen. Her face reminds her of Ma. The way the lines around her eyes and mouth used to get real deep when she

was lost in thought. Allison has her mother's face, she admits. The same brown hair and green eyes. The same narrow nose and small ears. But Allison never thought she'd look like the older version of Ma. That's what the face in the mirror makes her think of.

The older version.

It seems so unfair, though. To look like someone you've spent years trying to forget. She'd rather see hints of Daddy in her face. His sideways smile. His crooked front teeth. Anything but Ma. And what if looking like Ma means that Allison will act like her one day too? Will she also abandon the people who love her most? Will she shatter their hearts?

Not if she can help it.

Allison studies the lines on her face again, then looks at the meandering scar across her neck. Thin and narrow and slithery like a garden snake. *Ma never had one of these,* Allison thinks. Whatever scars Ma had from Mel seemed hidden. She never stuck around long enough for them to show.

All of a sudden Allison realizes that something is out of place. Something is missing.

Her scarf.

She glances at the floor and the countertop. It's not with the rest of her clothes. Maybe it fell off by the Jeep or in the passenger seat of her car, she thinks. She has to find it. She can't lose the scarf Bo gave her.

Bo.

Her time with him feels like it was part of another life.

They usually text-message two or three times a day, she and Bo, and he has probably left several messages on her useless cell phone by now. But what could she talk to him about, anyway?

The end of the world?

Her unfaithful heart?

Maybe she has more in common with Ma than she'd like to admit.

Allison turns off the faucet, and she can hear David talking to Sheriff Cooper on the phone. His words run together fast. David tried his cell in the car with no luck, so they raced here. It was the nearest place they could think of with a phone.

Besides, Allison was still hoping to see Ike sitting in front of David's door. Waiting for them with a Where-the-hell-have-you been? smirk on his face. Instead they pulled up to an empty hotel. No cars in the lot. No sounds, not even from the winds.

And no Ike.

Allison wipes her face again. Her eyes are puffy and red, but there's nothing she can do about that now. She grabs a thick towel from the back of the door and wraps it around her chest. It hangs a few inches above her knees.

She opens the door.

David's room is identical to Jade's and Emma's. The same comforter and cheap furniture. The same posters with purple and blue flowers. Something about the sameness makes Allison uneasy. So much has happened, so much has changed, she thinks, but you'd never know it from this room.

David is leaning over the end table. The phone cord is too short for him to stand up straight, and it looks like he's speaking into the lampshade. It's ridiculous and cute at the same time.

"It's just a couple of miles from here on Route Fifty-four," he says into the receiver. "I don't know . . . I don't know where he is either. . . ."

David switches the receiver to his other hand and reaches for his duffel bag on the puffy chair. He shuffles through a few things until he pulls out an inhaler.

"Room fifteen . . . Allison is with me."

*Hssst.*

He sucks in the medicine and holds it for a moment. His entire chest inflates. "Okay, we'll be here."

David hangs up and turns toward Allison. His eyes

widen at the sight of her wearing only a towel. "Um . . . Sheriff Cooper is on the way."

"I figured," Allison says, lingering by the bathroom. "Could you get my bag from the car? I need some new clothes."

"I figured," David says. He takes a step toward the door, then stops. "Who do you think survived the fire that night?"

"I don't know," Allison replies, shaking her head. "But if Linda's right, the whole town could be caught up in this somehow."

"With the killings?"

"Maybe they're just *letting* these things happen. . . ." Allison hesitates. "I don't know."

"Even the sheriff?" David's voice sounds hollow.

"Even the sheriff," she echoes.

David looks at her towel again. "I'll grab your stuff."

As he leaves the room with her keys, Allison glances outside. It's dark from the coming storm, and the gray clouds look like water balloons ready to burst. Suddenly the sky cracks with thunder. Loud and angry. The rumble shakes the walls of the Whispering Winds and fades into an echo.

Allison plops down on the edge of the bed. A few seconds later David comes back with her duffel bag in one hand and his inhaler in the other. He sits down next to her, putting the bag on the floor between them.

"Thanks," Allison says as she eyes his inhaler. "You still need that much? I haven't seen you use it yet."

"Hardly ever. I'm not sure why I keep it. A few years ago some doctor in Philadelphia told me that the prescription I had as a kid was a placebo. My pediatrician must have thought it was all in my head." He pauses. "Weird, huh?"

"What?"

"Thinking something is so real—life-or-death real—and finding out it's total bullshit."

Allison takes hold of David's hand. It's warm and moist.

"You mean Jacob?" she asks softly.

"I don't know. . . . Everything, I guess."

Another crack of thunder shakes the room, and David squeezes her hand. He looks into her eyes.

"I never told you what happened to me that day."

"When?"

"At the Confessional. I never . . . I just didn't want to think about it. But now . . ."

Allison puts her other hand on his.

"Now," he continues, "I can't get it out of my head."

At first David didn't mind the woods and the campsite because they were so quiet. It was like the exact opposite of his old house, which he considered the noise capital of North Carolina. That's because his mom was a yeller. Loud words and wild hand gestures—that's how she dealt with the world. It's not that she was particularly angry or upset twenty-four hours a day. Not at all. She was just loud.

That's the thing with yellers. They think the world can't hear them unless they're shouting at the top of their lungs. And after a while they don't even realize they're shouting anymore.

That was his mom.

So David figured that she wouldn't last five minutes in a quiet place like Jacob's camp. That he would be home before the first "Hallelujah" or whatever.

But the more Jacob talked, the quieter his mom got.

In fact, most adults seemed to clam up around Jacob, whether he was talking or not.

That eventually happened to the kids, too. During the final few months of the cult Jacob started having them write down their visions in silence. After that, Jacob took away their papers and never mentioned them again. This made David uneasy. What

if Jacob finally learned something from their dreams after all? Something terrible.

David couldn't remember much about his dreams back then. It was like they were gone as soon as Jacob read them. But not the day Allison came back. . . . On that day, he could remember every detail.

The words just poured out of him, like he couldn't write them fast enough. And when Jacob came to the cabin to collect their journals, David held on to his tight. He watched the cult leader move from the back bunks to the front. Taking everyone's pages.

"Thank you, Emma," Jacob said.

"Thank you, Jade. . . ."

He was standing in front of Harold when David reached under Ike's mattress. David knew that Ike kept a couple matchbooks there from his trips to town, so he grabbed one and ran. He didn't know where he was going or what he was going to do exactly.

But he couldn't give his dreams to Jacob anymore.

By the time David got to the well, his journal was totally crumpled. It was so cold out that he was shaking all over. The dampness made it hard to light the matches too. He tried a bunch of them, but none would take.

Finally David got one.

The pages flared up, and he waited until the whole thing was burning good before he dropped it into the well. Jacob saw that part. David's dreams in flames, falling into the waterless well.

"Why?" Jacob yelled.

"Because . . . they're mine!" David blurted out. It was the only thing he could think to say.

With that, Jacob turned around and left.

The Doctor didn't come for him until after dinner. He was waiting outside the dining hall. He didn't speak. He didn't have

to. David knew right away that it was his turn for the Confessional.

The Doctor always seemed to appreciate quiet things, David remembers. And they walked the entire path without a word. David felt grateful for the silence. It would've been a lot harder if the Doctor had said something. Sometimes talking just makes things worse. Most people don't understand that. But the Doctor did.

At the shed, he put his hand on David's shoulder, stopping him from going inside.

"No. Around back," he said. "Jacob is waiting for you there."

A thick blanket of leaves covered the ground. David could still make out the vivid colors in the twilight—reds, oranges, yellows, and browns. Ivy clung to the walls of the Confessional, and the whole thing was a lot longer than David had realized. It went right into the hill of black stone.

Then he saw Jacob standing there in his white suit—about fifteen or twenty feet in front of him. Not moving at all.

"Come," Jacob said, his voice cold and somehow magnetic.

David remembers taking one slow step, then another. And the whole time Jacob kept talking.

"Your visions, David, are not private things. They're not just your own." Jacob tilted his head back and looked up at the sky. "No. Your visions come from some place greater than this. From some being greater than us. And you have a responsibility to share them. . . ."

The leaves seemed to get deeper and thicker with every step.

"You had a real vision this morning, didn't you? Something important." Jacob lowered his head. "Something prophetic."

David took another step, and—

*Swoosh.*

The ground opened like a trapdoor.

Leaves and branches and dirt spilled on top of him as he tumbled into the opening. David tried to get up, but the back of

his head hurt bad from the fall. That's when he noticed the smooth surface beneath him. Not dirt, but something else. Wood. Some kind of plank.

Right then a door closed above him, and everything got pitch black.

He was trapped in a small, tight space. Walls on all sides of him. He could hardly move.

That's when he realized that it wasn't a door that had closed. It was a lid.

He was in a coffin.

David's lungs started to tighten. He remembers trying to catch his breath, but he couldn't stop coughing from the dirt. There wasn't enough air.

He started pounding and kicking and screaming. He pushed his hands and knees against the lid. But it wouldn't budge. There was a heavy weight on top. It got harder to breathe, and his head was spinning.

For a second everything got still, and he tried to listen for Jacob. For any sound at all. *Jacob will let me out, David told himself. He wouldn't just leave me. He couldn't.*

David started to cry out for help, but that's when he heard the sounds. Not from outside. Not from above. But from inside the coffin.

Scurrying and clicking . . .

They were everywhere. All at once, it seemed. Not just sounds, but movement—things crawling up and down his body. On his chest and arms. On his neck. His face.

David swatted at them. He tried to roll over, to get away, but there wasn't enough room.

Then he heard a loud crash on top of the lid. He made himself get still. There was a heavy noise right above him. He tried to listen.

*Thump.*

*It's Jacob,* David thought. *It's over. He's going to save me.*

*Thump.*

*Thump.*

Then David figured out the sound. He finally knew what was happening.

*Thump.*

Dirt was falling onto the lid in heavy clumps. Jacob wasn't going to save him after all.

He was going to bury him alive.

David could feel hot tears all over his face. His whole body seemed to be covered with moving, biting things.

Pinching and burning his skin.

He pounded on the lid again. He knew it wouldn't do any good, but still he kept pounding.

After that David shut his eyes, like closing the shutter of a camera. He figured if he didn't see it, if he didn't take a picture of it in his mind, maybe it wouldn't be real. Maybe he would survive. . . .

David stops talking. His body is still, and he looks at the floor. Allison can see tears on his nose and upper lip. She wonders if he wants to reach for his inhaler. If the memory of being buried alive is enough to bring on an attack. It would be for her. But he doesn't move.

The inhaler stays on the bedspread.

"I don't know what happened after that," David adds. "I woke up in the infirmary. The Doctor told me I had been asleep for almost two days. Then he asked if I'd had any new dreams, but I honestly didn't remember any."

The thunder outside crashes again. This time rain follows, pounding heavy and fierce against the rooftop and the ground outside.

"Sorry," he says. "It's weird talking about it after all this time."

"That's okay. I'm glad you told me."

Allison gazes at David's face. The hard angles and faraway stare are handsome and sad at the same time. She understands the sad part. You don't have to live long to know that the deepest scars can't be seen. Sure, being marked on the outside sucks. But at least people know something happened. An accident. An illness. The cruelty of another. With a scar like Allison's, people don't assume everything is fine all the time.

But not for David. Like Allison's mother, he carries his scars on the inside. And it's tough for most folks to understand what they can't see.

"So," she says, "what did you write in your journal? The one you burned?"

"Oh . . ." David hesitates for a moment. "It was about the night you tried to steal my asthma medication from Jacob's box."

David turns to her, letting go of her hand. "I always thought you hated me for that. For what Jacob did to you . . . Even on the way back here I wondered if you still did?"

He says the last part as a question, and she can see the uncertainty in his eyes. Allison never considered blaming David for anything. They have all carried around so much guilt for so long, she thinks. For killing Jacob. For the death of their parents. Allison can't believe that David has been holding on to this, too.

Yes, she wanted to help him that night. That's why she went. But the box was filled with things that Jacob had no right to. Things that belonged to all of them. Things she wanted to take back.

"No," Allison replies, "I hated Jacob."

She reaches for his face, to wipe away some of the wetness from his tears, and David kisses her.

His lips are warm. His mouth and tongue taste better than chocolate chocolate chip ice cream. Cool and sweet.

A guilty pleasure.

Being this close. Breathing him in. Kissing him. It all sends

chills down her body, and she wonders how she has lived her entire life without this feeling—when your whole body is so into someone that you can't think of anything else.

David touches her face now, and Allison presses her palms against his chest, mostly to keep from falling over with desire. One of his hands slides down to her shoulder, the other to her breast. He cups it gently.

She leans into him—

*THUD. THUD. THUD.*

The sound makes her jump.

"Police," a voice calls out from the other side of the door.

"Damn," Allison mutters, grabbing some clothes from her bag. "Turn around."

"What?" David asks.

"I gotta put something else on."

"Oh, yeah . . ." David looks at her, smiling, then turns his head. "I forgot."

"Sure you did."

Allison could just eat him up, she thinks as she sets a new world record for getting dressed when you don't want to get caught with a guy.

*THUD. THUD. THUD.*

"Coming," David calls out.

As she watches him walk to the door, she thinks she'd give just about anything in the world for a few more minutes of feeling his lips pressed against hers, for a few more minutes of forgetting about the fear inside her.

# 12

# THE PORTRAIT OF
# MRS. J. P. NORRINGTON

Allison hasn't seen David since they got to the Meridian Police Department. She can still taste him on her lips, though. She can feel his touch all over and picture the scar underneath his chin. She never noticed it before—the small, crescent-shaped scar. Maybe it's from those things that bit him in the coffin, Allison guesses. Maybe it's a nick from shaving or a fall from skateboarding. She wants it to be the kind of thing that happens to guys all the time. Something normal. Not a mark from Jacob's hand, just an ordinary scar. Something that an ordinary girl would notice about an ordinary boy she's falling in love with.

"David Holloway," she whispers. The syllables dance lightly on her tongue.

She is waiting in the same room, the same chair, where Sheriff Cooper took her statement about thirty minutes ago. It must have been a den when the last mayor lived here, Allison figures. Several oak bookcases are filled with novels and plays you wouldn't expect to find in a police station. Some stuff she's read in school, too—*The Crucible, The Old Man and the Sea, Catcher in the Rye, To Kill a Mockingbird*. There's a small oak table in the center with two matching chairs.

Across from her a portrait of an old woman hangs on the wall. She wears a plain gray dress and a silver necklace with a ruby pendant. Not the kind of outfit most folks would choose for a picture, Allison thinks. But she shouldn't talk. Back at the

hotel she threw on a wrinkled floral skirt and a white tank top. The blue scarf almost matches the blues in her skirt. Almost. Her hair is a damp mess from the rain, and she could use some serious makeup.

Deputy Archibald enters the room. His forced smile reminds Allison of someone who has to go to the bathroom. When he sits down, he makes a slight grunting sound. Raindrops have left dark stains on his light brown shirt. He doesn't wear a hat like the sheriff, and his blond hair falls flat and square across his forehead.

He leans back just far enough to see her whole body, especially her legs. She doesn't like his hungry eyes. She has seen that look on guys before—mostly when she's around her best friend, Heather, but sometimes it's for her, too. It's the kind of looking that feels like touching—when you don't want to be touched.

"It must be real hard bein' back here," he begins, his words heavy and thick like the humidity. "After all this time. Of course, I only moved to Meridian a few years ago, so I wasn't around when y'all were up at that campsite. I remember seeing it on the news, though. About the cult. The fire. All those dead bodies."

Allison remembers the strength of the flames that night. It was hot enough to knock a person over, but that was nothing compared with losing her daddy. That pain still burns too deep to extinguish.

"That's gotta do somethin' to a person," Deputy Archibald continues, glancing again at her legs. "All that loss. All that talk about the end of the world. You think it's true?"

Allison tucks her legs under her chair. "What?"

"You think the world's going to end?"

"No." Her voice sounds more confident than she feels.

Deputy Archibald nods, and the constipated smile comes

back to his face. "That's kind of strange, don't you think?"

"What?"

"You not believin' . . . but here you are anyway. You and your friends." He pauses, as if he just asked a question.

"I didn't come here for the end of the world. Where's the sheriff?" Allison asks abruptly. It's the only thing she can think of to get out of this room—to get away from the deputy's probing eyes and sagging voice.

"Don't you worry. He'll be right along."

"Well, I want to talk to him. Not you."

"I saw the Jeep, Allison," he says. "All that blood. Jade's hand. We still haven't found the rest of her, though. Of course, she might be alive. There might be time to save her—"

"So what are you waiting for?" Allison snaps.

Deputy Archibald's smile dries up. "For you to start telling the truth."

"About what? I didn't do anything—"

"Why are you back here?"

"Harold's funeral . . . ," Allison starts, but she doesn't know what to say next. She's no closer to understanding what happened to Harold and Emma and Jade. She's no closer to knowing if Jacob was right after all. Her hands start to shake. "To say good-bye."

"I see. . . . Well, there certainly has been a lot of that lately. With all your friends getting killed, I mean. Just like old times."

His words hit her like a slap.

"Screw you!"

He leans forward, resting his elbows on the table. "It seems like you have quite the temper, don't ya?"

"Just a low threshold for stupidity."

The deputy chuckles. "In that case, why don't we cut to the chase? Seeing as you're so smart and all."

Allison doesn't speak.

"I think . . . ," he begins slowly. "I think you wanted to kill all those people five years ago when you started that fire. And I think you have something to do with what's going on now."

"No."

"We found your clothes in the bathroom, Allison. Soaked in blood."

"But—"

"How long do you think it's gonna take us to match that blood with the blood we found in the Jeep?"

"David and I were there. We told you that. *We* called *you*!"

"There'll be plenty of time for excuses later. Right now you need to tell me the truth. About where Jade is. About your other friend, Icarus."

"Ike," Allison mutters.

"Pardon?"

"His name is Ike, not Icarus," Allison says, practically spitting the words. "And I have no idea where they are."

She stands up, holding the edge of the table.

"Sit down," the deputy commands.

Allison can see his body tense, but she doesn't move. "Jacob killed my daddy five years ago. Jacob killed all those people that night," she says, her voice shaking. "Not me. Not any of us—"

"Sit down, I said," he barks, and the sharpness of his voice makes Allison drop back into her seat.

"Everyone around here is afraid of what's happening," he says. "Too afraid to see what's right in front of them, but not me. I know what you're trying to do—"

"What do you mean, 'afraid'? Afraid of what?"

All of a sudden the door swings open and Sheriff Cooper hurries inside. His pudgy face is flushed and sweaty, as if he has just been running. "Deputy, I need to talk with Miss Burke for a minute. Alone."

"I'm not finished with my questions—"

"Yes, you are."

The Sheriff stands there, breathing heavy and resting his hands on his hips. He watches Deputy Archibald with eyes as cold as the old woman's in the portrait.

"We'll finish this some other time," the deputy says to Allison as he gets up. "I promise."

"Joshua," Sheriff Cooper calls out, and the deputy leaves the room with sluggish, reluctant steps. He closes the door behind him.

Sheriff Cooper doesn't sit. He lingers halfway between the door and the table. "It's time for you and your friend to go," he says.

"What do you mean?"

"It's time for you to leave town. Understand?"

"Yeah."

"Good. Because if I see you again after tonight, I'm gonna let Deputy Archibald arrest you for murder."

*Murder?* The word makes Allison feel like she's riding in a car with someone who just slammed on the brakes. It was the word folks used to describe what she and the other kids did back then. Maybe it's true, Allison thinks. Maybe killing Jacob makes her a murderer. But she did it to save herself and her friends. To save her daddy.

Shouldn't reasons count for something?

"You think I had something to do with Jade?" she asks, fighting back her tears and anger. "Or Emma?"

"Deputy Archibald does. And when he sinks his teeth into something, he's as stubborn as a pit bull." Sheriff Cooper motions with his hand for her to get up. "Come on, now. I'll drop you off at the hotel so you can pack up."

Allison pushes back from the table and glances at the elderly woman in the portrait. Her dry, long face and black eyes

seem more alive now—as if she has been watching all along.

"Sheriff?"

"Yes?"

"Who is that, anyway?" Allison asks.

The sheriff turns toward the painting. "That's Mrs. J. P. Norrington. At the turn of the nineteenth century she was mayor for a short while—until some folks around here started saying she was a witch."

"A witch?"

"Yup."

"So . . . what happened to her?"

"One night she was burned at the stake. Right in the middle of the town square." Sheriff Cooper looks back at Allison. "We've known a lot of sadness here."

Looking closer, Allison thinks that Mrs. J. P. Norrington has a smirk on her face. Kind of like the pictures she's seen of the *Mona Lisa*. Both of them seem to be women with secrets. Both of them seem to be women who like having secrets.

As Allison leans closer, the portrait bursts into flame. The canvas curls. The paint bubbles. And Mrs. J. P. Norrington's mouth opens in a silent scream. With her body burning, her face changes too. It becomes more youthful, more masculine—

Allison's body jolts. Her mouth is dry, and her tongue feels thick. She blinks several times to figure out what is real.

Suddenly the painting appears to be fine. Mrs. J. P. Norrington is elderly again. There is no fire.

Sheriff Cooper is watching Allison closely now. "Let's go," he says.

"Was she?" Allison asks.

"Was she what?"

"A witch?"

Sheriff Cooper pauses before opening the door for Allison.

"She was someone who didn't understand how fear changes people."

"So they were afraid of her?" Allison asks, not entirely sure what the sheriff is getting at.

"Most folks are afraid of what they don't understand. . . . Now, come on. I have to get you back to the hotel."

# 13

# WINGS OF WAX

David starts packing as soon as they get back to the Whispering Winds. He shoves his clothes into the duffel bag with a swoosh and tosses it on the bed—the bed where they kissed and sat close and felt like normal teenagers for a while. Now it just looks empty, Allison thinks. Empty and like nothing happened at all.

She doesn't have to listen hard to hear David's breathing from across the room. It reminds her of a squeaky cat toy now. Wheezing and whistling. The kind that John Donne, the Packers' big white fur ball, plays with.

"I don't understand," he says as he checks the dresser drawers again. "Why did they let us go?"

"We didn't do anything—"

"We were the last people to see them alive!"

"Ike could be fine," Allison says flatly.

In truth, she *needs* Ike to be okay. She needs David's calmness, too. His soft voice and easy way with the world.

David glances at her before opening the desk drawer and taking out the phonebook. "If the sheriff wants us out of town so badly, why didn't he wait around for us to pack and leave?" David asks without looking up. "It just doesn't make sense," he adds with an *I'm sorry I snapped at you* voice. "That's all."

"Not unless he believes."

"Believes what?"

"Deputy Archibald said something really weird," Allison

says, watching David as he flips through the book in front of him. "He said that everyone here was afraid."

"Afraid of what?"

"I'm not sure, but what if Sheriff Cooper . . . what if the people around here believe that Jacob was right? Like Linda was saying at the library."

"That God is doing this?"

Allison nods. "That the end is coming, and there's no stopping it."

David tears a page from the phone book in a quick motion. "I just thought of what Jade would say about that theory," he says.

"With or without the bad words?"

David laughs, but it's over quick.

They both get quiet.

"I say we make one last stop in Meridian," David suggests as he hands her the page and points to a name near the bottom: Marcum P. Shale, 2818 Ezekiel Lane.

Something about the address seems familiar to her, but she's not sure why.

"He's listed?"

"Looks like it," David says as he grabs both of their bags and walks over to the door.

"Why didn't I think of that?"

"You were too busy putting the moves on me."

Allison feels her cheeks flush. "Yeah, right."

Outside it's dark, and the damp wind raises goose bumps on Allison's arms and legs. She can't remember a September night ever being this cold. Usually you can feel summer all month long, holding on for dear life. But not tonight. Tonight the air is winter cold, and the gray clouds move across the sky like crowds of people pushing one another forward.

Allison gets to her car quickly.

The wind picks up all of a sudden, and it carries a strange noise from the wall of trees behind her. Not the whistling winds or an ominous melody. Something else. A muffled cry. A moan.

"Do you hear that?" Allison asks.

"Yeah."

The sound starts again. Louder this time. It reminds Allison of the nights she used to cry into her pillow so no one else could hear.

"Ike?" she calls out.

A branch cracks loudly—*snap*.

There is movement in the trees. Someone is running away. Fast.

"Ike!" Allison screams.

Without thinking, she runs into the forest.

It's much darker here. Wet branches and leaves slap her body. Scratching, biting, and clawing at her skin as she chases after the movement ahead.

"Slow down," David yells somewhere behind her.

But Allison can't stop herself. If Ike's out here and he's okay, then maybe she and David will be okay too. They have to find him. To help him.

She stumbles over a fallen trunk but doesn't lose her balance completely. The forest seems to be getting thicker and more aggressive, she thinks. Like it doesn't want her here.

*Urrrrr.*

The muffled yell is close now.

Allison pushes into a large, circular clearing. A tall, T-shaped post stands in the center with what looks like a scarecrow tied along the top. Its arms out. Frayed clothing hangs from its body.

The dark keeps everything in shadows.

*Urrrrr.*

The sound is coming from the scarecrow, Allison realizes.

Its head is moving side to side. She rushes forward and sees the disheveled, spiked hair. The round face. The wide eyes.

*Ike.*

"Ike," she says, happy enough to cry. "Don't worry. We'll get you down—"

Bright light and a wave of heat suddenly knock her to the ground. She can see Ike's sky blue eyes and freckled skin clearly now. His hair reminds her of orange flames. It illuminates his whole face.

But the sound . . . it isn't muffled anymore. It's piercing. A scream—a terrible, painful scream.

Ike's face shifts in the light. His skin is changing. Melting like Mrs. J. P. Norrington's. The white light turns red and orange. Fire scrambles up the pole. It's as bright as high noon in the desert. And hot—against her face, her legs. All over.

For a second Allison wonders if this is another trick, another seizure or vision, but no. It's different. The screams. The vicious heat . . .

It's real.

Ike is burning to death. Right in front of her.

"Allison!" David is pulling her back now, away from the fire. Toward the line of trees.

*No, no, no, no . . .*

Allison swings her arms to break free. David is saying something, but she can't hear anything over Ike's screams and the roar of the fire.

She starts to run. Back into the forest again. Faster than before. Frantic. Sweat gathers on her face and chest. Her skin is still warm from the memory of the flames.

She stumbles and falls. Hard. Something jagged cuts into the skin beneath her elbow. A stone.

She gets back on her feet, running again.

At the parking lot she hurries past the Dumpster and her

car. She remembers a fire extinguisher on the outside wall two doors down from David's room. *There.* There it is.

The rusty box opens easily. She grabs the heavy red canister and sprints back into the woods.

The light of the fire is spilling through the trees now, making the branches and leaves glow around her. Her heart is pounding. Her breath short and hard.

She stumbles back into the clearing again and struggles with the extinguisher in her hands—snapping the safety and removing the hose. She aims at the flames. . . .

Nothing.

She pulls the handle again.

Nothing.

She starts shaking the can.

"Come on!"

David is by her side. He takes the canister from her and points it toward Ike as well. No spray comes from the hose.

"It's broken," David says. "It's . . . it's too late. He's gone."

Allison falls to her knees. David's right, she realizes. There are no more screams. Only a shadowy outline of Ike hangs in the middle of the flames. It's not him anymore.

Allison starts clawing at the ground. The soil feels cool and forgiving against her skin. She wants to scream and cry, but can't. Everything is bright as day. The circle of trees huddle around like spectators. David is on his knees next to her.

They can't do anything now but watch. . . .

Allison gets up slowly and leads the way back to the hotel without a word. The smell of fire is thick in the air, and she can even see flakes of ash on the windshield of her car. She stands at the door, hands shaking as she reaches for the keys in her pocket.

"You're bleeding," David says.

Allison looks at the long stream of blood on her forearm. "I don't feel a thing."

"Come on." David touches her other arm gently, leading her back to room 15. "Let's take care of that."

Inside, Allison lingers by the door while David grabs a washcloth from the bathroom. He dabs it against the wound at first, then presses down strong.

"It's not that bad," he says, his voice shaky.

Allison looks at the keys in her hand and notices the crumpled page from the phone book there. Balled up. She opens it, staring at the name and address at the bottom. Something about it . . .

"What the hell happened back there?" David asks, still holding the cloth to her arm. "It's like he just burst into flames."

"Yeah," Allison says faintly, but she is far away now. Numb. She's not still picturing Ike in the clearing like David is. She's saying Marcum Shale's address over and over in her head. That number nags at her. There is something about it.

"We have to get out of here," David continues. "The cops are just going to blame us."

"Yes, we should go," Allison says.

David nods, obviously relieved. "Want me to drive first? I figure we can make it to Virginia in a couple hours, then—"

"No. We have to go here."

Allison hands David the paper. He stares at it for a few seconds.

"Are you out of your mind?"

"Maybe, but we have to—"

"Seriously. Are you fucking crazy? We have to get out of this town while we still can."

"While we still can?"

"Yeah!" David yells. "Before we end up dead."

"How far do you think we're going to get, huh?" Allison snaps back. "Five miles? Ten? It's not going to stop, David. We need answers, and this is the only place we're going to find them."

David turns away from her and exhales loudly.

"What makes you think this guy knows a damn thing?" he asks, forcing his voice to be calm.

Allison steps over to the nightstand and opens the drawer.

"What are you doing?"

"Read the address to me," she says.

"What?"

"Read Shale's address!"

"Twenty-eight eighteen Ezekiel Lane," David answers flatly.

Allison turns to him with the hotel Bible in her hands. "Ezekiel. Chapter twenty-eight, verse eighteen: 'Thou hast defiled thy sanctuaries by the multitude of thine iniquities, by the iniquity of thy traffic; therefore will I bring forth a fire from the midst of thee, it shall devour thee, and I will bring thee to ashes upon the earth in the sight of all them that behold thee.'"

Allison closes the Bible.

"He's gotta know something," she says.

# 14

# THE UNSPOKEN

The car ride is postfight quiet—the kind of quiet that feels almost as bad as fighting. Uneasy. Electric. It's not like they're really mad at each other, Allison admits. They're just hurting from what they've seen, from what's been happening to them. But that doesn't change anything now.

Allison presses the cloth against her arm. It's still bleeding a little—that's why David insisted on driving.

"You know where you're going?" she asks with the voice she usually reserves for Brutus Packer Jr. on bad days or for creepy Bill Stevens, who sits behind her in chemistry class and blows on the back of her neck.

"I'll just look for the fire and brimstone." David's voice is colder than the air.

She deserves it.

The front windshield starts to steam up from their angry breathing. Well, that and because the defroster doesn't work. It has always been broken, and Allison has never gotten around to fixing it.

David wipes his forearm on the windshield before turning off the highway and heading back into the heart of Meridian. The town circle is empty and without light. She forgot what it's like to be in a place without streetlights. A place where everything is so dark at night.

The Confederate soldier eyes them as they swing around the circle and turn onto Maple Drive. Allison wonders if he was

watching when the town chanted "Witch" and burned Mrs. J. P. Norrington at the stake. Would he have saved her if he could? Would he have looked for a fire extinguisher? Or just put a bullet in her head so she wouldn't have to suffer like Ike did?

Tears start to sting Allison's eyes, but she holds them back.

They pass several streets of quiet, dark houses. It's late for Meridian, Allison realizes as she glances at her watch. Almost ten o'clock. She can't believe it's the same day. Each minute has lasted a thousand years, and it's still not over. She turns to David, wanting to say something about the way time can be slow and stubborn. But he is staring at the road.

She closes her eyes.

Bedtime always came too early. At least that's how Allison remembers it. Both Melanie and her in pj's. Brushing teeth. Trying to hog the bathroom sink. Sometimes shoving each other when Daddy wasn't looking.

"Enough silliness, girls," he'd say, and they were off to bed.

Melanie in her room with the window overlooking the front yard. Allison in her room down the hall.

Daddy read stories to both of them before bed. Always in Mel's room—because she was the youngest, he'd say. His voice swayed when he read. Like the swing in their front yard. Back and forth and easy enough to carry you along.

Then they'd fold their hands for prayers.

"Keep our family safe from harm," he'd say, so soft that Allison always imagined God having to listen really hard to hear. Maybe that was the point. It's better to have someone listening close than only half listening. Or not at all.

"Bless Allison and Melanie, Ma and Daddy. Amen."

"Amen," the girls would echo.

Half the time Mel waited until she heard Daddy go to bed, then she'd sneak down the hall to Allison's room. The

door would open real slow before Mel hurried over and hopped into her older sister's bed.

Mel had lots of bad dreams. Mostly about sharks. About how they never stop moving, not even to sleep. About how they're always feeding off things. Sometimes she was underwater with them, swimming and breathing just fine, but she was always afraid in those dreams—afraid one would get her.

When Mel talked about the sharks, Allison would stroke her sister's long brown hair until they both fell asleep.

Or until she wanted Mel to leave.

"It's time to go," she'd tell Melanie.

"I wanna stay."

"You have your own room. Go on, now."

Mel would climb out of bed, pouting and dragging her feet. "Dork," she'd mutter.

"Loser."

"Booger head."

"Vagina."

That was Mel's least favorite word, so Allison usually saved it for last. Mel always left after that.

Sure, there were times Mel didn't come down the hall to talk about her dreams or anything else—if they'd had a fight that day or if Daddy was real serious about bedtime. But after Allison's first seizure and her vision of Mel dying, Allison wanted her sister close.

She wanted to keep an eye on her.

It was getting late the night it happened. Daddy tucked them in, and almost an hour went by without any sign of Mel. Allison kept looking at the clock. The numbers glowing red and moving soundlessly from one minute to the next: 9:54 . . . 9:55 . . . 9:56 . . . 9:57 . . .

Allison just couldn't stand it anymore. She got out of bed and crept down the hall. It was so dark and quiet and cold. The wood floors felt icy against her feet. No wonder Mel didn't want to go back to bed alone.

The door to Mel's room was slightly open. The moonlight spilled in through the window, giving everything big shadows and an eerie white glow. Allison was about to call out to her sister when she saw something move.

It hovered over Mel's bed. Bigger than Daddy. Bulky and mean looking. It exhaled in snorts like an animal.

Allison's eyes adjusted, and she could see the outline of a man. He was wearing a coat that gave his body a strange shape. One hand pressing hard against Mel's mouth. The other came to a sharp point.

The pointed hand moved fast across Mel's neck, then the man stood up straight. He was almost tall enough to hit the ceiling with the top of his head. Allison could tell that he was looking at her now. She just stood in the open door, clutching her yellow blanket. She couldn't speak. She couldn't move, either. It was like her feet had finally frozen to the floor.

That's when he smiled.

It was the ugliest smile she had ever seen. The kind that would make you never want to smile again in your whole life. It stayed on his face as he stepped over to her. His pointed hand hanging at his side.

Something was dripping from it.

He leaned down, bringing his face close to hers. His eyes were black, and she could feel the hotness of his breath on her face.

"Next time," he whispered, the words coming out slow.

All of a sudden Allison could feel a warmth between her legs. Urine running down her legs and pooling on the floor. She looked down.

The man dropped something at her feet. Something wiry and sharp.

A second later he was gone.

Allison isn't sure how long it took her to move or why she can't remember anything more about his face than those black eyes. But when she picked up the untwisted coat hanger and

felt the stickiness on her fingers, she could move again.

She ran to her sister.

Black blood covered her neck like a scarf. Her eyes were whiter than the moonlight. Allison screamed.

She screamed until Ma and Daddy burst into the room. But by then it was too late. Mel was gone.

A shark had gotten her after all.

Allison jolts up in her seat. At first she isn't sure if she just had a nightmare or a seizure. A sticky taste fills her mouth, but she doesn't feel dizzy or nauseous. No. It was a nightmare. A familiar one.

Later on the police explained that Mel had been strangled to death—that the coat hanger was used "after the fact." But knowing that has never made Allison feel any better. She still should've gotten to Mel sooner. She should've called out for help faster—

"You okay?" David asks.

Allison looks out the passenger window. There are fewer houses now and more trees along the roadside. She and David are getting toward the far end of town, she realizes. They're almost there.

"Yeah," she says. "Just thinking."

"About?"

"My sister." Allison continues to watch the road. "I've never been able to talk about what happened the night she died. Not really. It's like I can't, you know?"

David doesn't say anything. There is only the sound of the engine grumbling and the tires humming against the road. Every once in a while the glove box rattles like it always does.

"I think . . . ," David begins. "I think there's at least one thing in everyone's life that's too painful, too hard for words. For the right words, anyway. One thing that should stay . . ."

"Unspoken?"

"Yeah, unspoken."

Allison turns to David. "That's my unspoken, then. What happened that night."

David nods, then his expression changes. The car slows, and he pulls to the side of the road. Allison looks ahead. The headlights reflect off an old, weathered mailbox with the number 2818.

"I can't believe it," David says as he turns off the engine. "I was starting to think we wouldn't find it. That it wouldn't be a real address."

"Yeah."

They sit quietly for a few moments before David asks, "Now what?"

"I don't know," Allison replies. "I'm scared."

"Me too."

David reaches over and takes her face in his hands. Allison can tell that he is trying to say something—something to comfort them. Or something about her sister. Or maybe something about love.

But love can be an unspoken thing too, Allison thinks. Secret love. Forbidden love. Unrequited love. At least with love, there are other ways to communicate.

Allison leans in and kisses him.

His lips are surprised at first. Then warm and soft and eager. The back of her head tingles.

When they finally pull away, David is smiling. They both are.

"You ready?" he asks.

"For what?"

"I have an idea," he replies, reaching for the handle to open the door.

But as Allison gets out of the car, she can't help but wonder if that was the last kiss she'll ever have. If that was an end-of-the-world kiss.

# 15

# EZEKIEL LANE

Allison watches as David opens the trunk and grabs the tire iron.

"What's that for?" she asks.

"Insurance." David closes the trunk and looks at her. "Let's go up there and see what we can see. No rushing into anything, okay?"

Allison nods as they start walking up the dirt driveway. The broken stones and patches of mud make it hard not to trip. On both sides of the path trees and tall grasses buzz with sound—crickets, cicadas, and other moving things. It seems like too much noise for the dark, Allison thinks.

It takes a while before they see the front yard and the shadowy outline of a walnut tree. Its enormous branches spill outward from the trunk in all directions. Its leaves shake from the steady wind.

Somehow the tree seems blacker than the night sky.

Underneath there is a parked car. As Allison gets closer, she recognizes it from the funeral home and the hotel. It's rust colored. Marcum Shale must be the man with the flute, she figures. Her stomach knots fast with the memory of him walking toward her in the parking lot. The black coat wrapped around his body. His purple lips.

"Maybe this is a mistake," Allison mutters.

"You think?" David asks sarcastically, still moving forward.

"Seriously," she says.

David turns around. "It's like you said. This guy knows

something. And if he's responsible for what happened to the others . . ." His grip tightens on the tire iron. "We're just taking a look."

With that, David continues past the car and up to the front of the house. There isn't a single light coming from inside. The porch, which wraps around the first floor, is covered with scattered furniture—some beat-up chairs, a swing that looks ready to collapse at any second, boxes stacked here and there, a folded card table. It's not a porch for resting, Allison thinks. It's a place for discards. For junk.

"Let's check around back," David whispers.

All of the windows alongside the house seem boarded up—or at least covered by something on the inside. One has a shattered pane with only a few triangles of glass left. The siding is weathered and chipped. A tired roof sags over each side, and the storm gutters remind Allison of an open tin can. Rough and uneven.

As they move toward the rear of the house, she can see things more clearly. The shape of David's body. The plants and weeds at her feet. It's getting brighter, she realizes. A flickering light glows in the backyard.

All of a sudden David stops moving. He sees the light too. Allison hesitates.

"What is it?" she asks in a whisper, but he doesn't respond. She creeps forward to see for herself.

Inside the yard there is a circle of torches. Each one burns at the tip of a long staff. Six total. Gusts of cold wind push the flames sideways. Almost hard enough to snuff them out, but not quite. In the center there is a large pile of dirt.

"We have to get out of here," Allison says, grabbing David's arm. He was right back at the hotel, she thinks. They shouldn't be here. It's a mistake, a trap.

But David pulls away from her. He moves toward the dirt

with steady, plodding steps, as if he's in a trance.

*"David,"* she pleads, but he doesn't stop.

The flickering light animates all the shadows around them. The trees. The closed-up house. Everything in the darkness seems alive and watchful now.

David gets to the center and stands perfectly still, staring at something beneath him. She finally understands what. There isn't just a pile of dirt in the circle, but a deep hole in the ground.

A burial plot.

Allison rushes forward. She has to get him out of here. She reaches the edge of the pit and glances inside. There is enough light to see movement below—fast and shimmering. For a split second she wonders if it's a stream of muddy water.

Then she makes out the rats. Rats fighting one another and clawing at the walls. Rats trying savagely to get out.

This time Allison clasps David's wrist and pulls.

"Come on!"

David turns toward her as something hits both of them. More jarring than electricity. Allison falls to the ground, twisting her left ankle. At the same moment David tumbles into the pit.

He's gone.

Now the man in black is standing there. The man from the parking lot. He holds a shovel in his hand. The shovel he used to hit David on the back of the head.

"I've been expecting you," he says.

# 16

# THE END OF THE WORLD

The man tosses aside the shovel and bows his head, as if in prayer. His body is perfectly still. From here Allison can see his purple lips. The gray skin that seems so familiar. Hard and unforgiving.

The cold wind stings her face as she turns sideways and gets to her feet. Her ankle burns from the awkward fall, and her heart races with worry for David. She can't let this happen to him.

Not again.

She starts running toward the house and up the steps of the back porch, her ankle screaming in protest. Glancing over her shoulder, she can see the man behind her, still standing by the grave, but she doesn't slow down. She just pulls open the door and slams it shut behind her, turning the dead bolt.

*I have to do something,* she thinks as she looks around.

Inside the house isn't dark after all. The boarded-up windows make it seem that way from the outside, but several candles give off a low light. A few on the kitchen counter. Several in the dining room beyond that. Small, weak flames, but just enough to see.

The cabinets and counters look as worn as the exterior. Allison checks the drawers for a knife, for anything she can use to protect herself.

Nothing.

Each drawer is empty—as if they've never been opened before. The cabinets, too.

She doesn't see a phone.

The kitchen door rattles, followed by the dead bolt snapping open with a hollow clap.

*He's using a key,* Allison realizes as she limps quickly into the dining room.

A round table takes up most of the space here. It's almost completely covered with papers and yellow notepads. Three candles sit on a plate in the center—dark red and mostly hollowed out. The walls are lined with boxes and stacks of newspapers, just like the office at the library.

The living room is similar. Papers and books and boxes against most walls. Thick drapes cover the windows, which would otherwise look onto the massive walnut tree in the front yard. More than a dozen candles of different sizes glow on the mantel. A painting hangs on the wall above them. A painting of emptiness, Allison thinks. A barren landscape. Black and charred. Thin strands of smoke rising from the ground. Completely lifeless.

Allison can hear heavy footsteps in the kitchen now. The man is coming for her. Fast.

She darts into the hallway and heads for the door at the other end. The framed photographs covering the walls rattle as she rushes by. She can't make out the pictures in the dark, though. She holds out her hands, so as not to crash headfirst into anything. Then she reaches the door. The handle seems stuck at first. She twists it back and forth a few times before realizing that it's locked.

"Damn it!" she blurts out.

To her right the hall continues. To her left a staircase leads upstairs.

"Allison," the man calls out from the living room. He stands at the end of the hall, looking at her. His body thicker than the walls. His voice cold enough to freeze water. "You're the last one."

She takes the stairs two at a time, despite the pain in her ankle, despite the fact that she wants to run outside to David. He'll be okay, she tells herself. She can't be the last one.

"It's time," the man says, his voice already sounding too close.

At the top of the staircase Allison sees light coming from a room halfway down the corridor. There is another door at the far end, but it is closed. She hurries toward the light, slipping inside the nearby room and pulling the door shut behind her. Quietly. Her heart pounds. Her breathing is short and panicked.

This place is different from the rest of the house. It's clean and orderly. Nicely bound books fill several bookcases. The desk in the center is mostly cleared off. Two candles burn there, next to a jar filled with cloudy water and something else.

Allison picks it up.

The jar is heavy, and the glass is moist with condensation. She holds it over one of the candles to see more clearly.

Inside there is a hand soaking in formaldehyde. The fingers wiggle slightly from the movement.

Fingers with blue nail polish.

She screams, dropping the jar onto the desk. The glass shatters. Fluid spills onto the floor, and Jade's hand slides across the desktop.

The door swings open behind her.

"It's been a long time, Allison," the man says calmly as he pulls back his hood.

For the first time Allison can see his entire face clearly. The long, drooping face. The black eyes and gray skin. The half smile that makes you think you're safe when nothing could be further from the truth.

*"Doctor?"*

She moves to the other side of the desk, wanting to put something between herself and this ghost. Jacob's assistant.

The Doctor. The man who patched up wounds so Jacob could open them again.

"That is what you used to call me," he says, flat and cold.

"You survived the fire that night. *You.*" She thinks of the way his face looked when he bandaged her neck, when he said kind things on the way to the Confessional. None of that softness is there now.

She is seeing the *real* Doctor.

"You've been doing this all along," she says.

"No." He takes a step forward. "But I've been watching you for five years. All of you. Keeping track. Making preparations for the end."

"The end?"

"The prophecy is nearly fulfilled. You know this, Allison." The man nods slightly. "Praise be."

"Prophecy? That's what you call killing us one by one?"

"God is bringing about the end, not me. I'm merely . . . facilitating his plans."

"You really think God is going to end the world because some wacko said so five years ago? Jacob wasn't a prophet. He was . . . a liar. A liar and a killer. *Like you!*"

The Doctor starts to laugh, and his entire body shakes. It is an unsettling sound.

"Of course Jacob wasn't a prophet. Jacob was nothing. Less than nothing. When I found him, he was drunk and broke and eating out of garbage cans."

"What are you talking about!" she yells, her legs shaking as much as her voice.

"I knew there was something special about him, though. The way he could talk circles around most folks. A silver tongue, he had. A quick mind, too. He had been a teacher once—before he was fired for abusing some of his students. Jacob always had a bit of a temper," the Doctor says with a

smile. "But I was able to help, you see. I cleaned him up. I taught him about faith and the Bible. I taught him about the end time and the need to prepare for the new world. And after he got his son back from his ex-wife, we moved to Meridian. Well, he came here first."

"Jacob wasn't a prophet?"

"No."

"What . . . what about his visions?"

"The only vision Jacob ever had was from a bottle of scotch." The Doctor chuckles. "At a certain point he had you write out your dreams so I could read them," the Doctor continues, his voice scratchy and intense and faint at the same time—like someone with laryngitis. "Jacob was only interested in learning about your nightmares. About your fears."

The Doctor pauses.

"Think of him as a mouthpiece. A spokesman for the truth. I needed someone with his charisma, someone with his gift for words. To get people to listen."

Allison's head is spinning. How can she believe any of this? That Jacob was the biggest lie of all? That she and Daddy and everyone else who was part of the Divine Path had just been fools?

She feels nauseated.

"It was all a *lie*?"

"Oh, no. My visions of the end—what I've seen, what I came to understand from your dreams. It's all true, Allison. I simply chose Jacob to be the voice. Like God giving the Commandments to Moses."

"I don't believe you. . . ."

"Real power is never where you think it is. It's never what it seems to be."

"Lies," Allison mutters. "Jacob. God. All the things we were told to believe. *You—*"

The Doctor lunges forward so quick that Allison doesn't have time to react. He clamps his hand around her neck and shoves her against the wall. The bookcases rattle. Allison tries to pry open his grip, but he just squeezes tighter. With his other hand he tears down the drapes covering the only window in the room.

"See for yourself," he hisses, pressing her face against the glass pane.

She struggles to breathe.

"Look!" he bellows.

In the yard below Allison can see the circle of torches and the rectangular plot in the center. Something is happening. The dirt. It's filling the hole—pouring in as if someone were shoveling it. But no one is there.

The dirt is moving . . . *on its own*. Thick, steady clumps lifting from the pile. Burying David with each passing moment.

"No," Allison says, shaking her head. "I don't believe it. I don't believe you!"

He throws her across the desk. Shards of glass from the jar bite into her back and legs. Then she hits the floor.

"Believe? It doesn't matter what you believe." The Doctor spits out the words. "You and your friends are the final sign. The sacrificial lambs. And with your death, Allison, a great fire will consume the earth—"

"*No!*"

"Nothing can stop it. Even if I let you walk out of here right now, there are still ninety-three days until the year's end. Ninety-three days for your greatest fear to find you. To consume you. It is his will."

*Ninety-three days.*

The words buzz in her ears. She hadn't thought of it like that. After the e-mail about Harold, Allison figured she'd either

survive coming back to Meridian or she wouldn't. She never imagined another ninety-three days of being afraid. She shakes her head again.

"Still a doubting Thomas," the Doctor says, taking a step toward her. "How do you explain what happened to your friends, then? And what about your mother? Leaving you and your daddy for a nice little place in Florida, right outside of Tallahassee."

"What?"

"Well, I had to keep an eye on her, too. You never know when guilt will get the better of a person, when a mother might come looking for her daughter."

"You know where Ma is? You saw her?" Allison gets into a sitting position. Her right thigh is bleeding bad. A large fragment of glass is next to her. She takes it in her hand.

"Yes. And the man she had an affair with."

Tears start flooding Allison's eyes, making the room blurry. "That's not true."

"She got pregnant," the Doctor continues. "Of course, she got rid of the baby."

"Liar!"

"The problem was she didn't tell the father. That's why he came to your house that night—when he found out. That's why he killed Melanie. An eye for an eye, Allison."

"Stop. . . ." Allison gets to her feet, backing away from him. The anger and confusion pulsing through her body. Her lips quiver. Her arms and legs tense.

"I have something for you." The Doctor opens the desk drawer, and his hand lingers for a moment. Then he takes out a long wire, sharpened at one end.

An untwisted coat hanger.

"You recognize this, don't you?"

Allison backs into the hallway through the doorway,

shaking her head. She can feel the glass cutting into her hand, but she doesn't care.

"I had a chat with Mr. Hascom," he presses, walking toward her with the coat hanger in his right hand. "That was his name. Roger Hascom. He followed your ma to Florida, but she wouldn't have anything to do with him. Broken, he was. That can make a man dangerous. Having no hope left."

The Doctor stops in the doorway.

"I couldn't take the chance that Roger would come looking for you," the Doctor continues without moving. "That he would kill you like he killed your sister. To take away what your mother took from him. So I paid him a visit."

"You . . . killed him?"

"He is at rest now. It was the only way to protect you, Allison. To protect the prophecy."

"What about—"

"Your mother? She's still an empty shell. Too dazed by pain to be much good to anyone. All that guilt about the affair. About her own daughter's murder. It can eat a person from the inside out."

Allison's head is spinning. She runs toward the staircase, not sure what to do. The Doctor is following close behind her. She just reaches the first step when he shoves her against the wall. Her head smashing into the plaster. She can feel it give way.

She turns, and the sharpened coat hanger cuts across her neck. It digs into the skin, rough and uneven. The strength leaves her legs.

She collapses to the floor. Head spinning. Her vision blurry.

His black boots are caked with mud, and so is the bottom of his overcoat. He holds the coat hanger by his side now. She can see her own blood on it. Dripping in slow, heavy drops to the floor. Allison presses one hand against her neck. It is warm

with blood. The other burns from the glass shard that she still squeezes there.

The Doctor squats and presses the coat hanger against her cheek.

"I wonder what your sister was thinking that night," he whispers. "Was she too terrified to scream? Or was she waiting for you? For her big sister to save her?"

Allison can feel something surging inside her—rage and hatred. For this man. For all the guilt and pain. For Mel and Ma and Daddy. Suddenly Allison thrusts the broken glass into his neck. She drives it deep into the skin and keeps pushing, even as he falls backward onto the floor.

The Doctor drops the coat hanger and reaches for the glass in his neck. Air comes out of his nose and mouth like a high-pitched whistle. His eyes wide with surprise. His teeth clenched as he tries pulling out the shard.

Allison starts crawling toward the stairs, but the Doctor grabs her ankle. With one yank he pulls her back. Allison's face slams against the floor, and her skirt slides up around her waist.

She picks up the coat hanger.

The Doctor pulls her again. This time his clammy hands lock on to the backs of her thighs. His fingers digging deep into her flesh. He rolls her over.

He has removed the glass from his neck, and blood pours fast from the wound. His eyes wide as he looks up and down her body. At her bare legs and underwear. At her torn shirt. At the blood on her neck.

The Doctor is swallowing her up with his eyes, Allison realizes. He doesn't look at her the way a hungry man looks at food. He looks at her with greed. Like someone who is ready to take something that doesn't belong to him. For a split second she imagines him watching Emma and Jade and Harold

and Ike with those insatiable, thieving eyes.

He grabs both of her legs again and pulls her closer to his body.

Allison shoves the coat hanger into his left eye.

"Ahhh!"

Allison reaches the handrail and starts pulling herself down the stairs. To get away from the horrible screams. To get away from his body writhing on the floor. She slips and falls down two or three steps, landing on her knees.

When she gets to the bottom of the staircase, the Doctor has gotten silent.

She looks up.

His body is still.

Allison limps through the dark hall—past the living room and into the kitchen.

Outside the strong wind makes the torch flames cower and blink. It still carries some dirt into the hole, but not the same way. It no longer looks like an invisible force shoveling clumps into the open grave.

Allison rushes over to the pit. The lid of the coffin is closed, but some of the yellowish pine is visible through uneven layers of dirt. She can still get to him, she thinks. There's still time.

Allison grabs the shovel on the ground and lowers herself onto the coffin. She gets down on her knees and starts wiping away the dirt. There are a few inches of space surrounding the coffin, and Allison tries to push most of the dirt into those gaps.

"David!" she yells. "Can you hear me?"

She pounds her fists on the lid several times.

"David!"

She pounds again.

Nothing.

She stands up, grips the handle of the shovel with both hands, and starts to smash the metallic scoop into the wood. Up and down. With all the strength in her arms and shoulders. Smashing and pounding. Moving in a frenzy.

*Crack*—a board gives way.

*Crack. Crack.*

"David!" she yells as another board snaps beneath her.

There is a hole in the wood now, and she strikes it again. Out of the opening a rat scurries toward her.

Allison screams, swatting at it with the shovel.

Several more follow.

"David," she calls out again as the rats race toward the walls of the pit and try to climb out.

She wedges the shovel into the hole and moves the handle up and down. A piece of the lid snaps off—wide enough for a basketball to fit through.

Rats and beetles spill out from inside the shattered wood. They're everywhere now. All around her feet. Scrambling. Then she hears a thumping beneath her.

*"David?"*

A hand suddenly reaches through the opening, and he starts pushing against the lid. *He's alive,* she thinks.

"Hold on," she yells as she starts to claw at the loose dirt and grass, pulling herself up and over the edge.

David pushes open the lid in an instant, gasping for air as if he has been held underwater. He swats at the rats on his body.

"David," she says, holding out her hand.

But he pulls himself onto the grass next to her.

His face is scratched and bleeding from bite marks. He runs his fingers over his face and ears and neck. His movements are frantic. His eyes wide with fear.

"I can still feel them all over!"

"It's okay," Allison says.

But his body is shaking, and he still swats at his skin.

"It's okay," she says again, grabbing his shoulders. "It's over."

He looks at her, blinking fast.

"You're safe now."

"No . . ."

His body still twitches. He pushes back from her and stands up, brushing at his clothes. His eyes dart back and forth.

"David," she says, touching his cheek.

He starts to calm this time, and she can hear the squeakiness of his breathing as he gets more still.

"It's okay," she adds again.

"You're hurt," David mutters, moving his hand toward her neck, but he doesn't touch her there.

"I'm fine."

David looks over at the house. "What happened?"

"The Doctor hit you over the head," Allison tells him. "He was behind all of it."

"The Doctor? What do you mean?"

"Marcum Shale is the Doctor. He's the one who survived the fire."

David turns toward the open grave. His body as tall as the torches.

"Where is he?" David asks, still facing the place where he was buried for the second time in his life.

"Inside . . . I think I killed him."

David looks at her, his eyes cold as stone.

"I want to see," he says.

# 17

# NINETY-THREE DAYS

Allison follows David inside. The stillness in the house has an edgy, uneasy quality. Something is about to happen, Allison thinks. Something bad.

It's darker than before. A few candles have burned themselves out, but the thickest one on the kitchen table still glows. David picks it up.

"Which way?" he whispers.

Allison points toward the hall. "It happened upstairs."

She stays close to him as they pass the photographs on the walls, and this time Allison lingers for a better look.

Black-and-white images cover the walls. Mostly of bodies. Dead bodies. Some with parts stitched together—like Frankenstein. Others with leather masks. One masked figure has been nailed to a cross. Two grayish monkeys have been crucified next to him. Another photograph shows a naked woman lying on a table. Her eyes closed. Her mouth gagged. Needles sticking out from the skin on her chest and arms and legs.

"David," Allison gasps.

He holds the candle up to the wall. The flame flickers near a photograph of a row of decapitated heads on spears, their lips sewn shut. A grimace tightens on David's face.

"Okay," he says, "this guy totally needs to get out more."

At the end of the hall they turn left toward the staircase. The landing above it appears empty now.

Allison rushes past David, climbing several steps. Pain hits her knees and ankles like an electric shock. Her body stiffens. She stops halfway up the stairs, grabbing on to the handrail and turning to David.

"The body is gone," she says. "He was right here."

Thick pools of blood cover the wood floor. She takes a few more steps, with David right behind her. Some loose plaster crunches under their feet. At the top she doesn't see any light coming from the office. The entire corridor is dark.

"Look," David says, holding the candle over the blood. Red footsteps lead down the hall. The left foot smeared more than the right.

"We have to get out of here," Allison whispers.

But David is already moving—mixing his own blood-stained footprints with the Doctor's. He hurries toward the far door and the light of the candle seems to disappear.

Allison follows quickly, running her fingers along the wall so as not to stumble in the dark.

"David?" she calls out.

A white light blinds her suddenly. A flashlight, she thinks for a second. But brighter. Much brighter . . .

*Lampposts start glowing at twilight. Long rows of houses on both sides of the street. No cars along the curbs or in the driveways. No kids playing. Just houses—houses that Allison passes as she walks down the middle of the street.*

*She stops at one.*

*It's the Packers' house—the front door wide open. Welcoming.*

*It makes her smile, being home again. She listens for the sound of Brutus Packer Jr.'s drums, but everything here is quiet. She never realized how much the Packer house looks like all the other houses on the street. The same shingled rooftop. The same manicured lawn. The same trees scattered here and there.*

*At first the sound is barely noticeable. It's far away in the distance. A low, hungry rumbling. As it starts to get louder and louder, Allison can feel something beneath her feet. A shaking. The houses rattle. The trees rock back and forth. She glances at the Packer house again.*

*Suddenly the front door slams shut.*

*The rumbling is violent now. And loud. It almost knocks her over. She struggles to stay on her feet.*

*Then she sees it coming toward her—the cement street rolling like an enormous ocean wave. At its peak there is a fire like she's never seen. Bright red and orange. Molten. It devours the houses and the trees and the manicured lawns.*

*Destroying everything . . . everywhere.*

*It moves fast. Closer and closer.*

*Its fiery crest is about to break, to curl over and crash down onto her. It's about to reduce her body to ash.*

*She closes her eyes—*

"You okay?" David asks, helping Allison to her feet.

She feels dizzy and off balance from the seizure, but she is far more shaken by her vision. Fire consuming the earth. The end of everything just like Jacob . . . just like the Doctor predicted.

"Yeah," she mutters, nodding. "Did you find him?"

He hesitates, glancing at the door at the end of the hall.

"What?" Allison asks. "What is it?"

"I found something . . . strange."

David takes Allison's hand and leads her to a small, empty room.

The window is uncovered and open. A cold wind pushes through, and for the first time tonight it feels good against her face.

"It's empty," Allison says, unsure about what David wants her to see.

"Behind you."

A full-length mirror leans against the opposite wall—unhung—and Allison sees her reflection in it. Slanted and distorted by the glass. Her body is bruised and bloody. Her hair messy. Above the mirror two numbers have been written in thick blood: 93.

"What do you think it means?" David asks, looking closely at Allison. The candlelight makes the gold in his eyes sparkle.

"He's gone," Allison says.

"Yes, but what does ninety-three mean?"

Allison pauses. "It's a countdown."

David helps Allison down the stairs, her body aching, her head still spinning from the seizure. Everything seems to hurt. In the living room a few candles still burn above the mantel, lighting the painting of nothingness.

David struggles with the dead bolt on the front door for a few seconds before it unlocks. Then he opens the door and ushers Allison through. She steps onto the cluttered porch. The boards creak under the weight of her body. The shadowy walnut tree spreads its arms over most of the lawn. But something is missing.

The rust-colored car.

It's gone.

She turns to David and notices that he is lingering in the doorway.

"Wait right here," he says. "There's something I gotta do."

"What?"

He goes back inside the house without answering.

"David," she calls out, stepping into the living room again.

She doesn't see him at first. She doesn't hear him either. *What's he doing?*

She moves farther into the room, and suddenly everything

brightens. The dark corners. The stacks of papers and boxes and books. A light pushes from the hallway. Crackling.

"David?"

The fire crawls forward. Flames start clinging to the walls, lapping at the pictures there. Pushing into the living room.

David hurries into the living room, a candle in his hand. He holds it to a stack of papers on the floor. They light as quick as the snapping of fingers. David moves down the line, from one pile to another. Each one catching fire and burning.

Soon the whole room is bright, the heat of the flames growing.

"Come on," David says.

They rush out the door and down the front steps. Allison almost falls, but David holds her up. He keeps her moving fast. Away from the house and the walnut tree. Down the rocky driveway. Back to her car.

Years ago, on the night before the fire, Allison didn't sleep. She kept tossing and turning and going over the plan in her head.

Well, it wasn't much of a plan. It was a thing that needed desperately to be done. There was no other way.

For weeks Allison and David and Jade and Ike and Emma had been trying to convince their parents to leave the Divine Path once and for all. But something was different about the adults after Jacob's final prophecy: "We are the Chosen who will rise up from the ashes to govern the new world with justice and wisdom, with vengeance and mercy. . . ."

After that Daddy couldn't stand to hear talk about leaving.

"But Jacob did this to me," Allison pleaded, pointing to the still-raw cut on her neck.

"Al, we're part of something real important here. And you don't just run away from the important things in your life. Even when it gets hard. You just don't."

No, Daddy never did get over what happened with Ma. He just kept putting his faith in Jacob, no matter what happened. Allison figured it had to do with Mel and making sure that bad folks were punished in the next life.

Daddy might have given up on life by the time Jacob strolled into town. But Allison wasn't going to.

So when she came up with a plan for killing Jacob, they all huddled close together on Allison's bunk and voted on it. Even Harold nodded with the rest of them. They all knew that Jacob was causing too much hurt. That he had to be stopped. Harold thought so too, but he didn't offer to help with the plan after that.

And no one asked. There are some things in the world that a person just can't live with. And Harold couldn't kill his father.

As they were talking it over, a noise came from outside. The loud snap of a branch. They all tensed—terrified that it was Jacob, that he was only moments away from bursting inside and sending them all to the Confessional for their treachery. But it must have been nothing. Everything got still again. They listened to the silence for a few minutes, then continued.

"Once Jacob is gone, we can get our parents back," Allison said before they all left her bed and climbed into their own bunks. It was what they wanted most of all. For things to be like they were before Jacob.

No one slept easy for the next three nights. They had to wait until Wednesday, when one of the adults went into town to refill the gasoline can.

The night it happened, no one slept. David and Jade went first. They grabbed the gas can by the only generator at camp. It powered the four lightbulbs of the main hall. The rest of the buildings didn't have electricity.

Ike and Allison waited by Jacob's cabin with the matches, while Emma kept a lookout—just in case someone made a late-night run to the crappers and saw them. It seemed like forever and a day before David and Jade showed up, Allison remembers. She could hear the gas sloshing in the can before she saw them rushing toward her in the dark.

Then they started pouring it along the base of each wall. Letting it soak in real deep. Jade also splashed some on the walls and the door so Jacob couldn't get out. There was no room for error.

Allison and Ike started at opposite sides of the building. It was dry out, and the matches flared up fast, even with the wind. But that was nothing compared with how fast the wood burned. It seemed like the entire cabin went up in a single blaze.

The shingles on the rooftop burned brighter than the rest, and wind seemed to make the fire angrier. More hungry.

Allison hadn't thought about what would happen next. She just assumed the rest of the Chosen would wake up and come running. They would try to save Jacob, frantically throwing water onto the fire. There would be screams and tears and prayers. But when the smoke cleared, it would be over.

No more cult.

No more Jacob.

They could finally go home.

But no one came running. The fire burned and crackled and roared. The dark sky became bright. And when the wind started carrying the flames from Jacob's cabin to the other buildings, Allison ran to wake up Daddy.

He and the other adults were sound asleep.

Perfectly still and quiet.

Allison whispered at first, then she started shaking him hard. She yelled. She even slapped his face.

Nothing.

Jade and David were doing the same to their parents, but no one moved.

Everyone—their parents, all of the adults—were dead.

Back at Jacob's cabin, as she stood in a circle with the only friends she had ever known, Allison looked around at the six of them, heads bowed as if they were too ashamed to look at one another.

Jacob must have poisoned Daddy and the others, she thought. Maybe when they passed around the chalice that evening during service. Or maybe it was something in the food.

With the fire raging and her daddy dead and Ike Dempsey gripping her hand so tight that she couldn't feel her fingertips, she couldn't think anymore.

The heat from the blaze started to make her back sweaty, and she leaned forward. There were sirens in the distance. Fire trucks and police cars. The fire must have been visible for miles, Allison figured.

The sirens got closer, but none of those sounds were louder than Jacob's last words to her:

"In five years' time," he said, "your greatest fear will consume you. It will rob you of your last breath."

Listening to the fire sizzle and gasp behind her, Allison wondered if he hadn't just been trying to scare them.

"What if it comes true?" she asked to break the silence, her voice hoarse and unsteady.

But no one looked up or said a word. They just held hands as the air around them filled with smoke and the white ash of burning flesh. . . .

A fire blazes behind them now. David drives her car, and Allison slumps in the passenger seat. Every muscle and bone

in her body is dog tired. Sore. Her arms and neck still throb from the open wounds.

As the Doctor's burning house lights up the road and the trees all around them, Allison wonders why she doesn't feel more relieved. More safe at this moment. She and David survived. They're leaving Meridian for good, she thinks. But somehow she can't talk herself into feeling better.

She's always had an ear for words. When someone says something, she just can't get it out of her head. And right now she is replaying the Doctor's promise:

"Even if I let you walk out of here right now, there are still ninety-three days until the year's end. Ninety-three days for your greatest fear to find you. To consume you. It is his will."

Ninety-three days.

It's hard for her not to believe it now. Not after seeing Emma's eyes and the fire that devoured Ike and the way the wind blew dirt into David's grave. Not after having her own dream of the apocalypse. If all her other dreams have come true, then perhaps the Doctor is right. Perhaps there are only ninety-three days or less until she and the world die in fire.

"You know . . . I was just thinking," David begins, and Allison turns toward him.

"What?"

"This is the worst vacation I ever had."

Allison smiles. "Tell me about it."

"So . . . where do you want to go?"

"Anywhere but here."

"How about Philadelphia?"

"Philadelphia?"

"It's where my foster family is. I think you'll like it," David says, and she can tell that he really means it.

"You should meet the Packers, too," Allison adds. "They're a little crazy, but nice."

"Okay."

As the car speeds along, Allison tries to picture Philadelphia and the steps that Rocky ran up and down in that movie. She thinks that seems like a good place to imagine a better future—to hope for one, at least.

Right then David reaches for her hand on the leather seat and squeezes it. She squeezes back.

And for a second, just a split second, Allison thinks that the world might not end after all.